# The Value of the University Armed Service Units

Rachel Woodward, K. Neil Jenkings and Alison J. Williams

]u[

ubiquity press
London

Published by
Ubiquity Press Ltd.
6 Windmill Street
London W1T 2JB
www.ubiquitypress.com

Text © The authors 2015

First published 2015

Cover design by Amber MacKay
Images used in this cover design were sourced from http://www.defenceimagery.mod.uk and are licensed under the Open Government Licence v3.0
Front cover image by Bombardier Murray Kerr © Crown Copyright 2012
Back cover image by Sgt Si Longworth RLC © Crown Copyright 2014

Printed in the UK by Lightning Source Ltd.

ISBN (Paperback): 978-1-909188-57-0
ISBN (PDF): 978-1-909188-58-7
ISBN (EPUB): 978-1-909188-59-4
ISBN (Kindle): 978-1-909188-60-0

DOI: http://dx.doi.org/10.5334/baq

This work is licensed under the Creative Commons Attribution 4.0 International License. To view a copy of this license, visit http://creativecommons.org/licenses/by/4.0/ or send a letter to Creative Commons, 444 Castro Street, Suite 900, Mountain View, California, 94041, USA. This license allows for copying any part of the work for personal and commercial use, providing author attribution is clearly stated.

Suggested citation:
Woodward, R, Jenkings, K N and Williams, A J 2015
*The Value of the University Armed Service Units*. London: Ubiquity Press.
DOI: http://dx.doi.org/10.5334/baq. License: CC-BY 4.0

To read the online open access version of this book, either visit http://dx.doi.org/10.5334/baq or scan this QR code with your mobile device:

# Contents

| | | |
|---|---|---|
| List of tables | | vi |
| List of figures | | vii |
| List of abbreviations | | x |
| Note on terminology | | xi |
| Acknowledgements | | xiii |

**Chapter 1. The University Armed Service Units: Background and Context**     1

| 1.1 | Introducing the university armed service units | 1 |
|---|---|---|
| 1.2 | The university armed service units missions | 5 |
| 1.3 | The UK higher education sector | 19 |
| 1.4 | Policy issues framing the university armed service units | 22 |
| 1.5 | The purpose and structure of this book | 30 |

**Chapter 2. Studying the Value of the University Armed Service Units: Research Rationale and Methods**     31

| 2.1 | Rationale and background to the research | 31 |
|---|---|---|
| 2.2 | Research methodology | 35 |
| 2.3 | Conclusions on rationale and methodology | 42 |

**Chapter 3. The Student Experience of University Armed Service Unit Participation**     45

| 3.1 | Demographic characteristics of the university armed forces units survey sample | 46 |
|---|---|---|
| 3.2 | University attendance, qualifications, degree subjects and other activities | 48 |
| 3.3 | Joining a university armed service unit | 56 |
| 3.4 | University armed service units and skills development | 63 |

| 3.5 | Progression through university | 80 |
| 3.6 | Career choices | 83 |
| 3.7 | Seeking and gaining employment after graduation | 91 |
| 3.8 | Opinions about the armed forces | 95 |
| 3.9 | Overall experiences of university armed service units | 97 |
| 3.10 | Conclusions: the value of the university armed service units for participating students | 99 |

## Chapter 4. Graduate Evaluations of the University Armed Service Units Experience — 101

| 4.1 | The sample of graduates | 101 |
| 4.2 | The value of university armed service units experience in the workplace | 106 |
| 4.3 | Defence-minded for life? | 116 |
| 4.4 | Considering a career in the armed forces | 120 |
| 4.5 | The value of the individual to their university armed service unit and the armed forces | 124 |
| 4.6 | Graduate perceptions of the value of the university armed service units | 131 |
| 4.7 | Conclusions: the value of the university armed service units to graduates | 135 |

## Chapter 5. The Value of the University Armed Service Units to the Armed Forces — 139

| 5.1 | The commanding officers | 139 |
| 5.2 | The university armed service units and the universities | 142 |
| 5.3 | The value of the university armed service units to universities | 148 |
| 5.4 | The value added to university armed service units and the armed forces from the university relationship | 149 |
| 5.5 | Commanding Officer perceptions of the value of the university armed service units | 150 |
| 5.6 | Conclusions: the value of the university armed service units to the armed forces | 152 |

## Chapter 6. The Universities and the University Armed Service Units — 155

| 6.1 | Knowledge of the university armed service units within universities | 155 |

| 6.2 | University armed service units-university communication and liaison | 157 |
| --- | --- | --- |
| 6.3 | Perceptions of the value of university armed service units to students | 159 |
| 6.4 | The benefits to universities of the university armed service units | 161 |
| 6.5 | Conclusions: the value of the university armed service units to universities | 163 |

## Chapter 7. Conclusions: the Value of the University Armed Service Units 165

| 7.1 | The reach of the university armed service units across higher education | 165 |
| --- | --- | --- |
| 7.2 | Equalities, politics and access to information about university armed service units | 166 |
| 7.3 | The comparability of university armed service units and other extracurricular student activities | 167 |
| 7.4 | The university armed service units and recruitment to the UK armed forces | 169 |
| 7.5 | Knowledge of the university armed service units within the higher education sector | 170 |
| 7.6 | Knowledge of university armed service units amongst employers | 171 |
| 7.7 | Researching the university armed service units | 172 |

Appendix 1: Questionnaire used for survey of student USU participants, spring 2013 — 175

Appendix 2: Semi-structured interview schedule for graduate interviews — 186

Appendix 3: Semi-structured interview schedule for Commanding Officer interviews — 188

Appendix 4: Semi-structured interview schedule for university representative interviews — 190

Appendix 5: Student survey participation by university and service unit — 191

Appendix 6: Students' assessments of skills development through university armed service unit participation — 200

Appendix 7: Students' assessments of skills development through degree programme — 204

# List of tables

| | | |
|---|---|---|
| Table 1.1 | Officer Training Corps units and participating universities | 8 |
| Table 1.2 | University Air Squadrons, training locations and participating universities | 11 |
| Table 1.3 | University Royal Naval Units, ship and base, and participating universities | 15 |
| Table 1.4 | Military Education Committees, associated USUs and participating universities | 18 |
| Table 3.1 | Proportion of USU participants by JACS subject codes, by percentage | 52 |
| Table 3.2 | Awareness of USUs prior to arriving at university, by percentage | 56 |
| Table 3.3 | Awareness of USUs prior to arriving at university amongst women, by percentage | 57 |
| Table 3.4 | Motivations for joining by service unit, by percentage | 60 |
| Table 3.5 | Motivations for joining a USU by service unit and gender, by percentage | 61 |
| Table 3.6 | Pre-university views on an armed forces career, by percentage | 83 |
| Table 3.7 | Student views on an armed forces career, by percentage | 85 |

# List of figures

| | | |
|---|---|---|
| Figure 3.1 | Age profile of USU survey participants, by percentage | 46 |
| Figure 3.2 | Gender profile of USUs sample, by percentage | 47 |
| Figure 3.3 | Proportion of sample attending independent school, by percentage | 47 |
| Figure 3.4 | Length of time in unit at point of survey, by percentage | 49 |
| Figure 3.5 | Proportion of USU participants by degree type, by percentage | 50 |
| Figure 3.6 | University stage on joining USU, by percentage | 51 |
| Figure 3.7 | Percentage of USU participants registered on degree programmes in medicine, subjects allied to medicine and biological sciences | 53 |
| Figure 3.8 | Percentage of USU participants registered on degree programmes in physical sciences, maths, computing and engineering | 53 |
| Figure 3.9 | Percentage of USU participants registered on degree programmes in social studies, law, business and mass communications | 54 |
| Figure 3.10 | Percentage of USU participants registered on degree programmes in languages, historical studies, creative arts, education and combined studies | 54 |
| Figure 3.11 | Significant sources of information about USUs, by percentage | 58 |
| Figure 3.12 | Motivations for joining by service unit, by percentage | 60 |
| Figure 3.13 | Motivations for joining OTC, by gender | 62 |
| Figure 3.14 | Motivations for joining UAS, by gender | 62 |
| Figure 3.15 | Motivations for joining URNU, by gender | 63 |

Figure 3.16  Critical thinking: student evaluations of USU and university degree — 64

Figure 3.17  Numeracy: student evaluations of USU and university degree — 65

Figure 3.18  Literacy: student evaluations of USU and university degree — 65

Figure 3.19  Information literacy: student evaluations of USU and university degree — 66

Figure 3.20  Synthesising information: student evaluations of USU and university degree — 66

Figure 3.21  Organisation and planning: student evaluations of USU and university degree — 67

Figure 3.22  Project planning: student evaluations of USU and university degree — 68

Figure 3.23  Decision-making: student evaluations of USU and university degree — 68

Figure 3.24  Initiative: student evaluations of USU and university degree — 69

Figure 3.25  Independence: student evaluations of USU and university degree — 69

Figure 3.26  Adaptability: student evaluations of USU and university degree — 70

Figure 3.27  Problem-solving: student evaluations of USU and university degree — 70

Figure 3.28  Time management: student evaluations of USU and university degree — 71

Figure 3.29  Budgeting: student evaluations of USU and university degree — 71

Figure 3.30  Communication skills: student evaluations of USU and university degree — 72

Figure 3.31  Verbal interaction: student evaluations of USU and university degree — 73

Figure 3.32  Presentation skills: student evaluations of USU and university degree — 73

| | | |
|---|---|---|
| Figure 3.33 | Leadership: student evaluations of USU and university degree | 74 |
| Figure 3.34 | Teamwork: student evaluations of USU and university degree | 74 |
| Figure 3.35 | Knowledge of the armed forces: student evaluations of USU and university degree | 76 |
| Figure 3.36 | Maturity: student evaluations of USU and university degree | 76 |
| Figure 3.37 | Self-confidence: student evaluations of USU and university degree | 77 |
| Figure 3.38 | Social skills: student evaluations of USU and university degree | 77 |
| Figure 3.39 | Self-confidence: assessments of USU skills development by gender | 78 |
| Figure 3.40 | Time management: assessments of USU skills development by gender | 78 |
| Figure 3.41 | USU skills learned through other activities | 80 |
| Figure 3.42 | USU participation: positive effects on degree progression, by percentage | 81 |

# List of abbreviations

| | |
|---|---|
| BA | Bachelor of Arts |
| BSc | Bachelor of Sciences |
| CO | Commanding Officer |
| COMEC | Council of Military Education Committees |
| DBIS | Department for Business Innovation and Skills |
| DTOEES | Defence Technical Officer and Engineer Entry Scheme |
| ESRC | Economic and Social Research Council |
| HESA | Higher Education Statistics Agency |
| JACS | Joint Academic Coding System |
| MA | Master of Arts |
| MEC | Military Education Committee |
| MEng | Master of Engineering |
| MoD | Ministry of Defence |
| MPhil | Master of Philosophy |
| MSc | Master of Science |
| NCO | Non-Commissioned Officer |
| NUMEC | Northumbrian Universities Military Education Committee |
| OTC | Officer Training Corps |
| OTR | Officer Training Regiment |
| PhD | Doctor of Philosophy |
| RAF | Royal Air Force |
| SaBRE | Support for Britain's Reservists and Employers |
| TA | Territorial Army |
| UAS | University Air Squadron |
| UCAS | Universities and Colleges Admissions Service |
| UK | United Kingdom |
| UOTC | University Officer Training Corps |
| URNU | University Royal Naval Unit |
| USU | University (Armed) Service Unit |

# Note on terminology

In this book, we list the units alphabetically rather than by seniority of service, in the order: Officer Training Corps, University Air Squadrons, University Royal Naval Units. This reflects both the sizes of the three service units and alphabetical order. It is a convention within defence-related documentation where all three armed forces are discussed, to list these in the order Royal Navy, Army, Royal Air Force, and we are aware that we are at variance with that.

In this book, we refer to 'university armed service units' in order to clarify for those working outside the armed forces, potentially with very little knowledge of the units, that the Officer Training Corps (OTC), University Air Squadron (UAS) and University Royal Navy Unit (URNU) are part of the UK armed forces, despite the fact that students are not liable for deployment and are not armed (although they may receive weapons training). We use this terminology to distinguish the units from other providers of services within universities, and in recognition that many student-centred university organisations and activities provide some kind of civic or public service, either for students or in a wider voluntary charitable capacity beyond the university campus. However, because the term 'university service unit' is more commonly used within defence circles and the armed forces, we use the abbreviation USU throughout this book.

We use the term Officer Training Corps and OTC throughout, in preference to University Officer Training Corps and UOTC, to reflect both common usage of the term OTC and to help the reader distinguish easily between the three service units. We use the term 'units' to denote individual units within the OTC, UAS or URNU, and 'service units' to denote the OTC, UAS or URNU as distinct branches of the armed forces. The term Royal Navy rather than Naval Service is used, whilst recognising that the latter is often used in official defence documentation to include both the Royal Navy and the Royal Marines. The Royal Marines does not have a separate university service unit.

We use the term Commanding Officer and abbreviation CO to refer to commanding officers across the three service units, although we recognise that in the Royal Air Force the term Officer Commanding is more commonly used for the individual charged with responsibility for individual UASs.

We use the term Reserves in the text, but have kept to original wording when quoting individuals who have talked about the Territorial Army, to reflect the name of the organisation referred to at the time of data collection.

# Acknowledgements

This research was funded by the UK Economic and Social Research Council (ESRC) through grant reference ES/JO23868/1.

The origins of this project lie in conversations with members of the Northumbrian Universities Military Education Committee (NUMEC), about the possibilities of conducting research on the value of the OTC, UAS and URNU experience for students, and for wider social understanding of military issues. We are very grateful for the support received from NUMEC in the earliest stages of this research, and in particular for the advice and input of Air Commodore Ian Forster OBE RAF (Rtd), Air Vice-Marshal Sandy Hunter CBE AFC MA LLB DL (Rtd), Captain Professor Iain Moffat RD DL RNR (Rtd) and Professor Trevor Page FREng. NUMEC and the Council of Military Education Committees (COMEC) have proved effective sounding-boards for the research as it has progressed, and we would like to thank the members of these two organisations for their input. The project steering group, a small group of 'critical friends' providing advice and constructive input, was established in 2013. Membership included representatives from the Ministry of Defence, Royal Military Academy Sandhurst, RAF College Cranwell, Britannia Royal Naval College, COMEC, NUMEC and the Newcastle University Careers Service. Our steering group members gave generously of their time and expertise, and the research benefitted greatly from their input. The analysis contained in this book reflects the views of the authors and not necessarily those of the project steering group, their parent organisations or the individuals listed above.

This book draws on data collected from a very large number of people involved in various ways, both in the present and past, with the USUs. In work of this nature, interviewees and questionnaire respondents are, necessarily, anonymous. We would like to thank all our research participants for their input to the project, not least in terms of their time. The richness of the data collected is an accurate reflection of the care and consideration with which our interviewees and respondents patiently answered our questions. Again, the conclusions drawn remain our own, and do not necessarily reflect the views of individuals or organisations consulted for the purposes of data collection.

We would like to thank our colleagues at Newcastle University, particularly members of the Power, Space, Politics research cluster in Geography, our colleagues across the School of Geography, Politics & Sociology, and members of the university's Military, War and Security Research Group, for sharing their views and observations about our research. The research reported here was undertaken in a wider academic context of ongoing conversations about the nature and politics of research on militarism, militarisation and military forces. Newcastle University has emerged as a leading centre in the UK for critical scholarship on these issues; we are proud to be part of that intellectual movement within the social sciences, and are thankful to our colleagues at Newcastle University and further afield for providing us with the best possible mix of support and challenge as we proceeded with this research.

Finally, our thanks go to Alison Copeland, Joe Painter, Ralph Parlour and Billy Williams for assistance and advice on data analysis and presentation, to Heather McGrath and Lasairfhíona Swift for research administrative support, to two anonymous academic peer reviewers for comments on the manuscript, and to Tim Wakeford, Sam Hall and Paige MacKay at Ubiquity Press for their input in the production of this book.

CHAPTER 1

# The University Armed Service Units: Background and Context

This chapter introduces the university armed service units (hereafter USUs), and the reasons for studying them. It outlines the key features and missions of the three service units, the Officer Training Corps (OTC), the University Air Squadrons (UAS) and the University Royal Naval Units (URNU), and introduces the Military Education Committees (MEC). It provides an overview of the higher education sector in the UK, the context in which USU participation takes place. The chapter concludes with an assessment of the key policy issues currently facing the USUs, and outlines the structure of the book.

## 1.1 Introducing the university armed service units

### 1.1.1. What are the university armed service units?

The USUs comprise the OTC, UAS and URNU.[1] These units are overseen and managed through their respective parent services, the British Army, the Royal Air Force (RAF) and the Royal Navy, and funded through public expenditure via the defence budget. The USUs exist to provide military training and an experience of military life to students attending UK universities. Participation is open to British and Commonwealth students, and is selective, subject to specific medical and physical criteria. Participation is paid, but does not involve payment or subsidy of university tuition fees. Students who join a USU do

---
[1] See Note on terminology.

**How to cite this book chapter:**
Woodward, R, Jenkings, K N and Williams, A J. 2015. *The Value of the University Armed Service Units.* Pp. 1–30. London: Ubiquity Press. DOI: http://dx.doi.org/10.5334/baq.a. License: CC-BY 4.0.

so voluntarily, can leave at any time, and are under no obligation to join the armed forces when they graduate from university. Participation takes the form of weekly attendance at drill nights, and activities undertaken at weekends and during university vacations, which involve a combination of specific training activities (including land-based exercises for the OTC, flying for the UAS or ship-based activities for the URNU) and adventurous training opportunities in the UK and overseas. Although encouraged, it is not a requirement that cadets attend every drill night or weekend, though many do.

As of 1 April 2014, Ministry of Defence (MoD) statistics record a total of 6,370 students enlisted across the USUs: 4,420 in the OTC, 1,090 in the UAS and 850 in the URNU.[2] To put this into context, the total UK student population in the academic year 2013–14 (the most recent figures available) was 2,299,355, comprising 1,759,915 students registered for undergraduate degrees, commonly Bachelor of Arts (BA) and Bachelor of Sciences (BSc), and 539,440 students registered for postgraduate degrees at a Masters of Arts or Sciences level (MA, MSc) or for a Masters or Doctor of Philosophy degree (MPhil, PhD).[3] USU members comprise around 0.28% of the total UK student population, a very small percentage of this group.

USU members are enlisted as Category B reservists but cannot be mobilised for active service. They are considered as part of the total strength of the UK armed forces in some iterations of MoD statistics, although not all. As of September 2014, the total strength of the UK armed forces, including trained and untrained, Regular, full-time and Reserve personnel (but excluding OTC, UAS and URNU participants), was 195,980 (120,800 for the British Army, 37,170 for the RAF and 38,020 for the Royal Navy).[4] As with the UK student population, USU members are a minority organisation, one-thirtieth the size of the full UK armed forces, although this proportion is likely to have grown over the past decade with the overall reduction in the size of the armed forces.

### 1.1.2. Why study the university armed service units?

It could be argued, given the relatively small size of the USUs relative to both the UK student population and the UK armed forces, that this is a minor, possibly even insignificant organisation in terms of the wider interests of the defence and higher education sectors, and wider debates about student experience and

---

[2] **Ministry of Defence**. (2014). *TSP7 UK Reserve Forces and Cadets*. Retrieved from https://www.gov.uk/government/uploads/system/uploads/attachment_data/file/314795/uk_reserve_force_cadets_2014.pdf

[3] **Higher Education Statistics Agency**. (2015). *Statistical First Release 210*. Retrieved from https://www.hesa.ac.uk/stats

[4] **Ministry of Defence**. (2014). *UK Armed Forces Quarterly Personnel Report (1st October 2014)*. Retrieved from https://www.gov.uk/government/uploads/system/uploads/attachment_data/file/373115/af-quarterly_personnel_report_oct14.pdf

student employability. We disagree. The USUs are significant and merit scrutiny for the following reasons.

First, the UK armed forces are undergoing a substantial programme of restructuring in the wake of the 2010 Strategic Defence and Security Review and the Future Force 2020 programme, and anticipate further changes with the anticipated 2015 Strategic Defence and Security Review, which is under development at time of writing.[5] The longer history of the units suggests that their planning, organisation and strategic development has always been closely tied to wider UK defence structures and objectives. Given current debates about the size, structure and function of the UK armed forces under conditions of tight public expenditure controls, and given that the USUs are part of the wider UK defence picture in that they are maintained by the three parent armed forces, there is a case for close scrutiny of the value of the USUs as part of the wider debate on the future structure of the armed forces.

Second, knowledge and understanding of the role and function of USUs, and of the nature of the USU experience for participants, is uneven within the armed forces. Those with experience of USU command, or indeed personal experience of membership as students themselves, will be alert to the existence and function of the units. There is reason to believe that within the wider defence community in the armed forces and MoD, knowledge of the units, what they do and what their value might be, is not as widely shared. This book is our contribution to expanding the knowledge base within that defence community.

Third, the UK higher education sector is also undergoing a period of quite distinct structural change. Specific initiatives include the recent introduction of payment of full tuition fees by undergraduate students (up to £9,000 per year for full-time study, at time of writing), coupled with the development of broader moves within higher education to make explicit the value of graduate-level skills and the demonstrable employability of graduates. Such developments have in turn introduced a greater awareness across the sector and within higher education institutions of the need to make explicit the value of a university degree. This broader debate about the value of a degree necessarily needs to include informed understanding about the full range of activities undertaken by students, and the benefits that these activities may bring to their employability. So whilst USU participation may be a minority pursuit within the UK student body, there is evidence that an understanding of the USUs brings an

---

[5] For a summary of changes initiated and proposed under the Future Force 2020 plans, see https://www.gov.uk/government/uploads/system/uploads/attachment_data/file/62487/Factsheet5-Future-Force-2020.pdf. A key element of the Future Force 2020 plans is a restructuring of the Reserves, including a significant increase in the size of the Army Reserve (formerly the Territorial Army) to a trained strength of 30,000, 1,800 for the Royal Auxiliary Air Force and 3,100 for the Maritime Reserves. These proposals were set out in the Government White Paper: **Ministry of Defence.** (2013). *Reserves in the Future Force 2020: Valuable and Valued* (Cm 8655). Retrieved from https://www.gov.uk/government/uploads/system/uploads/attachment_data/file/210470/Cm8655-web_FINAL.pdf

additional and potentially valuable contribution to that wider debate. We are also alert to the potential utility of this book in raising awareness of the existence and core functions of the units within the higher education sector more generally, where informed knowledge amongst academics, administrators and students is unevenly distributed, and sometimes non-existent.

Fourth, despite their long history (the OTCs were first established in 1908, and some units trace their origins back over much longer timescales) there have, to date, been very few published accounts of the units.[6] This book is an attempt to fill that gap. It is also worth noting that for those involved with USU organisation and administration, and for their participants, the units can be a very significant element of their university or military career. Furthermore, given the long history of some units, and the continual throughput of students within the units over time, what looks initially to be a pursuit undertaken by a very small proportion of students is in fact a far more widely-shared experience than per annum participation numbers initially suggest. Therefore this book provides both a knowledge base about the current state of a much older organisation, and a summary of the units and the unit experience for a wider interested readership who may have previous or current experience of unit participation.

Finally, there are any number of anecdotal understandings about the units which have informed the genesis of the research underpinning this book, and which merit investigation in their own right. These include: questions about the reach (or otherwise) of the units across the higher education sector, including the question of the disproportionate inclusion of students from elite or Russell Group universities; considerations of whether USU graduates have a greater chance of success in the graduate labour market; interest in the significance of the USU experience for those seeking careers in the armed forces; questions about employer awareness of the units; what the experience may bring to graduates; questions about the influence of USU graduates in civil society as they pursue non-military careers after university; questions about whether USU participation is, could or should be included in mechanisms formally recording student activities whilst at university and questions about whether the USUs constitute a form of militarisation of universities.

This book does not constitute a formal assessment of the USUs for strategic defence planning purposes, and has been produced independently of the UK MoD (which funds the USUs) and the three armed forces. Neither does it constitute a formal evaluation of the skills and employability aspects of USUs for the purposes of university audit, or an assessment of the USUs for the purposes of

---

[6] See **Strachan, H**. (1976). *The History of the Cambridge University Officer Training Corps.* Tunbridge Wells: Midas Books; **Mileham, P**. (2012). *University Service Units: What are they really for?* (Council of Military Education Committees of United Kingdom Universities occasional paper no. 1). Retrieved from http://www.comec.org.uk/documents/occasional_paper_no_1_small_file1.pdf; **Harrop, M. D.** (2013).*The University Air Squadrons: A valuable organisation and an organisation that adds value?* (Unpublished MSc thesis, Cranfield University, Bedford).

student-centred organisations. However, it has been written with a view to its potential utility in informing current debates on the future role, purpose, impact and organisation of the units across the defence and higher education sectors.

## 1.2 The university armed service units missions

### 1.2.1. The Officer Training Corps

'The mission of the UOTC is to develop the leadership potential of selected university students and raise awareness of the Army ethos. Each UOTC is an independent [unit] with its own cap badge, customs and traditions. Members of the UOTC are paid to participate in training activities, but have no obligation to join the Armed Forces when they leave.'[7]

The OTC is the largest of the three service units, with a membership of 4,420 in 2014. The size of the OTC nationally has remained fairly constant over the past decade.[8] There are 18 units in total; some include multiple sub-units to account for geographical distance between units. One of the 18 (Yorkshire) is designated an Officer Training Regiment (OTR) following proposals from an internal OTC review (the Roskelly Study) in 2010. Originally structured as two separate OTCs, the Yorkshire OTR was stood up in 2011, combining Sheffield and Leeds OTCs.[9] The units and their participating universities are listed in Table 1.1. OTC units range in size from around 120 to over 400 actual strength.

As Table 1.1 shows, all OTCs take students from a number of different universities. Unit catchment areas can be geographically large, and some OTCs have local detachments to facilitate participation from geographically distant universities within a region or across federal universities (for example, London and Wales OTCs). It is also significant that each unit takes students, potentially at least, from universities across the range of providers in the higher education sector (see 1.3.2. below). So whilst all units offer a broadly similar training programme, they do so to a potentially diverse range of students. Units will not necessarily have, in any one year, students from all the universities listed in Table 1.1. Also, access to units by students from different universities will be uneven in terms of travelling distance.

---

[7] **Ministry of Defence.** (2014). *TSP7 UK Reserve Forces and Cadets*, pp. 28. Retrieved from https://www.gov.uk/government/uploads/system/uploads/attachment_data/file/314795/uk_reserve_force_cadets_2014.pdf. Omission of 'unit' in original text.

[8] **Ministry of Defence.** (2014). *TSP7 UK Reserve Forces and Cadets* gives figures of 4,700 for 2004, 4,140 for 2010, 4,120 for 2011, 4,360 for 2012 and 4,400 for 2013, with the cautionary note that a discontinuity in the time series means that figures for the pre-2012 period include support and training staff, and from 2012 includes students only.

[9] Although a second OTR for the North West of England was proposed through the merger of the Manchester & Salford and Liverpool OTCs, these two OTCs remain as distinct units.

| Unit name | Participating Universities[1] |
|---|---|
| Aberdeen UOTC | University of Aberdeen<br>Robert Gordon University |
| Birmingham UOTC | Aston University<br>Birmingham City University<br>University of Birmingham<br>Coventry University<br>Harper Adams University<br>Keele University<br>Newman University<br>Staffordshire University<br>University College Birmingham<br>University of Warwick<br>University of Wolverhampton<br>University of Worcester |
| Bristol UOTC | University of Bath<br>Bath Spa University<br>University of Bristol<br>University of the West of England |
| Cambridge UOTC | Anglia Ruskin University<br>University of Cambridge<br>University of East Anglia<br>University of Essex<br>University of Hertfordshire<br>Bedfordshire University |
| City of Edinburgh UOTC | University of Edinburgh<br>Edinburgh Napier University<br>Heriot-Watt University<br>Queen Margaret University |
| East Midlands UOTC | De Montfort University<br>University of Derby<br>University of Leicester<br>University of Lincoln<br>Loughborough University<br>University of Northampton<br>University of Nottingham<br>Nottingham Trent University |
| Exeter UOTC | University of Exeter<br>Peninsular College of Medicine and Dentistry (Plymouth)<br>Plymouth University<br>University of St Mark and St John Plymouth |

| Unit name | Participating Universities[1] |
|---|---|
| Glasgow & Strathclyde UOTC | University of Glasgow<br>Glasgow Caledonian University<br>University of Strathclyde<br>University of the West of Scotland |
| Liverpool UOTC (includes both Liverpool and Lancaster detachments) | University of Chester (Warrington campus)<br>University of Cumbria<br>Edge Hill University<br>Lancaster University<br>University of Liverpool<br>Liverpool Hope University<br>Liverpool John Moores University<br>University of Central Lancashire |
| Manchester & Salford UOTC | University of Manchester<br>Manchester Metropolitan University<br>University of Salford |
| Northumbrian UOTC | Durham University<br>Newcastle University<br>Northumbria University<br>University of Sunderland<br>Teesside University |
| Oxford UOTC | University of Buckingham<br>Cranfield University<br>University of Gloucestershire<br>University of Oxford<br>Oxford Brookes University<br>University of Reading<br>Royal Agricultural University Cirencester |
| Queen's UOTC (Belfast) | College of Agriculture Food and Rural Enterprise<br>Queen's University Belfast<br>University of Ulster |
| Southampton UOTC (includes Brighton detachment) | Bournemouth University<br>University of Brighton<br>University of Chichester<br>University of Portsmouth<br>University of Southampton<br>Southampton Solent University<br>University of Sussex<br>University of Winchester |
| Tayforth UOTC (detachments in Dundee, St Andrews and Stirling) | Abertay University<br>University of Dundee<br>University of St Andrews<br>University of Stirling |

*(Continued)*

| Unit name | Participating Universities[1] |
|---|---|
| University of London UOTC (includes Canterbury Company) | Includes the colleges and institutes of the federal University of London[2] Brunel University Canterbury Christchurch University City University London University of Greenwich University of Kent Kingston University St Mary's University |
| Wales UOTC (Detachments in Aberystwyth, Bangor, Cardiff, Swansea and Wrexham) | Aberystwyth University Bangor University Cardiff University Cardiff Metropolitan University University of Chester (Chester campus) Glyndŵr University Swansea University University of South Wales University of Wales Trinity Saint David |
| Yorkshire Officer Training Regiment (detachments in Leeds, Sheffield and York) | University of Huddersfield University of Hull University of Leeds Leeds Beckett University University of Sheffield Sheffield Hallam University University of York York St John University |

**Table 1.1:** Officer Training Corps units and participating universities.

[1] The university titles given are the trading names of the institutions concerned as of February 2014.
[2] Birkbeck, University of London; Courtauld Institute of Art; Goldsmiths, University of London; Heythrop College; The Institute of Cancer Research; King's College London; London Business School; London School of Economics and Political Science; London School of Hygiene and Tropical Medicine; Queen Mary University of London; Royal Academy of Music; The Royal Central School of Speech and Drama; Royal Holloway, University of London; Royal Veterinary College; St George's, University of London; School of Oriental and African Studies (SOAS), University of London; University College London; School of Advanced Study, University of London.

OTCs follow a standardised training syllabus laid down by the Royal Military Academy Sandhurst. In year one, students complete basic training (known as MOD1) which covers key military skills including drill, map reading and field craft, as well as weapons handling, camouflage techniques and first aid training, and includes a number of exercises and often an extended training visit to a British Army base. In year two, students progress to leadership training (known as MOD2) which focuses on learning to manage small groups of officer cadets, organising and planning battlefield tactics, giving orders and debriefing after exercises. Both MOD1 and MOD2 are assessed and students are required to pass a series of written and practical exercises in order to progress satisfactorily. In year three, students can be chosen to take on additional responsibilities as senior cadets, leading platoons and providing some training for more junior students.[10]

### 1.2.2. University Air Squadrons

'University Air Squadrons (UAS) offer flying training to undergraduates and a chance to experience life in the Royal Air Force. Undergraduates are paid for any training activities they take part in, however there is no obligation to sign up to the Royal Air Force upon graduation.'[11]

In 2014, 1,090 students were enlisted into UAS units, and numbers have been broadly stable over the previous decade.[12] There are 14 UAS units in the UK. Potentially, students from any of the universities listed below can participate in a UAS unit, although geographical distance and ease of access may be a factor shaping participation. Each UAS takes around 70 students. Table 1.2 lists the units, their locations for air training and participating universities.

Although there are fewer UAS than OTC units, they are distributed across the full extent of the UK, with 2 squadrons operating in Scotland, 1 in Wales and 11 in England. Of course, access to an airfield is not as even as the location of universities, and thus in some cases, UAS are located in cities that are tens of miles from their home airfield (London UAS for example). However, all UAS offer a weekly meeting, usually at a location close to their home city, with weekend visits to the airfield that houses their aircraft. The UAS fly Grob training aircraft and students can participate in flight training, although this element has been reduced in recent years and students are no longer streamed as air or ground trade officer cadets. This means that all UAS participants can receive flying training, although limits in the availability of suitably qualified personnel to support UAS flying instruction has limited the amount of flying each student is able to undertake to 10 hours per year.[13]

---

[10] For further details, see the UOTC Military Training information on the British Army website, available at: http://www.army.mod.uk/UOTC/32104.aspx
[11] **Ministry of Defence.** (2014). *TSP7 UK Reserve Forces and Cadets*, pp.28. Retrieved from https://www.gov.uk/government/uploads/system/uploads/attachment_data/file/314795/uk_reserve_force_cadets_2014.pdf
[12] **Ministry of Defence.** (2014). *TSP7 UK Reserve Forces and Cadets* gives figures of 1,030 for 2004, 1,200 for 2010, 1,080 for 2011, 1,100 for 2012 and 1,110 for 2013.
[13] Details on the University Air Squadrons are available at: http://www.raf.mod.uk/universityairsquadrons/aboutus/

| University Air Squadron | Training location | Participating Universities |
|---|---|---|
| Birmingham UAS | RAF Cosford | Aston University<br>University of Birmingham<br>Birmingham City University<br>Coventry University<br>Keele University<br>Staffordshire University<br>Warwick University<br>University of Wolverhampton |
| Bristol UAS | Colerne Airfield | University of Bristol<br>University of the West of England<br>University of Bath<br>University of Exeter<br>University of Plymouth |
| Cambridge UAS | RAF Wyton | Cambridge University<br>Anglia Ruskin University<br>University of Essex<br>University of East Anglia |
| East Midlands UAS | RAF Cranwell | Nottingham University<br>Nottingham Trent University<br>Loughborough University<br>Leicester University<br>De Montfort University<br>University of Lincoln |
| East of Scotland UAS | RAF Leuchars | The University of Aberdeen<br>University of Abertay [Dundee]<br>Edinburgh Napier University<br>University of Edinburgh<br>Heriot Watt University<br>Robert Gordon University<br>The University of St Andrews<br>The University of Dundee<br>Queen Margaret University |
| Glasgow & Strathclyde UAS | Prestwick Airport | Glasgow University<br>University of Strathclyde<br>University of Stirling<br>Glasgow School of Art<br>Glasgow Caledonian University<br>University of the West of Scotland |
| Liverpool UAS | RAF Woodvale | Bangor University<br>University of Chester<br>University of Cumbria<br>Edge Hill University<br>Glyndwr University |

| University Air Squadron | Training location | Participating Universities |
|---|---|---|
|  |  | Lancaster University<br>University of Central Lancashire<br>University of Liverpool<br>Liverpool John Moores University<br>Liverpool Hope University |
| London UAS | RAF Wittering | University of London (all colleges)<br>University of Kent |
| Manchester & Salford UAS | RAF Woodvale | University of Manchester<br>Manchester Metropolitan University<br>Queen's University Belfast<br>Salford University |
| Northumbrian UAS | RAF Leeming | Durham University<br>Newcastle University<br>Northumbria University<br>Sunderland University<br>Teesside University |
| Oxford UAS | RAF Benson | Oxford University<br>Oxford Brookes University<br>Reading University |
| Southampton UAS | MoD Boscombe Down | Bournemouth University<br>Portsmouth University<br>Southampton University<br>Southampton Solent University |
| Yorkshire UAS | RAF Linton-on-Ouse | Leeds College of Music<br>Leeds Metropolitan University<br>Sheffield Hallam University<br>University of Bradford<br>University of Huddersfield<br>The University of Hull<br>University of Leeds<br>University of Sheffield<br>University of York<br>York St John University |
| Wales UAS | MoD St Athan | Aberystwyth University<br>Cardiff University<br>Cardiff Metropolitan University<br>University of Wales Trinity Saint David<br>University of South Wales |

**Table 1.2:** University Air Squadrons, training locations and participating universities.

The first UAS were set up in 1925 to provide initial flying training for would-be RAF pilots.[14] Whilst this remit still exists to an extent, the range of activities offered by UAS now extends to cover not only basic military training and procedures and RAF-specific training relating to both aircrew and ground-based roles, but also includes adventurous training and a range of sporting activities, as well as annual camps and opportunities to visit RAF stations. Officer cadets in the UAS are officially members of the RAF volunteer reserve, but are under no obligation to join the RAF, nor can they be deployed during their university careers.

### 1.2.3. University Royal Naval Units (URNU)

'The aim of the URNU is to provide an insight into Naval life for undergraduates. Each URNU has land based facilities close to the university plus a dedicated training vessel. Members get paid for any training activities they participate in, however there is no obligation to join the Naval Service upon graduation.'[15]

There are 14 University Royal Naval Units, with 850 enlisted students in 2014.[16] Although historic figures are unavailable, anecdotal evidence suggests that, as with the OTC and UAS, total URNU strength has remained stable over the past decade. Historically, the URNU has not seen recruitment to the Royal Navy as part of its core mission, although increasingly the development of awareness of opportunities within the Royal Navy has become more significant.

The URNU train on dedicated vessels, P2000 class fast inshore patrol craft, and the URNU ships are counted as part of the Royal Navy's total fleet strength, comprising 14 out of a total of 66 ships in service in the Royal Navy in 2013.[17] As the Royal Navy's website notes, the mission of these ships is:

'To provide high-quality sea training experiences to undergraduates from universities, developing seamanship, teambuilding and leadership skills in a maritime environment. These ships also support the Fleet in

---

[14] Details on the history of the University Air Squadrons are available at: http://www.raf.mod.uk/universityairsquadrons/history/index.cfm

[15] **Ministry of Defence.** (2014). *TSP7 UK Reserve Forces and Cadets*, pp.27. Retrieved from https://www.gov.uk/government/uploads/system/uploads/attachment_data/file/314795/uk_reserve_force_cadets_2014.pdf

[16] **Ministry of Defence.** (2014) *TSP7 UK Reserve Forces and Cadets*. Retrieved from https://www.gov.uk/government/uploads/system/uploads/attachment_data/file/314795/uk_reserve_force_cadets_2014.pdf. Historic figures for URNU strength are not available in this publication.

[17] **Ministry of Defence.** (2014). *UK Defence Statistics Compendium 2014*. Retrieved from https://www.gov.uk/government/uploads/system/uploads/attachment_data/file/378301/2014_UKDS.pdf

a range of tasking around the UK and European waters, showing the White Ensign in places that larger vessels cannot reach.'[18]

As with the OTC and UAS, the potential number of universities in the catchment area for each URNU is large, but as with the UAS, in practice the feasibility of access to one of the 14 units will be a factor shaping recruitment in some regions; although physical distance from the sea is not an issue, as URNU weekly training nights are held at locations near to host universities, except for access to their ship. Each URNU has about 60 members. Table 1.3 lists the URNU units, ship and shore base and participating universities.

URNUs are located across the UK, with a similar distribution to the UAS, with 1 unit in Wales, 2 in Scotland and 11 in England. Training for URNU members focuses on basic military drill, skills and procedures both on land and at sea, via the Royal Navy Patrol boats that are assigned to each unit. Until recently the officer commanding each URNU also commanded its allocated vessel, but recent staffing changes have led to this command being split, with a dedicated ship commander now being assigned. This doubling of command opportunities also enables a wider range of staff to be allocated to the shore command role, offering students the opportunity to work with a broader contingent of Naval Service staff.

URNU members are offered the opportunity for deployment at sea, to develop their navigation and seamanship skills on their assigned ship at weekends and during most university vacations. In addition to military-specific training and activities, as with their OTC and UAS colleagues, URNU members are given opportunities to undertake sporting and adventurous training activities, and there is a formalized social calendar, including Trafalgar Night celebrations. UNRU members hold the rank of honorary Midshipmen in the Royal Navy Reserve, but have no commitment to serve and cannot be called upon for deployments.

### 1.2.4. Military Education Committees

OTC, UAS and URNU, with some small discrepancies, recruit from the same universities within their geographical area. In 1908 when the first OTC was established under the Haldane Reforms[19] to promote military skills and supply officers to the British Army, particularly in wartime, it was agreed that some form of oversight and conduit for communication between the units and their host universities was required, and to do this the MECs were established.

---

[18] See http://www.royalnavy.mod.uk/our-organisation/the-fighting-arms/surface-fleet/patrol/archer-class/hms-ranger

[19] **Strachan, H.** (1976). *The History of the Cambridge University Officer Training Corps.* Tunbridge Wells: Midas Books

| University Royal Naval Unit | Ship and base | Participating universities |
|---|---|---|
| Birmingham URNU | **HMS Exploit** HMS Forward, Birmingham's Royal Naval Reserve Training Centre. | Aston University University of Birmingham Birmingham City University Coventry University University of Leicester Loughborough University De Montfort University Newman University Nottingham University Warwick University |
| Bristol URNU | **HMS Dasher** HMS Flying Fox, Bristol's Royal Naval Reserve Training Centre | Bath University Bristol University University of the West of England |
| Cambridge URNU | **HMS Trumpeter** Cambridge University Royal Naval Unit, Chaucer Road, Cambridge | Cambridge University University of East Anglia Anglia Ruskin University |
| Edinburgh URNU | **HMS Archer** Edinburgh Universities Royal Naval Unit, Hepburn House, East Claremount Street, Edinburgh | University of Edinburgh Edinburgh Napier University Heriot-Watt University Queen Margaret University |
| Glasgow and Strathclyde URNU | **HMS Pursuer** HM Naval Base Clyde and University Place, Glasgow | Glasgow University University of Strathclyde Stirling University Glasgow Caledonian University University of the West of Scotland |
| Liverpool URNU | **HMS Charger** RNHQ Merseyside, East Brunswick Dock, Sefton Street, Liverpool | Lancaster University Liverpool University Liverpool John Moores University Liverpool Hope University |
| London URNU | **HMS Puncher** HMS President St Katharine's Way London | All London Colleges |
| Manchester and Salford UNRU | **HMS Biter** Crawford House, The Precinct Centre, Oxford Road, Manchester | Manchester University Manchester Metropolitan University Salford University University of Central Lancashire |

| University Royal Naval Unit | Ship and base | Participating universities |
|---|---|---|
| Northumbrian URNU | **HMS Example** HMS Calliope, South Road, Gateshead | Durham University Newcastle University Northumbria University Sunderland University Teesside University |
| Oxford URNU | **HMS Smiter** Falklands House Oxpens Road Oxford | Oxford University Oxford Brookes University Reading University |
| Southampton URNU | **HMS Blazer** National Oceanography Centre Waterfront Campus European Way Southampton | Southampton University Portsmouth University Southampton Solent University |
| Sussex URNU | **HMS Ranger** University of Sussex, Falmer, Brighton | Sussex University Brighton University |
| Wales URNU | **HMS Express** HMS Cambria, Sully, South Glamorgan and Penarth Marina, Cardiff Bay | Cardiff University University of South Wales Swansea University |
| Yorkshire URNU | **HMS Explorer** 22 Pearson Park, Hull | Leeds University Hull University Sheffield University Sheffield Hallam University |

**Table 1.3:** University Royal Naval Units, ship and base, and participating universities.

Currently there are 20 MECs: 1 in Wales, 1 in Northern Ireland, 4 in Scotland and 14 in England. Not all MECs have a full complement of USU units attached to them (Queens Belfast MEC, for example only has responsibility for an OTC). Table 1.4 shows the current provision of MECs and the units they oversee.

The 20 MECs commonly represent combined university interests in a locality or region on one committee.[20] They vary considerably in terms of their

---

[20] The full list of Military Education Committees (there are 20 in total) can be found on the Council of Military Education Committees website at: http://www.comec.org.uk/military_education_committees

| MEC | Associated USU units | Participating universities |
|---|---|---|
| Bristol MEC | Bristol OTC<br>Bristol UAS<br>Bristol URNU | Bath University<br>Bristol University<br>University of the West of England<br>University of Plymouth |
| Cambridge MEC | Cambridge OTC<br>Cambridge UAS<br>Cambridge URNU | Cambridge University<br>University of East Anglia<br>Anglia Ruskin University<br>Bedfordshire University<br>Essex University<br>Hertfordshire University |
| East Midlands MEC | East Midlands OTC<br>East Midlands UAS | De Montfort University<br>Leicester University<br>Loughborough University<br>Nottingham Trent University<br>Nottingham University<br>University of Derby<br>University of Lincoln<br>University of Northampton |
| Edinburgh MEC | Edinburgh OTC<br>East of Scotland UAS<br>Edinburgh URNU | University of Edinburgh<br>Edinburgh Napier University<br>Heriot-Watt University<br>Queen Margaret University |
| Glasgow & Strathclyde MEC | Glasgow & Strathclyde OTC<br>Glasgow & Strathclyde UAS<br>Glasgow & Strathclyde URNU | Glasgow Caledonian University<br>Glasgow School of Art<br>Glasgow University<br>Stirling University<br>University of Strathclyde<br>University of the West of Scotland |
| Leeds MEC | Yorkshire URNU<br>Yorkshire OTR<br>Yorkshire UAS | Hull University<br>Leeds College of Music<br>Leeds Metropolitan University<br>Leeds University<br>The University of Bradford<br>The University of Huddersfield<br>The University of Leeds<br>The University of York<br>York St John University |
| London MEC | London OTC<br>London UAS<br>London URNU | All London colleges[1] |

| MEC | Associated USU units | Participating universities |
|---|---|---|
| Manchester and Salford MEC | Manchester and Salford OTC<br>Manchester and Salford UAS | Manchester Metropolitan University<br>Queen's University Belfast<br>Salford University<br>The University of Manchester<br>University of Central Lancashire |
| MEC for Wales | Wales OTC<br>Wales UAS<br>Wales URNU | Aberystwyth University<br>Bangor University<br>Cardiff University<br>Glyndŵr University<br>Swansea Metropolitan University<br>Swansea University<br>Trinity College Carmarthen<br>University of Chester<br>Cardiff Metropolitan University<br>University of Wales Trinity Saint David<br>University of South Wales |
| Northumbrian Universities MEC | Northumbrian OTC<br>Northumbrian UAS<br>Northumbrian URNU | Durham University<br>Newcastle University<br>Northumbria University<br>Sunderland University<br>Teesside University |
| Oxford University – Delegacy of Military Instruction | Oxford OTC<br>Oxford UAS<br>Oxford URNU | Oxford University<br>Oxford Brookes University<br>Reading University<br>Royal Agricultural College<br>University of Gloucestershire |
| Queen's Belfast MEC | Belfast OTC | Queen's University Belfast<br>University of Ulster<br>Stranmillis University College |
| Sheffield MEC | Yorkshire OTR<br>Yorkshire UAS<br>Yorkshire URNU | Sheffield Hallam University<br>Sheffield University |
| Southampton MEC | Southampton OTC<br>Southampton UAS<br>Southampton URNU | Bournemouth University<br>Portsmouth University<br>Southampton Solent University<br>Southampton University<br>The University of Winchester |
| Universities of Sussex and Brighton Services Liaison Joint Committee | Sussex URNU | Sussex University<br>Brighton University |

*(Continued)*

| MEC | Associated USU units | Participating universities |
|---|---|---|
| Tayforth MEC | Tayforth OTC | University of Abertay Dundee<br>University of Dundee<br>University of St Andrews<br>University of Stirling |
| Universities of Aberdeen MEC | Aberdeen OTC | Aberdeen University<br>Robert Gordon University |
| University of Exeter MEC | Bristol OTC<br>Bristol UAS<br>Bristol URNU | Exeter University |
| University of Liverpool MEC | Liverpool OTC<br>Liverpool UAS<br>Liverpool URNU | Bangor University<br>Edge Hill University<br>Glyndwr University<br>Lancaster University<br>Liverpool Hope University<br>Liverpool John Moores University<br>Liverpool University<br>University of Central Lancashire<br>University of Chester<br>University of Cumbria |
| West Midlands MEC | Birmingham OTC<br>Birmingham UAS<br>Birmingham URNU | Aston University<br>Birmingham City University<br>Coventry University<br>De Montfort University<br>Harper Adams University College<br>Keele University<br>Loughborough University<br>Newman University College<br>Nottingham University<br>Staffordshire University<br>University of Birmingham<br>University of Leicester<br>University of Wolverhampton<br>University of Worcester<br>Warwick University |

**Table 1.4:** Military Education Committees, associated USUs and participating universities.

[3] Birkbeck, University of London; Courtauld Institute of Art; Goldsmiths, University of London; Heythrop College; The Institute of Cancer Research; King's College London; London Business School; London School of Economics and Political Science; London School of Hygiene and Tropical Medicine; Queen Mary University of London; Royal Academy of Music; The Royal Central School of Speech and Drama; Royal Holloway, University of London; Royal Veterinary College; St George's, University of London; School of Oriental and African Studies (SOAS), University of London; University College London; School of Advanced Study, University of London.

statutory or non-statutory status within university governance structures, and vary also in terms of their membership. We know of a number of MECs where representation from some member universities is limited, and others with enthusiastic representation from across participating universities. All have parent service representation on them, usually via the commanding officers (COs) of the local OTC, UAS or UNRU. Where a Defence Technical Officer and Engineer Entry Scheme (DTOEES) unit is hosted by a university, that unit's CO may also be a member of the MEC.[21] University representation may include senior administrative and academic executive staff, and may also include individual administrative and academic staff with an interest in military issues. MECs may be serviced by university central administration, or run on a more informal basis without formal resourcing. A national Council of Military Education Committees (COMEC) oversees and coordinates collective MEC activities, and includes senior representation from the MoD and the three armed forces.[22]

## 1.3 The UK higher education sector

The university armed service units draw their participating students from across the UK higher education sector. As already noted, the total UK student population (2013–14) was 2,299,355 including both full and part-time students, comprising 1,759,915 students registered for undergraduate degrees, and 539,440 postgraduates.[23] The two features of the higher education sector most pertinent to the context for USUs are participation rates in higher education, and the diversity of provision across the sector.

### 1.3.1. Rates of higher education participation

Changes in government policies have encouraged wider participation in higher education, reflecting both changing social attitudes towards higher education and structural changes in the UK economy necessitating a higher proportion of the workforce to be educated at graduate level. This, combined with the expansion of the sector following reconfiguration of former polytechnic institutions after 1992, has led to a significant increase over the past two decades in the proportion of UK Home students (defined as those who meet UK residency qualifications for payment of tuition fees at the Home student rate) gaining a university-level qualification. Although statistics accurately reflecting rates

---

[21] Details on the Defence Technical Officer and Engineer Entrance Scheme are available at: http://www.da.mod.uk/dtoees
[22] Details on the Council of Military Education Committees are available at: http://www.comec.org.uk/home
[23] **Higher Education Statistics Agency.** (2015). *Statistical First Release 210.* Retrieved from https://www.hesa.ac.uk/stats

of higher education participation are difficult to produce with any accuracy, the Department for Business Innovation and Skills (DBIS), which has responsibility for higher education in England, estimate that higher education participation rates for 17–30-year-old English-domiciled first-time participants attending UK institutions in 2012–13 was 43%.[24] The Higher Education Funding Council for England has estimated that the young participation rate (those aged 18 and 19) has risen from 30% in the mid-1990s to 36% at the end of the 2000s.[25] What is significant for our purposes here is the point that participation in higher education has increased over the last three decades, and has changed fundamentally and dramatically over the post-war period. A university education is no longer the preserve of a small elite. This increase in the student population of course intensifies the pressure on USU places, which are limited (especially in the URNU and UAS) by restrictions relating to access to ships, aircraft and other training materiel.

This increase in participation includes an increase in diversity among the student population, including a greater proportion of women entering higher education. Data for 2013–14 indicates that of the full-time undergraduate student population, 762,065 (55%) were female and 629,410 (45%) were male. At postgraduate level this female majority is also in evidence, with 162,470 women and 141,925 men in full-time postgraduate study (53% and 47% respectively).[26] Within the UK undergraduate population of full-time first degree students (a core group in the USUs), about 23% also identify as being from an ethnic minority.[27] Although entry to higher education remains structured quite markedly by economic background and social class, there has been a slight increase in the proportion of young people entering higher education from disadvantaged neighbourhoods over the past three decades.[28]

The UK has long had a buoyant market for entry to its universities from international students at undergraduate and postgraduate levels. This is relevant to the USUs because students who are UK or Commonwealth citizens or Irish nationals can join USUs, so whilst USU membership is not open to the

---

[24] **Department for Business Innovation and Skills.** (2014). *Participation Rates in Higher Education: Academic Years 2006/7–2012/13(Provisional).* Retrieved from https://www.gov.uk/government/uploads/system/uploads/attachment_data/file/347864/HEIPR_PUBLICATION_2012-13.pdf. Note that participation rates for 2012–13 reflect the introduction of full tuition fees payable by undergraduates.

[25] **Higher Education Funding Council for England.** (2010). *Trends in Young Participation in Higher Education: Core Results for England* (January 2010/03). Retrieved from http://www.hefce.ac.uk/media/hefce/content/pubs/2010/201003/10_03.pdf

[26] **Higher Education Statistics Agency.** (2014). *Student Introduction 2013/14: Student Population.* Retrieved from https://www.hesa.ac.uk/content/view/3484/#eth

[27] **Higher Education Statistics Agency.** (2014). *Student Introduction 2013/14: Student Population.* Retrieved from https://www.hesa.ac.uk/content/view/3484/#eth

[28] **Higher Education Funding Council for England.** (2010). *Trends in Young Participation in Higher Education: Core Results for England* (January 2010/03). Retrieved from http://www.hefce.ac.uk/media/hefce/content/pubs/2010/201003/10_03.pdf

full student body at UK universities, there is a significant proportion of international students who are potentially able to access the USUs.

The USUs have long existed in an evolving landscape of increasing higher education participation. Although participation across higher education, and within certain parts of the sector, remains structured by socioeconomic factors, participation in higher education is no longer the preserve of a small elite. This is relevant to the USUs because it signals the potential diversity of student participants in terms of social background, and if recruitment to the armed forces (whether Regular or Reserves) follows USU participation, this has a potential effect on the social diversity of recruits to the British armed forces. Yet whilst the increase over the past two decades in total student numbers provides a larger potential recruitment pool for USUs, the number of students able to participate in a unit is becoming an ever smaller percentage of the overall student population because the size of the service units has remained fairly static.

### 1.3.2. The diversity of the higher education sector

Higher education provision in the UK has expanded considerably over the past three decades, and these changes sit within a much longer history of the development of the sector. The sector is marked by a range of types of institutions when defined by date of establishment, including universities with medieval origins, universities emerging from the requirements of 19th-century industrialisation for a technically-trained elite (the 'red brick' universities), universities developed in the wake of the Robbins Report of 1963 which recommended expansion of the sector (the 'plate glass' universities) and the former polytechnic institutions granted university status following the Further and Higher Education Act 1992 (the 'new' universities). Institutions in the sector differ in terms of governance and organisation, mission and core educational market for the degrees they offer, patterns of research intensity and of course, size. Bradshaw and Hamilton's exercise in mapping OTC provision against the different segments of the UK higher education sector illustrates this diversity.[29]

The higher education sector in the UK also shows huge variety in terms of provision across degree programme subjects and structures of degree programmes, with the Universities and Colleges Admissions Service (UCAS) estimating that there were over 37,000 undergraduate degree programmes offered in 2014 across over 300 providers. Admissions requirements vary, and recruitment to the increasing number of providers in the sector is often highly competitive.

A number of lobbying or mission groups exist within the sector, to promote the interests of their representatives. Universities UK is the largest grouping with a membership of 133 institutions, speaking for institutions across the

---

[29] **Bradshaw, R.** and **Hamilton, H.** (2010). *UOTCs and the UK Higher Education Sector.* Unpublished paper, East Midlands Military Education Committee.

sector. The Russell Group of 24 research-intensive universities represents perhaps the most visible group of universities, those that have international reputations as leading research institutions, and including those that housed the original USU units. GuildHE provides a formal representation function for its 38 members who are drawn from across the specialist, further education and post-1992 universities sector. University Alliance represents 20 universities, mostly from within the post-1992 sector, whilst Million+ is a think tank representing 17 universities from across the post-1992 sector.

The organisation and structuring of higher education provision in UK is the responsibility of the universities themselves, shaped by policy guidance from the DBIS and the higher education funding councils for England, Scotland and Wales, and the Department for Employment and Learning Northern Ireland. The defence sector has no direct involvement in these matters. However, defence has a necessary interest in higher education because, like employers across the UK, the defence sector draws on graduates as a key component of its recruitment pool: in civilian roles through the MoD, as employees within the wider defence industrial and service sectors and as recruits for (predominantly) officer training in the three armed forces. Entry for officer training is not restricted to graduates, but (reflecting the expansion of higher education provision in the UK over the past three decades) the majority of entrants to officer training programmes are graduates from UK universities. Furthermore, reflecting innovations in other labour market sectors, the defence sector's interest in higher education is reflected in the provision of university-level training specifically targeted at the employment needs of certain parts of that sector; this is evident in the DTOEES, administered by the UK Defence Academy with training provided through specific universities.[30]

## 1.4 Policy issues framing the university armed service units

The two preceding sections have given a very broad introduction to both the USUs and to the higher education sector in which they sit. In this section we identify six key policy issues which, in our view, frame the empirical research findings detailed in the remainder of this book. Neither the USUs, nor individual universities, sit in isolation from these policy issues.

### *1.4.1. Student fees*

Students at most UK universities now have to pay fees for their studies. In 1998 a fee of £1,000 per year of study was introduced. By 2004 this had risen to

---

[30] Details on the Defence Technical Officer and Engineer Entrance Scheme are available at: http://www.da.mod.uk/dtoees

£3,000 and in 2012 the maximum fee was raised to £9,000 (although the full sum payable per year varies between institutions) for UK students studying at English universities. Scotland-domiciled students studying at Scottish universities pay no fees, after the Scottish government abolished them. Wales-domiciled students pay full fees if attending a university in Wales, but are entitled to a maintenance grant that can be used to offset some of the costs. Students paying fees usually cover these costs through a loan. In 1990, the government replaced the grants system with the student loans system, which provides students with the ability to receive a loan during their studies, to be paid off once they enter graduate employment. The effect of both the introduction of student fees and the replacement of grants with loans is that students in UK higher education tend to incur debt. Although students have traditionally had limited financial resources, these changes mean that the majority of students now graduate from university with considerable debt (for example, a minimum of £27,000 if attending an institution which charges the full fees of £9,000 per year). In this climate, payment for USU participation continues to be significant, and there is anecdotal evidence to suggest that when in recent years one or more of the USU units temporarily suspended paying its students, participation rates dropped. Another potential implication of the higher fees environment is that it might encourage students to aim higher after graduation, to look for better paying graduate jobs in order to be able to cover the costs of repaying their fees and maintenance loans,[31] and this may have consequences for recruitment to some sectors within the graduate labour market (which includes officer training in the armed forces).

### 1.4.2. Graduate employment and employability

The employability of graduates is a key concern within the higher education sector. This is, in part, a consequence of the need for universities to make visible the value of a university degree to students incurring substantial debt in order to complete their education at this level. Concern also reflects a wider public debate about the expansion of higher education, and the correspondence (or otherwise) between the skills required in the graduate labour market and the availability of suitably skilled graduates. Although a long-standing issue within higher education, the 1997 Dearing report, *Higher Education in the Learning Society*, made recommendations in this regard, linking graduate employability to the development of transferable skills.[32] A joint report by

---

[31] The converse may also be true, as repayments are only made beyond a specified earnings threshold.
[32] **The National Committee of Inquiry into Higher Education.** (1997). *The Dearing Report 1997: Higher Education in the Learning Society.* Retrieved from http://www.educationengland.org.uk/documents/dearing1997/dearing1997.html

Universities UK and the Confederation of British Industry made explicit the necessity for universities to attend to the employability of their graduates.[33] Institutions across the higher education sector have responded with a range of measures aimed at enhancing graduate employability, including graduate skills frameworks, institution-specific accreditation for extracurricular activities (which may include skills training) and initiatives within curricula aimed at highlighting the transferable skills development inculcated within degree programmes.[34] There are a number of examples of these sorts of opportunities. The Durham Award, run by Durham University, provides students with the opportunity to apply for recognition of the transferable skills that they can develop as part of their degree programme and as part of being a student at Durham University.[35] The Sheffield University 'Skills for Work' scheme offers students the opportunity to have work experience recognised through the awarding of a certificate.[36] Other institutions run skills-specific modules that provide students with the opportunity to have work experience placements assessed as part of their degree programme; for example, Newcastle University's 'Career Development' module.[37]

The graduate employability agenda is significant for the USUs because there is considerable potential intersection between the skills development offered in units, and the skills development activities encouraged by universities. Whilst explicit focus on skills development and employability by the USUs may not always have been a deliberate intention, what has become apparent during the course of this research is the extent to which (both intentionally and inadvertently) the training experience offered by units, and as understood by participants, delivers skills and competencies which closely match those required by graduate recruiters. This is especially true in relation to key transferable graduate skills, such as time management, self-organisation, team-working and project preparation and management. USUs are increasingly aware of the transferable skills agenda within the graduate employment market, and many now offer accreditation for their students in order to provide recognition of the skills that USU participation offers. For example, USU members can use their

---

[33] **Universities UK and the Confederation of British Industry.** (2009). *Future Fit: Preparing Graduates for the World of Work*. Retrieved from http://www.cbi.org.uk/media/1121435/cbi_uuk_future_fit.pdf

[34] See, for example, **Cole, D.** and **Tibby, M.** (2013). *Defining and Developing your Approach to Employability: A Framework for Higher Education Institutions*. The Higher Education Academy. Retrieved from https://www.heacademy.ac.uk/sites/default/files/resources/Employability_framework.pdf

[35] Details on the University of Durham, Durham Award are available at: https://www.dur.ac.uk/careers/daward/

[36] Details on the University of Sheffield Skills for Work certificate are available at: http://www.sheffield.ac.uk/careers/students/advice/sfwc

[37] Details on the Newcastle University Career Development module are available at: http://www.ncl.ac.uk/careers/develop/cdm/index.php

participation to apply for the Chartered Management Institute Level 5 Award in Management and Leadership.

It should be noted that the USU experience is just one of many activities students undertake at university beyond their academic studies. Most students will at least have the opportunity to develop their employability and transferable skills through, for example, part-time work, involvement with charitable or voluntary work, sports and university clubs and societies.

### 1.4.3. The student experience

The idea of the 'student experience' and its associated terminology has gained traction in the UK higher education sector for two reasons. First, following the introduction of full fees, much public debate followed about the financial worth of a university degree, and what specifically students might anticipate getting in return for this payment (including enhanced employability in the graduate labour market). Although much of that debate is not of particular significance here, there is one element which is particularly pertinent. Across the higher education sector, universities are making very deliberate attempts to highlight how, in return for fees, they provide an education which delivers a curriculum appropriate to the degree programme, with appropriate levels of support and resources to facilitate student learning. In other words, the idea of the student experience includes increased visibility of the support structures in place at universities which underpin teaching and learning. Whether or not these structures are new (as a result of fees) or established (having already been in place) is not for us to comment on here. The point is the increased visibility of educational support in university marketing to potential applicants, and communications to current students, highlighting that universities take the student experience of education very seriously.

The second reason for the development of a language around the student experience is the need for universities to show explicitly that they have an awareness of the significance of the wider social experience of a university education. This is not just about the marketing of universities as places where (predominantly young) adults can enjoy a full and active life, although there is an element of that identifiable in much university recruitment material. This is primarily about making visible to a wider public the sector's awareness that individuals and groups experience their university participation in often quite markedly different ways, and that understanding of and support for those differences is necessarily a responsibility of institutions as part of their efforts to create the conditions of possibility for a positive student experience.

The increased focus on the student experience is significant for the USUs because it influences how students understand and reflect back on their university education. The material practices that are directly under university control and shape the student experience include health and welfare provision, additional educational support (for example, in literacy and numeracy), infrastructure and facilities for both educational and recreational purposes (ranging from free Wi-Fi to sports facilities) and the ready availability of social activities (which are not provided by institutions themselves, although institutions shape the conditions of their provision in, for example, indirect support for Student Unions and sports facilities). The efforts of institutions to enhance the student experience are influential, even when students are unaware of them. The practices universities have in place to enhance the student experience are significant to USUs because of the comparisons students will necessarily draw between their educational experience and that of their USU participation. Whether those comparisons are favourable or unfavourable, the point remains that the USU experience for students is structured relative to their university educational and social experience.

### 1.4.4. Recruitment rates to the UK armed forces

Recruitment into the armed forces has been an ongoing issue over the past decade, manifest in current levels of deficit against personnel requirements of 4.4% for the Army, 5.8% for the RAF and 0.3% for the Royal Navy/Royal Marines.[38] Although significant numbers of personnel have been made redundant under successive tranches of the Armed Forces Redundancy Programme (part of the Future Force 2020 restructuring), particularly from the Army, achieving the required levels of personnel is a delicate task involving a match between recruitment, retention and redundancy.

One of the key issues affecting armed forces recruitment (apart from the availability of jobs in specialties to which applicants want to apply), is the attractiveness or otherwise of an armed forces career. This is an issue very relevant to the USUs: for the OTC and UAS (although far less so for the URNU), the recruitment function of the units has become more central to their mission over the past few years. We should make clear that the service units do not exist solely as recruitment tools for the UK armed forces. However, it has long been recognised (as the research underpinning this book confirms) that they have a role to play in recruitment, particularly at officer level, and recruitment policy and practice within the three armed forces are increasingly alert to the significance of USUs in the context of concerns about declining levels of recruitment.

There are multiple factors shaping the receptiveness or otherwise of UK graduates to the idea of a military career (whether or not they are USU participants, as entry for officer training is not contingent on USU participation), including: the state of the graduate labour market for new entrants and its susceptibility

---

[38] **Ministry of Defence.** (2014). *UK Armed Forces Quarterly Personnel Report (1ˢᵗ October 2014).* Retrieved from https://www.gov.uk/government/uploads/system/uploads/attachment_data/file/373115/af-quarterly_personnel_report_oct14.pdf

to shifts in local, regional, national and international economies; demographic changes including declining birth rates having an effect on the number of people within a particular age cohort; perceptions about job insecurity in the armed forces as a consequence of redundancies and restructuring; the possibility of effects of the estrangement between the armed forces and civil society as a consequence of shifts over decades in the proportion of people with personal or relational experience of military participation; and antipathy towards the idea of military participation as a consequence of the recent wars in Iraq and Afghanistan, and the very real possibility of serious injury or death as a consequence of that participation. These factors are also thought to impact unevenly on different groups of potential recruits, and there is currently concern that recruitment levels are particularly low amongst women, and amongst certain religious and ethnic groups, which continue to be grossly underrepresented in the UK armed forces.

The armed forces have been proactive in tackling these issues, with a number of high-profile marketing campaigns in recent years aimed at increasing awareness of the range of occupations that the Army, Navy and Air Force can offer. Whilst the USUs are not explicitly recruiting organisations, recruitment pressures have led to a shift in approach, with more focus on the development of students who are looking to continue to officer training, and within the OTC especially, promoting future Reserves participation.

### 1.4.5. *The expansion of the Reserves*

The reduction of Regular forces and concomitant expansion of the Reserves as part of the Future Force 2020 programme has significant implications for the UK armed forces. These changes originate in a host of factors, including tight controls over levels of public expenditure on defence, the changing nature of the threat (and changing perceptions of those threats) to UK security, the emergence of new modes of warfare and of ways of responding (for example, to terrorist or cyber-warfare threats), and the constant and ongoing negotiations around the UK's strategic commitments and operational practices with respect to its allies. The ongoing expansion of the Reserves is only one of a whole range of measures outlined in the 2010 Strategic Defence and Security Review, and put into operation in the years since.[39-40]

---

[39] **Ministry of Defence.** (2010). *Securing Britain in an Age of Uncertainty: The Strategic Defence and Security Review.* Retrieved from https://www.gov.uk/government/uploads/system/uploads/attachment_data/file/62482/strategic-defence-security-review.pdf; **Ministry of Defence.** (2013) *Reserves in the Future Force 2020: Valuable and Valued.* Retrieved from https://www.gov.uk/government/uploads/system/uploads/attachment_data/file/210470/Cm8655-web_FINAL.pdf

[40] As an entirely separate enterprise, the research team sought and obtained funding for research investigating the workplace and identity issues pertaining to individuals pursuing

Although the USUs may seem quite distant, irrelevant even, to both profound changes in the nature and conceptualisation of security by successive UK governments, and to the restructuring around the Whole Force Concept (the label applied to the UK's reform of its military) currently underway across the British armed forces, by virtue of the fact that the USUs comprise an element of the Reserves, they are connected to these broader changes. At the time of writing, there is no way of telling exactly how the expansion of the Reserves in particular will shape strategic and practical organisational issues within the USUs. What is clear, however, is that the USUs are part of that broader conversation. There has always been a relationship between USU participation and subsequent Reserves participation, and the units' role in current Reserves expansion (particularly the OTC) will undoubtedly be subject to close scrutiny. We have already noted the Roskelly study of the OTC undertaken in 2010, which established the OTRs and also established pathways through which individuals could receive training within the units sufficient to commission individuals as officers in the Reserves. We would expect scrutiny of the USUs by the MoD and the three armed forces to continue, in terms of a return on the financial investment (however that return might be defined). Thus USU participation can be a stepping stone during a university career for those with an interest in continuing military participation but who do not wish to pursue a full-time military career.

### 1.4.6. Armed forces on campus

The first OTCs were established in 1908, as part of the Haldane reforms, meaning there has been an official UK armed forces presence within the UK university system for over 100 years. This historic, long-standing association is formalised through the MECs, but is probably made most visible at the annual Freshers' Fair events. Apart from these recruitment events at the beginning of each academic year, USUs are not particularly visible on campus; although some units have drill nights in buildings on campus, most are based at military facilities away from their host universities' estates. Although some universities have DTOEES units comprising students studying under the Defence Technical Undergraduate Scheme (DTUS), these students are rarely evident collectively (and in uniform) on campus; they take part in teaching and learning activities as any student on their degree programmes would, and their military commitments (such as drill nights) usually take place away from campus.[41] In

---

both paid civilian employment and employment with the Reserves, see: **Woodward, R., Edmunds, T., Higate, P., Hockey, J.** and **Jenkings N. K.** *Keeping enough in reserve: the employment of hybrid citizen-soldiers and the Future Reserves 2020 programme* (Economic and Social Research Council grant reference ES/L012944/1). Retrieved from http://www.future-reserves-research.ac.uk/

[41] Details on the Defence Technical Undergraduate Scheme are available at: http://www.da.mod.uk/dtoees

this respect, the question of armed forces recruitment and presence on university campuses is fundamentally different in the UK compared with the United States, where the Reserve Officer Training Corps has a more explicit presence on college campuses, and requires its students to sign up to military service on graduation.[42]

In the UK, there is some history of resistance by some student organisations to the presence and the idea of the presence of USU units on university campuses, usually articulated by specific Student Unions at specific universities. Student Unions are autonomous organisations, completely independent of the universities in which they operate, and exist to provide a framework for organising student services such as welfare support, and student activities including sporting, social, cultural and political activities. Most are affiliated to the National Union of Students, which provides a national voice for and representation of students in the UK. A number of Student Unions have a long history of initiating debate over military issues, including the deployment of armed forces and discussions over wider issues of militarisation on and beyond campus.

We have included this here as a policy issue to flag up that it is through Student Union policy, that questions around the armed forces on campus become an issue from time to time, primarily over the presence of USUs at Freshers' Fairs and similar events to advertise societies and activities on campuses. Some Student Unions have prevented USUs from participating in Student Union society recruitment events, although this can change from year to year at a single institution depending on the political make-up of the sabbatical officers that run each union, or may be a longer-standing and more embedded policy.[43] Some student organisations may also articulate a politics particularly critical of the relationships between university research and defence funding (particularly from multi-national arms manufacturers), and around university investments in the arms trade and associated sectors.[44] Arguments against the presence of USU recruiters at student events appear to rest either with a broader anti-militarist politics, or with concerns over student vulnerability.[45] We return to this issue of recruitment, and in particular of Freshers' Fairs, in Chapter 3.

---

[42] **Neiberg, M.** (2000). *Making Citizen Soldiers: ROTC and the Ideology of American Military Service*. Harvard: Harvard University Press; **Axe, D.** (2007) *Army 101: Inside the ROTC in a Time of War*. Columbia: The University of South Carolina Press.

[43] **Young-Powell, A.** (2013, 9 December). Armed forces make over 300 visits to UK universities in two years. *The Guardian.* Retrieved from http://www.theguardian.com/education/2013/dec/09/armed-forces-universities-recruit

[44] Note that this is also the focus of research and debate by academics working on military, defence and security issues; see for example **Stavrianakis, A.** (2006). Call to arms: the university as a site of militarised capitalism and a site of struggle. *Millennium, 35* (1), 139–154.

[45] **Iordanou, G.** (2013, 27 October). Get the armed forces away from universities *The Huffington Post*. Retrieved from http://www.huffingtonpost.co.uk/george-iordanou/armed-forces-universities_b_4161976.html?utm_hp_ref=uk

## 1.5 The purpose and structure of this book

The purpose of this book is to explore the value of the USUs, and in doing so we draw on data generated through a research project on precisely that issue. Throughout the research, and in this book, we have focused on value in non-financial terms, and indeed one of the research questions guiding the project concerned how the concept of 'value' might be understood. This book examines the value of the USUs from the perspectives of four key groups. These are: student participants in the USUs; graduates who had a USU experience as students, and who subsequently went on to pursue civilian careers; the three armed forces which provide strategic overview, funding, and daily organisation, staffing and management of the units; and the universities which provide student participants and have an interest in the workings of the USUs because of this. Throughout our discussions of the question of value to these groups, we also consider how a further group, employers of graduates, might also be understood as having an interest in the value of the USUs.

The book is structured as follows. In Chapter 2, we explain in more detail the rationale for the research, the methodology used to generate and analyse data, and consider what was and was not included in the study. Chapter 3 draws on a survey of USU members conducted during spring 2013 to explore the question of value from their perspective. Chapter 4 discusses findings from interviews with graduates of USUs, to provide an assessment of value of the USU experience from the perspective of those looking back to their student experience, and subsequent use (or otherwise) of the USU experience across their working lives. Chapter 5 explores the question of the value of the USUs from the perspective of the armed forces, and in particular the COs charged with the strategic and daily managerial direction of the units. Chapter 6 assesses the value of the USUs to universities. Chapter 7 concludes the book by summarising key findings and highlighting areas for further debate within the defence and higher education communities on the value of the USUs.

CHAPTER 2

# Studying the Value of the University Armed Service Units: Research Rationale and Methods

In this chapter, we introduce the research underpinning this book by noting the origins and rationale for that research. We explain the research methodology used, and discuss areas of investigation deliberately excluded from the study.

## 2.1 Rationale and background to the research

The origins of the research lie in conversations between members of the research team and individuals associated with the Northumbrian Universities Military Education Committee (NUMEC), about the possibility of undertaking a study of the value added to students and value returned to the armed forces of the USUs.[46] The research team were receptive to the idea, given their existing interests in the sociology and politics of the armed forces, and their roles in higher education as members of academic staff at Newcastle University. We noted at the time the absence of information in the public domain about the university armed service units, both generally beyond those who had direct experience of USUs, and more specifically within the academic military sociological literature.

---

[46] The initial proposal was for a study solely of the UAS.

---

**How to cite this book chapter:**
Woodward, R, Jenkings, K N and Williams, A J. 2015. *The Value of the University Armed Service Units*. Pp. 31–43. London: Ubiquity Press. DOI: http://dx.doi.org/10.5334/baq.b. License: CC-BY 4.0.

### 2.1.1. *The pilot study*

In the academic year 2009–10, Dr Alison Williams applied for and was awarded funding from Newcastle University's Catherine Cookson Foundation to undertake a pilot project exploring graduate skills and the USU experience.[47] This study focused on the three service units in the North East of England, the Northumbrian Universities Royal Naval Unit, Northumbrian Universities Officer Training Corps and Northumbrian Universities Air Squadron, which draw students from the five local universities of Newcastle, Durham, Northumbria, Sunderland and Teesside. This research showed the extent to which students identified the skills development they received through their USU experience as valuable, and suggested the viability of a bigger, national study.

### 2.1.2. *The Value of the University Armed Service Units* study

On the basis of the pilot project, funding for further study was sought from the Economic and Social Research Council (ESRC) to support a more comprehensive and ambitious national project. The ESRC is one of seven UK research councils, and provides research funding through grants at full economic cost to (primarily) higher education institutions in the UK for social science research. The ESRC is funded through the DBIS but is entirely independent of government in terms of its distribution of funds. Applications under the response mode scheme are not limited by topic, theme or approach. They are peer-reviewed, and the process is highly competitive. The application was submitted in December 2011 with Dr Alison Williams as Principal Investigator and Dr K. Neil Jenkings and Professor Rachel Woodward as Co-Investigators, was awarded in August 2012, and the research commenced in December 2012. Given the length of time between submission of the application and the start of the research, it is perhaps unsurprising that policy changes emerged between the start of the project planning and the start date of the actual research, and this was evident with the emergence of the Future Force 2020 agenda and its inclusion of strategies to reduce the overall size of the three armed forces and increase the proportion of reservists, particularly in the British Army.

The research had two core objectives. The first objective was to assess the value of the military experience provided by the USUs. We examined this with reference to student participants, graduates in civilian employment who had had a USU experience as a student, the armed forces, the universities and

---

[47] **Williams, A., Egdell, V.** and **Woodward, R.** (2010). *Graduate Skills and the University Armed Service Units Experience.* Retrieved from http://research.ncl.ac.uk/military-research/assets/docs/'Graduate-Skills-and-the-University-Armed-Service-Unit-Experience.pdf

employers and the wider labour market. The methodologies used to assess this question of value are outlined in section 2.2 below, and included a quantitative survey of participating students, and semi-structured interviews with graduates, unit COs and university and employer representatives. The intention was to establish whether, and if so how, value was understood, working with a preliminary understanding of value in non-financial terms and as manifest through individual, social and institutional benefits. Exploring respondents' understandings of what value might constitute in context of the USUs was an important element to this. This book focuses on research findings which speak to the first research objective.

The second research objective was to explore how this notion of value around the USU experience might then be used to extend and inform more conceptual debates about militarism, militarisation and civil-military relations. Informed by the analysis of empirical data around the value of the USUs, we were interested in questions such as how the relational categories of 'military' and 'civilian' are brought into being and performed within the USU context, and how current conceptualisations within the social sciences of militarism and militarisation might be confirmed, extended or challenged by consideration of the USU experience as a process which facilitates the extension of military presence, ideas and understandings into civilian life. We were particularly interested in the spatialities of militarism, looking explicitly at education and the workplace as locations where processes of militarisation might or might not be identified on the basis of USU influence.[48] These more conceptual issues are not discussed here, but are the focus for academic journal articles.

### 2.1.3. Research ethics

The research was conducted in accordance with ESRC guidelines for the ethical conduct of social science research. Ethical reviews were conducted as part of the ESRC research grant application process, and subsequent to award by the Newcastle University Faculty of Humanities and Social Sciences Research Ethics Committee. This ensured that the research was compliant with research ethics policies covering research validity, risk assessment, researcher safety, participant recruitment strategy, consent procedures, vulnerable groups, confidentiality and review of ethical issues within the project as it proceeded. Because this research was not funded by the MoD or armed forces, it was not subject to review by the MoD Research Ethics Committee.

---

[48] For further discussion of the geographies of militarism and militarisation, see: **Woodward, R.** (2004). *Military Geographies*. Oxford: Blackwell; **Rech, M. F., Bos, D., Jenkings, K. N., Williams, A. J.** and **Woodward, R.** (2015). Geography, military geography and critical military studies. *Critical Military Studies*, *1* (1), 47–60.

### 2.1.4. Steering group

The research was conducted according to the guidelines and expectations of ESRC. Included in these is an expectation that where research results are of potential utility or interest to research users or beneficiaries, those research users where possible should be involved in the preparation and execution of that research. This expectation recognises the independence of ESRC-funded research, whilst also recognising the benefits that follow to that research from research user engagement. Accordingly, the initial research design benefitted from consultations with the following: representatives from the Reserve Forces and Cadets division working under the Deputy Chief of Defence Staff Personnel & Training, who have responsibility for the USUs; from representatives at the Royal Military Academy Sandhurst, Britannia Royal Naval College and RAF College Cranwell with responsibilities for the units and for officer training; from the Council of Military Education Committees and from our local Northumbrian Universities Military Education Committee. These organisations subsequently joined a steering group which met three times over the period of research data collection. The steering group also included a representative of the Newcastle University Careers Service. We would like to record our thanks for the input of our steering group members; the research benefitted in many significant ways from their advice, and we are grateful for their time and input. However, the results and conclusions are our own, and do not necessarily reflect those of our steering group members or their respective organisations.

### 2.1.5. Conceptualising value

This project was about value, and investigating the concept of value was one of our research objectives (see section 2.1.2 above). As a concept underpinning the research, we understood value in terms of utility, benefit and advantage. The research did not set out to quantify value in economic or financial terms, and was not an exercise in cost-benefit analysis. Rather, the research explored what value might mean and might be defined as, with regards to the multiple ways in which that value might be manifest, observed or experienced by the groups on which we focused. We were concerned with value rather than values, and although a number of ethical and moral issues emerged in the data which indicated that the idea of value might incorporate ideas about values, our focus was emphatically on the former rather than the latter.

### 2.1.6. The research team

The research team comprised Dr Alison Williams (Principal Investigator), Dr K. Neil Jenkings (Co-Investigator and full-time project researcher) and

Professor Rachel Woodward (Co-Investigator), all based at the School of Geography, Politics & Sociology, Newcastle University, UK. The research team brought to the research their combined and considerable teaching experience in higher education contexts, experience in university administration and experience as social science researchers. Alison Williams' research has focused on political geography and geopolitics, aerial geographies (particularly in military contexts) and graduate and transferable skills education.[49] K. Neil Jenkings' research has focused on the sociology of workplace practices, social interactions and the relationships between armed forces and society in social and cultural contexts.[50] Rachel Woodward's research has focused on the sociology of the military, military geographies and military identities and relations (including gender identities and relations) in armed forces contexts.[51] One member of the research team had prior experience of employment with the British armed forces, and one had prior experience as a member of a USU for a short period of time whilst at university.

## 2.2 Research methodology

The research used a mixed methods approach, deploying both quantitative and qualitative methods of data collection and analysis. The advantage of a mixed methods approach is that it provides different types of data, generated using different methods of collection and subject to analysis using different techniques. Quantitative methods analyse numerical data from either primary sources (collected to answer a specified research question) or secondary sources (data collected for other purposes which can be used for specific purposes possibly unintended at time of generation). Quantitative methods are used to test hypotheses and deploy deductive reasoning from the general to the specific. Qualitative methods analyse textual, oral and visual data, and again may be used on either primary or secondary data sources. Qualitative methods are used to explore meaning and individual understanding in social contexts, and deploy inductive reasoning from the specific to the general. There is increasing consensus within the academic social science research community about the utility of using both quantitative and qualitative methods in combination, particularly when analysing complex social phenomena. Because of the complexity and range of issues pertaining to the key question about the value of the USUs, a mixed methods approach was identified as most appropriate for this research.

---

[49] Alison Williams' profile is available at: http://www.ncl.ac.uk/gps/staff/profile/alison.williams1
[50] K. Neil Jenkings' profile is available at: http://www.ncl.ac.uk/gps/staff/profile/neil.jenkings
[51] Rachel Woodward's profile is available at: http://www.ncl.ac.uk/gps/staff/profile/rachel.woodward

### 2.2.1. *The survey of current student university armed service units participants*

A quantitative survey was conducted of current student participants in USUs, in order to generate data on the demographics of the group, their perceptions of their USU experience, their motivations for joining a unit, their understanding of the benefits and disbenefits of their USU experience and their intentions with regards to a future career with the armed forces. A copy of the questionnaire is included in Appendix 1. Questions were either closed (requiring either a yes/no answer or selection from a list of potential responses), used a Likert scale (requiring a response on a sliding scale) or were open (requiring respondent completion using free text), and generated both numeric and textual data. In the interests of maximising participation, individuals completing the survey were able, if they chose, to skip a question and move to the next. Although an instrument which demands that participants complete all questions sequentially has the advantage of ensuring responses to all the questions, it has the disadvantage of lowering response rates if respondents have difficulties with a particular question. An additional compounding factor is overexposure to surveys, creating lower response rates; a particular methodological issue when researching students given the significant numbers of student opinion surveys conducted at module, degree programme and institutional level, and more generally for commercial purposes.

The survey instrument was a web-based online questionnaire, and was developed using SurveyMonkey software. Respondents to the survey were required to use a web link to gain access. Given the ubiquity of internet access, particularly amongst the target group, the use of an online survey instrument was felt to be the most appropriate mechanism to use, and no paper copies of the survey were distributed. This limited completion of the questionnaire to those who had access to the web link, which was distributed by COs, with agreement from the central leads for each service unit. Because of variations across the three services, and between units within each service, it is possible that approaches towards distributing the link varied across the sample. We also recognise that although the information given to the students made clear that the survey was being conducted by independent researchers, it is possible that because this information was distributed by COs it may still have been perceived by students as an official defence survey. However, the use of central gatekeepers (unit COs) was necessary because of data protection legislation and protocols preventing the sharing of student email addresses between third parties. COs were able to provide briefings to their students about the survey, and thus some variation in the description of the form and function of the survey was inevitable. The voluntary nature of participation was made clear to students, and a small prize offered as an inducement to participate.

The survey was distributed to all serving USU participants (in the OTC, UAS and URNU) and in all units, between January and April 2013. The timing of the survey was deliberate in order to capture the experiences of newer members who may only have joined a unit in the previous three or four months, and of established members who may have had a much longer period of participation (up three and a half years for those on four-year degree programmes) and who were in the process of completing their education and determining future career objectives.

A total of 1,798 students completed the survey. Of this total, 842 respondents (47%) were from OTC units, 656 (36%) were from UAS units and 285 (16%) were from the URNU. As a proportion of all students across all USUs for the academic year 2012–13, and using Defence Statistics estimates for that total USU population (see 1.1.1. above), we calculate the proportion of responses per each of the three services to be 19% for OTC (4,400 members, with a sample of 842), 59% for UAS (1,110 members, with a sample of 656) and 34% for URNU (850 members, with a sample of 285). Expected response rates for online surveys targeted at students vary quite markedly according to the demographic composition of a student body and institutional characteristics, and the response rates achieved in this case lie within an expected range. However, the figures for total USU population available through Defence Statistics will include both active participants, and those who are enlisted as members but who, for whatever reason, are not active in their units. The calculated response rate is likely to be an underestimation in terms of responses from active participants, and accordingly we would estimate our total and unit-specific sample to be higher than that indicated above.

The data collected through the questionnaire survey was 'cleaned' and entered into both SPSS version 21 (an IBM software package for the statistical analysis of social science data) and Excel, for analysis. Given the intended uses of the analysis and the research questions and hypotheses framing this, a decision was taken to focus analysis of numeric data on simple statistics rather than more complex forms of parametric and non-parametric statistical testing. Non-numeric data was manually coded where appropriate, for responses to questions requiring or providing the option of a free-text response and for responses requiring identification of university, degree programme and unit.

The statistical data used in this book is all taken from the survey of student USU participants, except where indicated. For the purposes of clarity, all percentages have been rounded up or down to the nearest whole number. Percentages have been calculated on the basis of total valid responses to a question, rather than on total response rates overall, to account for the fact that some questions did not generate a full response (for example, were missed by 10 to 20 participants).

### 2.2.2. Interviews with graduates of university armed service units

Qualitative interviews were conducted with individuals who had participated in a USU as a student but had not gone on to pursue a career in the armed forces. The purpose of these interviews was to explore the value of the USU experience from the perspective of former participants who had now embarked on careers in the civilian workplace (including those who had retired). We wanted to establish whether their USU experience had had value for them in their working lives and beyond, and the wider understanding of former members of the value (or otherwise) of their USU experiences in their lives to date.

Although we recruited participants on the basis of USU experience, in fact a number of respondents revealed during the course of their interview that they also had experience with the Reserve forces. We did not exclude these individuals from our analysis, because of the valuable insights that this sub-group were able to bring to the issue of the relationship between USU and Reserves participation (see section 1.4.5. above). At the time of the interviews, there was substantial and ongoing press coverage of the Future Force 2020 programme.

Interviewees were recruited through social media networks, including unit alumni pages and through snowballing from initial contacts. The original intention had been to interview up to 40 former USU participants. In fact, we interviewed 54 individuals, a reflection of the wide range of insights these individuals were able to share and the richness of the data that the interviews generated. We interviewed 24 former OTC members, 13 former UAS members and 17 former URNU members. Some individuals had experience with more than one service (for example, changing service unit when graduating from one university and entering another for postgraduate study), and we have allocated those individuals to the service unit they first joined. It would not have been possible to get a meaningful representative sample across categories such as unit location, degree subject or class or other sociodemographic factors. The sampling strategy therefore aimed to be broadly representative across age span and gender, and with the aim of generating interviewees across a range of localities and occupations (so not, for example, just recruiting individuals working in London for large corporations).

Further details about the sample are given in Chapter 4. In brief, all respondents at the point of interview were either in paid employment, were taking leave or other time out for childcare or were retired. Respondents ranged in age from their early 20s to their mid-70s, with the majority in their mid-20s to late 30s. Respondents were self-selecting. It has been suggested that there might be participation bias in the sample, with only those positively inclined towards the USUs ready to come forward for interview. However, a feature of data collection using semi-structured interviews is the fact that the technique is designed to tease out the range of ideas, knowledge, experience and understanding from interviewees, something that rests to no small degree on the skill and expertise of the interviewer. Furthermore, it would of course be extremely poor research practice to select a sample on the basis of a pre-determined assessment of their positive or negative views towards a specific social phenomenon. Nor did we attempt to recruit a sub-group within the sample who had had very limited experience of USUs (for example, individuals who had enlisted and participated for a very limited time before leaving) or a stated and overtly critical view of the units on the basis of either no experience or very limited experience. As noted above, the purposes of the interviews was the generation of understanding from an informed perspective, about how USU participation might be of value in post-graduate life. It was clear from the interviews that our respondents had a range of motivations for participating in the research, including positive experience, critical assessment and curiosity about the viability and future of the units.

Interviews were structured around a schedule (see Appendix 2), which established a core set of questions and answers, and facilitated further probing and exploration of issues as they arose during the interview. They were either conducted face-to-face at a venue of the respondent's choosing, or via telephone or Skype. All interviews were audio recorded. All interviewees were given an outline of the project prior to the interview, and were required to provide signed confirmation of their informed consent to the interview, its recording and subsequent analysis of data. The interviews were transcribed and the transcripts cleaned to ensure accuracy and respondent anonymity. Only one member of the research team had access to information matching each interview transcript to an individual's name and contact details.

Once transcribed, the interviews were coded using NVivo version 10 software (QSR International), enabling all respondent answers to a specific question to be collated together. These were then coded using the constant comparative method by members of the research team-working directly with the coded collated transcripts on specific questions.[52]

### 2.2.3. Interviews with representatives from the armed forces

The purpose of these interviews was to generate data on the value of the USUs from the perspective of those charged with their organisation, management and individual strategic direction. We chose to focus on unit COs (or Officers Commanding in the case of UASs) because we were interested in the detail of practical experience coupled with the wider expertise, experience and insight of officers working with USUs at that level (that is, officers of the rank of Lieutenant Colonel for OTCs, Squadron Leader for UASs and Lieutenant for URNUs). We did not, therefore, pursue either more junior officers or senior non-commissioned officers (NCOs) involved in unit management and training, nor more senior officers working within the three services or MoD with strategic overview but without direct unit responsibility. That said, our insights

---

[52] **Glaser, B. G.** and **Strauss, A. L.** (1967). *The Discovery of Grounded Theory: Strategies for Qualitative Research.* Aldine De Gruyter, New York; **Strauss, A. L.** and **Corbin, J.** (1990). *Basics of Qualitative Research: Grounded Theory Procedures and Techniques.* Sage Publications: Newbury Park, CA.

about the value of the units for the armed forces were enhanced through more informal conversations with senior and junior personnel in the course of doing the research, and we are grateful to those individuals for sharing their observations with us.

Given the number of units (46 in total: 18 OTCs/OTRs[53], 14 UASs and 14 URNUs), we identified five different localities around the UK from which to sample interviewees. We have maintained the anonymity of respondents and units by not naming these localities here. The five localities included a range of different types of university ('ancient', 'red brick', 'plate glass' and 'new') with different student socioeconomic and academic (pre-entry qualification) profiles, from regions around the UK with markedly different regional demographic, economic, social, cultural and geographical characteristics, and different regional traditions of military presence and military recruitment. Within these five localities, we interviewed the commanding officers for the local OTC, UAS and URNU, generating a total of 15 interviews. All unit COs who were approached agreed to be interviewed, and we are very grateful to them all for sharing their time and insights with us.

The same protocols for informed consent, interview schedules, data recording, data coding and data analysis were followed as with the graduate interviews. The interview schedule is reproduced in Appendix 3.

### 2.2.4. Interviews with representatives from universities

The purpose of these interviews was to generate information and understanding about the value of the USUs from the perspective of the universities. Although units may not be located in or near university campuses and facilities, and may not have close contacts with universities beyond MEC representation, the universities have a distinct interest in the question of the value of the units because of student participation. Universities are not responsible for the organisation, administration or strategic direction of the USUs, which is properly the responsibility of the parent services. However, universities have a potential interest in military and defence matters because of the employment destinations of their graduates (which will include the armed forces and the broader defence sector), because of links which may exist through research interests in defence or military issues, and because of cultural and political factors shaping the public reputation or perception of individual universities.

We explicitly did not seek to interview representatives who we knew had experience of USUs through their MEC participation. We focused our interviewee recruitment on senior university administrative officers with responsibility for

---

[53] Note that this is the number of units, and some have one or more additional detachments to account for the geographical extent of their catchment area.

student recruitment, student progression and student experience. Most commonly, these were academic registrars (although not all universities use this title). We were interested in this group because we were interested, in part, in levels of knowledge about and understanding of USUs at this level. We explore further features of our sample in Chapter 6 below. In brief, although having initially intended to match our CO sample with interviews with university representatives associated with those units, having generated a greater number of graduate interviews than originally intended, we confined ourselves to one geographical region which had within it both representation from all three units and universities across the range of the sector.

We contacted registrars from the five institutions represented in that region. One declined to be interviewed on the grounds that the individual concerned felt they knew nothing about the units (despite students from that universities participating in USUs) and preferred not to participate. However, within the sample we also had another university occupying a similar position in the higher education sector, so overall this omission was not felt to be detrimental to the sample. Another interviewee initially declined to be interviewed on similar grounds, but was persuaded that their self-perceived lack of knowledge about the units was in fact of interest to the research team, given that students from that institution participated in USUs and yet there appeared little knowledge of the units at a high level within that institution. The same protocols for interview schedule, informed consent, recording, coding and analysis was followed as described above for the interviews with graduates and with COs. The interview schedule is reproduced in Appendix 4.

### 2.2.5. Interviews with employers

Included in the first objective for this research (see 2.1.2 above) was an intention to interview a sample of employers. The interviews were to be conducted by telephone, using a short interview schedule. The sample was to be derived from *The Times Top 100 Graduate Employers*. However, this element of the research did not proceed as planned. It proved virtually impossible to make contact directly with senior company representatives with responsibility for recruitment, not least because of the absence of available contact information, particularly for large (often international) companies. In addition, it transpired that a number of recruiters screened initial graduate applications via recruitment agencies. Although the possibility was raised of using contacts via the Support for Britain's Reservists and Employers organisation (SaBRE), this would have resulted in a skewed sample, potentially generating interview contacts who were known to already have knowledge and understanding of the transferability (or otherwise) of skills derived in military contexts to civilian employment contexts.

However, the other data collection strategies we used with students, graduates, and, to an extent, COs and university representatives, did generate sufficient data to enable us to explore some of the issues around perceptions by graduate recruiters of the value (or otherwise) of the USU experience in terms of the inculcation of graduate skills. The student survey asked students about their experiences of engagement with the recruitment process, and generated quantitative and qualitative data on this. The interviews with graduates included a substantial focus on the experience of applying for and being recruited to organisations, and of being a recruiter, and thus generated qualitative data on the use of the USU experience by individuals seeking employment. Given the time constraints of the project, a decision was made to focus our efforts on the analysis of this data, rather than continuing with the seemingly fruitless task of trying to contact recruiters directly.

## 2.3 Conclusions on rationale and methodology

Despite the issues encountered in exploring directly the opinions of recruiters and employers of the value of USUs, the research project proceeded as intended, and the remainder of this book sets out the empirical results in full.

Prior to, and during the course of the research, a number of questions were raised by the research team and others concerning issues that the research did not explore; we include them here both for clarification and because they might indicate areas for future research on the broad topic of USUs and their value.

The first concerns the potential for a longitudinal element to the student survey. The survey provided a snapshot of a set of experiences and explanations from the surveyed cohort at a particular point in time. There was no intention at the time to repeat the survey and thereby develop a longitudinal data set able to capture continuity and change over time. That said, we include the original survey instrument in Appendix 1 should a repeat survey be thought feasible and useful at a future point in time.

The second concerns the capture of information from those with USU experience who went on to pursue careers in the Regular armed forces. Because the intention of the research was to focus on the value of the USU experience for those who did not join the Regulars, we made no attempt to capture data from this group. That said, it became clear during conversations (particularly with unit COs) both that there may be utility for the armed forces in being able to track whether a USU experience proves beneficial to those who pursue military careers, and that there is an absence of knowledge, beyond the anecdotal, within the armed forces of a more basic set of indicators about the presence or absence of a USU background amongst those pursuing military careers. Of particular interest were questions about the utility to individuals of the USU experience in providing military and transferable skills which then proved beneficial to the armed forces recruitment and training process and thence in career development, and questions about the utility to the armed forces in terms of the existence (or otherwise) of a cohort of individuals pursuing careers as officers who had previously had a USU experience. We note here that research to collect reliable data on USU experience and military career progression would be relatively straightforward to undertake.

The third concerns the comparability between the USU experience and that derived from other non-academic student activities. As this book will show, a significant element of this research examined the skills and wider experiences generated by one specific type of university activity. Although our student survey asked USU participants to evaluate their skills development in USUs in comparison with those from other activities, we did not set out to examine a control group who did not have USU experience to deliberately compare USU and non-USU value. This was partly because of time and resourcing (the research was deliberately focused on active USU participants), and also because of the difficulty of finding, amongst the plethora of student non-academic activities, a suitable sample of control activities against which the USU experience could be compared. Again, with sufficient care and attention to the methodological difficulties in establishing a control group, this is potentially an issue where future research could be undertaken.

The fourth concerns the experience of students who may have had a brief USU experience (that is, may have joined a unit following selection, but subsequently withdrew after a period of a few months). We can hypothesise that there would be a set of reasons for withdrawal, including negative views of the USU and its mission, health and medical reasons, and competing academic and other commitments. We made no attempt to engage with this disparate group, either amongst current students or amongst graduates, because we were interested in active participants and thus the value that they as students and graduates felt that they were getting or had gained through their participation. It is possible that this may be an area for further research, although the insights gained from such an exercise would most likely generate little further than confirmation of the hypotheses outlined above.

The final point to make about the research rationale and methodology is that although they are presented here as quite discrete exercises in data generation targeting four quite different groups, in fact the student questionnaire and the interview schedules were deliberately designed to explore similar themes from the perspectives of the different groups (students, graduates, COs and university representatives). There is thus, in the overall dataset, considerable potential for comparative analysis of particular themes such as value, skills development, workplace performance, employability and university benefit. In the following four chapters, we focus in turn on the data and results of data analysis for each group, and bring together key findings from all four groups in the concluding chapter.

CHAPTER 3

# The Student Experience of University Armed Service Unit Participation

In this chapter, we bring together the key findings from the survey of student participants in USUs, undertaken in spring 2013, in order to capture quantitative and qualitative data on the value of the USUs from the perspective of student participants. The questionnaire is reproduced in Appendix 1, and details on the distribution and analysis of the survey are given in section 2.2.1 above. A total of 1,798 responses were received. Of these, 842 identified as being in the OTC, 656 in the UAS and 285 in the URNU.[54] In this chapter we explore the results of the survey in terms of the demographics of the units, the university and educational profile of the sample, motivations for joining a USU, the role of USU participation in skills development, student perceptions of the effect of USU participation on progression through university, the influence of participation on student career choices including careers in the armed forces, student understandings of the potential utility of the USU experience in seeking and gaining employment after graduation, student opinions about the armed forces on the basis of their USU participation and overall student assessments of their USU experience. Key findings are highlighted in the concluding section, and the wider implications of these are discussed in the concluding chapter.

In the following analysis of the survey results, all calculations have been made on the basis of total completed responses to a specific question, and all percentages have been rounded to the nearest whole number. We have not

---

[54] As noted in Chapter 2, some respondents did not complete all the questions. For example, 15 respondents failed to identify which service unit they were members of.

**How to cite this book chapter:**
Woodward, R, Jenkings, K N and Williams, A J. 2015. *The Value of the University Armed Service Units*. Pp. 45–100. London: Ubiquity Press. DOI: http://dx.doi.org/10.5334/baq.c. License: CC-BY 4.0.

attempted to disaggregate responses within each service unit because of variations in response rates between units within each service.

## 3.1 Demographic characteristics of the university armed forces units survey sample

### 3.1.1. Age

The age profile of the sample, shown in Figure 3.1, reflects the expected profile for UK undergraduate students. On average, just under three quarters of the participants were aged 19, 20 or 21 on 31$^{st}$ March 2013.

### 3.1.2. Gender

Although across the total UK student population slightly more women than men participate in higher education, Figure 3.2 confirms an anticipated finding: that fewer women are USU participants. Across the sample, URNUs had the highest proportion of women of the three service units, and OTCs had the lowest.

### 3.1.3. Educational background

Respondents were asked about their educational background pre-university, because of significant anecdotal evidence which suggested that USUs attract a higher proportion of students who were educated in the independent (fee-paying) school sector than both the national average, and the average for their particular university. Figure 3.3 shows the proportion of USU participants, both

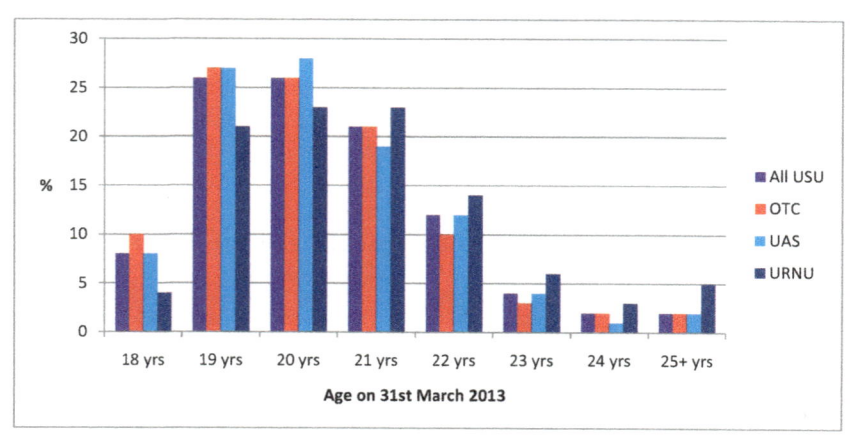

**Figure 3.1:** Age profile of USU survey participants, by percentage.

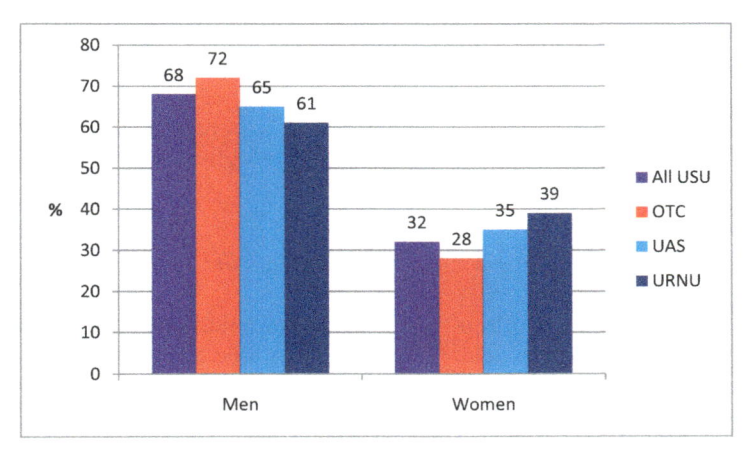

The Student Experience of University Armed Service Unit Participation  47

**Figure 3.2:** Gender profile of USUs sample, by percentage.

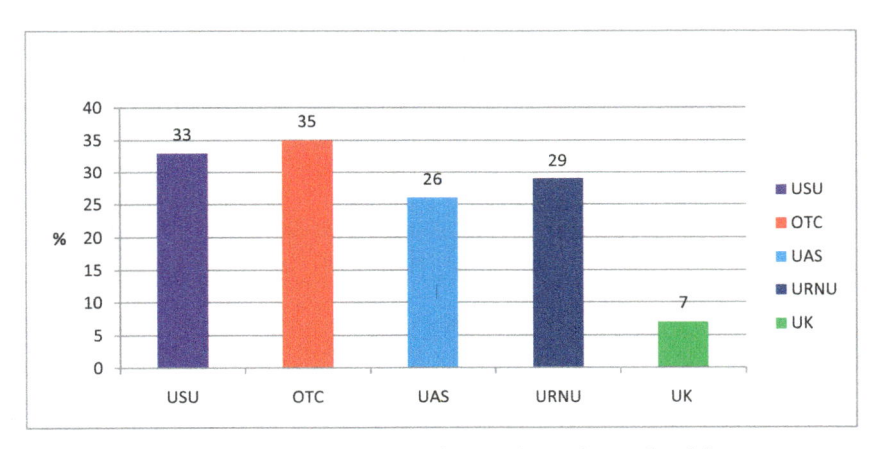

**Figure 3.3:** Proportion of sample attending independent school, by percentage.

overall and by service unit, who attended an independent sector (fee-paying) school or college (including both boarders and day pupils) whilst studying for A levels or equivalent.

The UK average for pupils attending schools in the independent sector for A level (or equivalent) education is about 7%.[55] As the survey data shows, the proportion in each USU from this educational background prior to university is far higher than the national average. We were unable to compare educational

---

[55] **Social Mobility** and **Child Poverty Commission.** (2014). *Elitist Britain?* Retrieved from https://www.gov.uk/government/publications/elitist-britain

backgrounds by service units against averages for individual universities because of the differentials in response rates from individual units and thus specific universities.[56] The disproportionate number of USU participants with an educational background in the independent sector raises wider points about the extent of the provision of the USUs across the higher education sector, and we discuss this in more detail in Chapter 7.

### 3.1.4. Length of time in unit

Figure 3.4 shows the length of time student respondents had spent in their units. There is a common picture across the three service units of a higher proportion having up to one year's experience. We have included this information here, as it may be useful in illuminating some of the experientially-based responses discussed later in this chapter. It also indicates quite clearly the different participation patterns across the three units, which include patterns of training according to service unit syllabi.

In conclusion, in terms of the demographic characteristics of the survey sample, we have made a working assumption for the analysis which follows that the sample is broadly representative of the service units as a whole, but that because response rates from some specific units were low, appropriate caution needs to be exercised in the interpretation of some survey results.

## 3.2 University attendance, qualifications, degree subjects and other activities

In this section we consider the type of university attended by our survey respondents, the qualifications and degree subjects for which they were registered and information about other activities undertaken at university.

### 3.2.1. Representation across the higher education sector

Student participation in USUs is uneven across the higher education sector. Anecdotally, it is widely recognised by those responsible for the USUs within the MoD and armed forces that the proportion of USU participants attending a Russell Group university is far higher than those attending from other mission group universities or types of institution, particularly from the post-1992 new universities. Overall, our survey showed that 53% of respondents attended a Russell Group university (which number 24), 14% attended a University

---

[56] Note that it might be feasible to do this at a very crude level, given that universities routinely collect information about their entrants' educational backgrounds. Any meaningful comparison would require full coverage from across the USUs, something which we cannot claim to have in this survey.

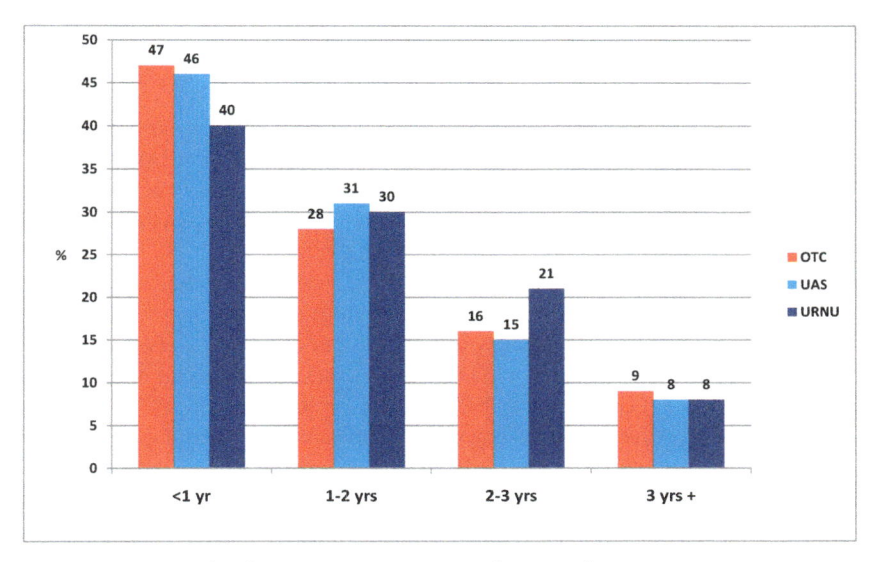

[Bar chart showing length of time in unit at point of survey by percentage for OTC, UAS, URNU:
- <1 yr: OTC 47, UAS 46, URNU 40
- 1-2 yrs: OTC 28, UAS 31, URNU 30
- 2-3 yrs: OTC 16, UAS 15, URNU 21
- 3 yrs +: OTC 9, UAS 8, URNU 8]

**Figure 3.4:** Length of time in unit at point of survey, by percentage.

Alliance institution (which number 20) and 2% attended a GuildHE institution (which number 30).[57]

Yet the survey also gave a good indication of the reach (and thus potential reach) of the USUs across the whole university sector. A total of 108 higher education institutions were represented in terms of student responses in the survey, which included responses from all 46 USUs. Note that the UK national body representing universities across the higher education sector, Universities UK, has 133 members. The sample produced responses from OTC participants attending 82 different institutions, UAS participants from 83 different institutions and URNU participants at 54 institutions. The full list of institutions represented by student participants is given in Appendix 5. The key point here is about the reach of the USUs in terms of providing a *potential* opportunity for students across the higher education sector, and the limits to that reach in terms of actually drawing students in from across the sector. The data clearly shows that the USUs have reach beyond their traditional home in the established (primarily Russell Group) universities, and the limits to that reach. We discuss in Chapter 7 the wider issues the data on representation of the USUs and issues of reach raises for participation.

---

[57] Details on Russell Group membership are available at: http://www.russellgroup.ac.uk/our-universities/. Details on University Alliance membership are available at: http://www.unialliance.ac.uk/member/. Details on GuildHE membership are available at: http://www.guildhe.ac.uk/members/

### 3.2.2. University degree type and stage of joining the university armed service units

A very common perception of the USUs is that they are the preserve of undergraduate students, particularly students in the first two years of study for a BA or BSc (undergraduate or Bachelors) university degree (typically of three years' duration in England, Wales and Northern Ireland, and four years' duration in Scotland). The data in Figure 3.5 supports this perception.

Reflecting the specialist training delivered in some universities in particular subjects (typically sciences, including engineering), included amongst the possible response choices to the survey question about degree type was a four-year degree leading to the award of a Masters qualification (such as an MEng.), and Figure 3.5 shows the differences between the service units in the proportion of members surveyed undertaking such degrees. The option of postgraduate diploma was also included as a potential option for response; only one URNU and one OTC participant selected this option, and these data are not included in Figure 3.5. The proportion registered for a PhD was very small. A point to note on the basis of the data in Figure 3.5 is the potential that the USU experience may offer for students across different stage cohorts to mix, something shared across many student activities but often very limited through degree programmes.

It is also commonly assumed that the majority of USU participants join in their first year of study, and the data shown in Figure 3.6 supports this.

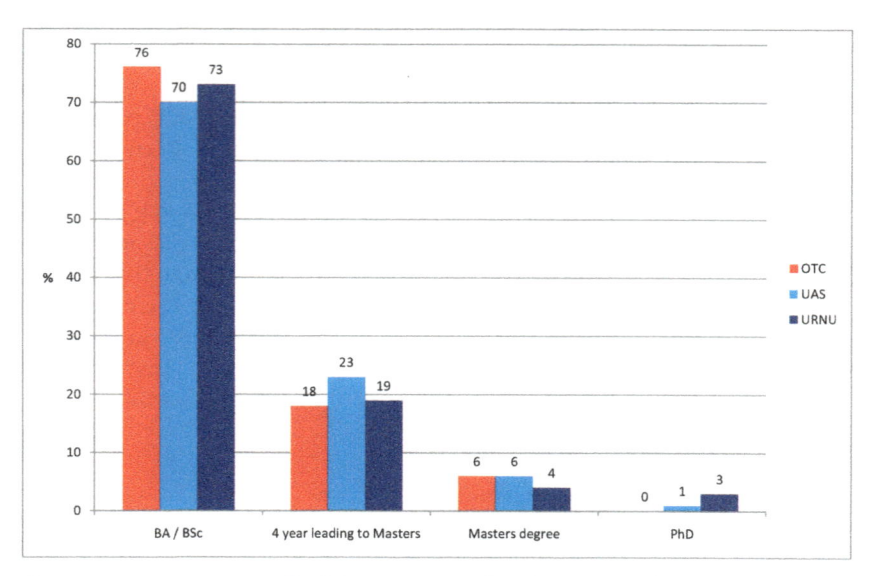

**Figure 3.5:** Proportion of USU participants by degree type, by percentage.

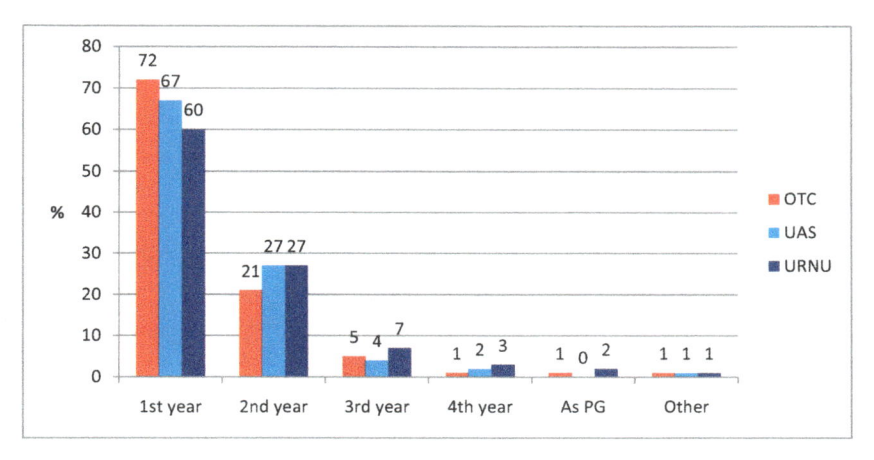

**Figure 3.6:** University stage on joining USU, by percentage.

Taking the data indicated in Figures 3.5 and 3.6 together, we can conclude both that participating in a USU is primarily an undergraduate activity, and one which for the majority commences in the first year of study, but also that this is not an absolute pattern. In terms of USU recruitment debates, two points follow from this. The first concerns the potential for expanded participation or more inclusive participation that may exist with a greater focus on students beyond the first year of undergraduate study at the point of joining. The second concerns the limits to participation amongst students in later stages of study (particularly at Masters level) because of the difficulties of combining academic and USU commitments.

### 3.2.3. University armed service units participation and degree subject

The USUs offer the experience of participation to university students regardless of subject studied and degree programme followed. We were interested to explore whether USU participation mapped on to particular degree subjects, and how any pattern of USU participation by degree subject corresponded to national patterns in the higher education sector. We asked survey respondents the title of their degree programme, and manually coded the data against Joint Academic Coding System (JACS) codes used by the Higher Education Statistics Agency (HESA) for all UK degree programmes.[58] Table 3.1 and Figures 3.7, 3.8, 3.9 and 3.10 show the results of this analysis (with the figures omitting subject areas where USU participation was minimal or negligible).

---

[58] The Higher Education Statistics Agency JACS3 codes are available at: https://www.hesa.ac.uk/component/content/article?id=1787

|   | JACS subject area | OTC | UAS | URNU | National UK |
|---|---|---|---|---|---|
| 1 | Medicine and dentistry | 5 | 10 | 11 | 3 |
| 2 | Subjects allied to medicine | 4 | 2 | 5 | 12 |
| 3 | Biological sciences | 14 | 11 | 11 | 9 |
| 4 | Veterinary science | <1 | <1 | <1 | <1 |
| 5 | Agriculture & related subjects | <1 | <1 | <1 | 1 |
| 6 | Physical sciences | 9 | 11 | 10 | 4 |
| 7 | Mathematical sciences | 1 | 3 | 1 | 2 |
| 8 | Computer science | 2 | 2 | 2 | 4 |
| 9 | Engineering & technology | 16 | 30 | 22 | 7 |
| A | Architecture, building & planning | 1 | <1 | 1 | 2 |
| B | Social studies | 14 | 11 | 12 | 9 |
| C | Law | 3 | 3 | 2 | 4 |
| D | Business and administrative studies | 8 | 5 | 4 | 14 |
| E | Mass communications & documentation | <1 | <1 | 1 | 2 |
| F | Languages | 4 | 2 | 5 | 5 |
| G | Historical & philosophical studies | 10 | 4 | 5 | 4 |
| H | Creative arts & design | 2 | 1 | <1 | 7 |
| I | Education | <1 | <1 | <1 | 8 |
| J | Combined | 3 | 3 | 4 | 3 |

**Table 3.1:** Proportion of USU participants by JACS subject codes, by percentage.

Note that for some subject areas, this was a crude exercise. Some subjects (such as geography) will be coded by HESA either as '6' (for physical geography) or 'B' (for human geography), but many geography degrees combine instruction in both physical and human geography and many students will not be aware of the HESA and/or institutional code assigned to their particular degree programme. We have made an educated assumption when coding this subject (with the caveat that two of the research team have considerable experience as geography lecturers in higher education). We have coded any combined honours subject as 'J', where the degree programme title indicated by the student showed a division across two of the JACS subject areas. The JACS codes themselves are broad, grouping together more traditional degree subjects with more applied courses of study, so for example, biological sciences includes biology, zoology and biochemistry, along with applied programmes in sport and exercise. Social studies combines economics and anthropology alongside emergent academic disciplines such as criminology

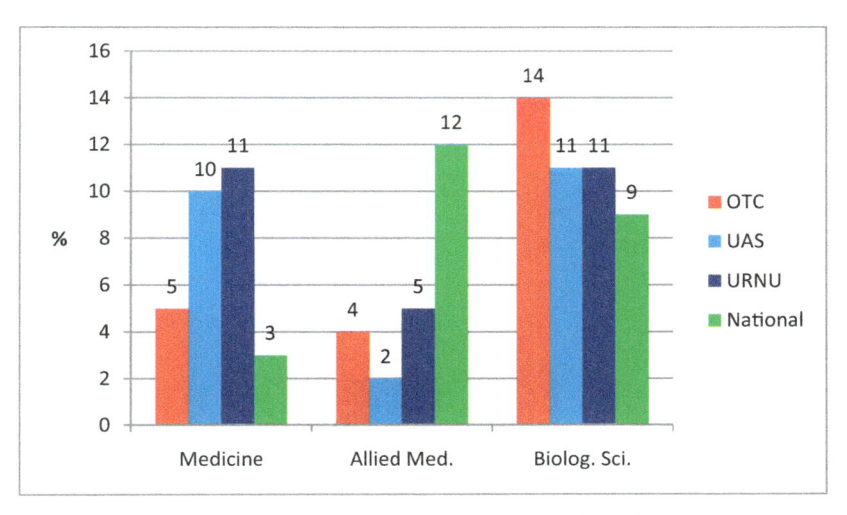

**Figure 3.7:** Percentage of USU participants registered on degree programmes in medicine, subjects allied to medicine and biological sciences.

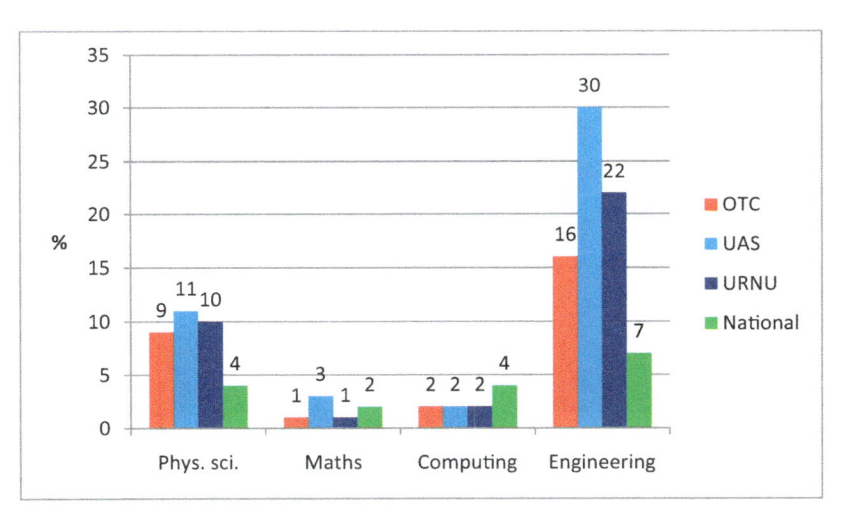

**Figure 3.8:** Percentage of USU participants registered on degree programmes in physical sciences, maths, computing and engineering.

and development studies. Note also that the HESA data used includes both full-time and part-time students (although the proportion taking part-time study is reducing nationally), and includes both undergraduate and postgraduate degrees.

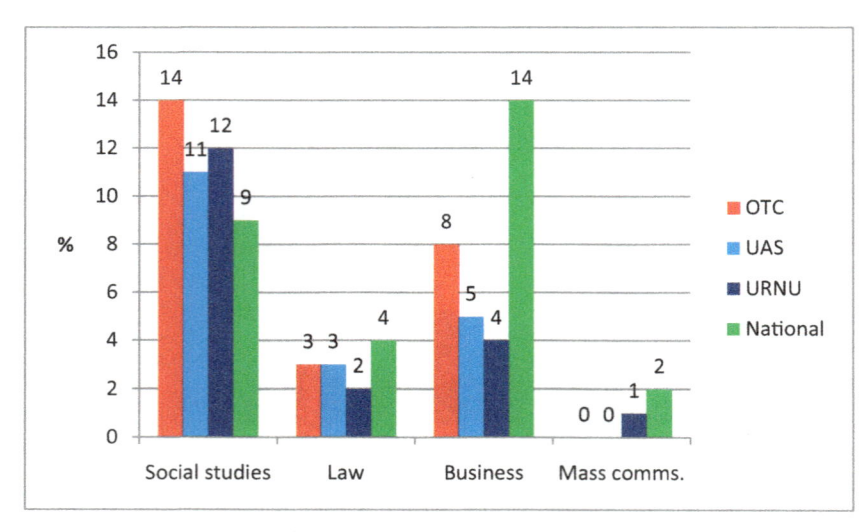

**Figure 3.9:** Percentage of USU participants registered on degree programmes in social studies, law, business and mass communications.

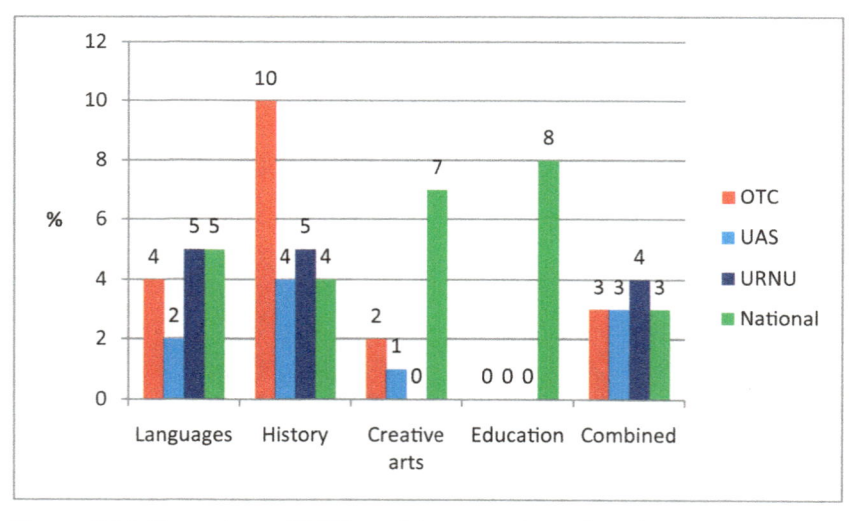

**Figure 3.10:** Percentage of USU participants registered on degree programmes in languages, historical studies, creative arts, education and combined studies.

In terms of comparisons between the service units, and against national rates of participation in degree programmes, some interesting points emerge. The proportions of USU participants taking degrees in medicine or biological sciences is above the national figure, and the reverse is the case for those taking subjects allied to medicine. The proportion of USU participants taking degrees in physical sciences or in engineering and technology is above the national figure, significantly so in the case of engineering, with 16% of OTC participants, 30% of UAS participants and 22% of URNU participants taking these subjects. The proportions taking social studies degrees is higher amongst USU participants, particularly those in the OTC, but lower for law, business and administrative studies, and in mass communications and documentation. The contrast between the proportion of OTC participants studying historical and philosophical studies compared with the other service units and the national picture is striking, as is the very small (and negligible) proportions of USU participants taking creative arts and design or education degrees.

Two points follow from this data, with the proviso that the indications given are potentially quite crude. The first is that there may be a correlation between the high proportions (particularly for UAS and URNU participants) taking engineering degrees, and the aspirations of those students for careers in aviation and marine engineering (within or beyond the RAF or Royal Navy). Students, in other words, may be making a strategic choice to participate in a USU as part of a package of activities undertaken at university aimed towards the pursuit of a particular career. The second point (see also 3.2.1 above) is that the degree subject patterns indicated above for USU participants may correlate quite directly with the dominance in the sample and in the USUs of students attending Russell Group universities, where certain subjects and approaches to subjects will dominate. This may also reflect the dominance of more traditional academic subjects studied by these students, where a significant proportion were educated in the independent sector where such subjects have continued to maintain purchase.

### 3.2.4. *Membership of other clubs and societies*

Across the USU survey participants, 60% indicated that they were members of other university or Student Union clubs or societies, and 40% indicated that they were not. This is of passing interest because it shows the extent to which USU participants engage across a range of other activities beyond their USU commitments. Sports activities dominated the list, with a much smaller proportion mentioning religious, political, music or degree subject-related societies, or voluntary or charitable activities. Sports clubs and activities arguably give a similar type of experience to students in terms of physical activity, and potentially too in terms of opportunities for the development of personal management and organisational skills. What is also notable is the relatively small number who included volunteering or community-based activities amongst USU members. We return to the question of the comparability or otherwise of the USU experience with other student activities in Chapter 7.

## 3.3 Joining a university armed service unit

In this section, we consider pre-university awareness of the USUs, the mechanisms by which students find out about USUs and student motivations for joining.

### 3.3.1. Awareness of university armed service units before arriving at university

Students were asked about their awareness of the existence of the USUs prior to arrival at university, and if so, whether pre-existing knowledge was a factor in their choice of university (Table 3.2).

| Where you aware of USUs before arriving at university? | OTC | UAS | URNU |
| --- | --- | --- | --- |
| No | 31 | 23 | 39 |
| Yes, but it was NOT a factor in my choice of university | 52 | 44 | 49 |
| Yes, and it was a factor in my choice of university | 17 | 32 | 11 |

**Table 3.2:** Awareness of USUs prior to arriving at university, by percentage.

URNU members show the lowest levels of pre-entry awareness of the service units, and constitute the lowest proportion who considered the USUs to be a factor in their choice of university. There was greatest pre-university awareness amongst UAS members, with three quarters of them having existing knowledge, and just under one third seeing the existence of a squadron as influential in their choice of university. This may be explained by pro-activity on the part of potential members in seeking out access to flying experience because it is a scarce resource, coupled with awareness of the opportunities UAS participation might provide for entry into either a RAF career in aviation or in civilian aviation. Qualitative comments from the 207 respondents who identified the existence of a USU as a factor in their university choice illustrate this, with comments such as 'I wanted a place at a university linked to EMUAS', 'I confirmed my chosen university was affiliated to a USU' and 'I did not apply to any universities without an UOTC'. For some, it was a key part of their decision-making:

> 'I knew I wanted to join the UAS so I found all the universities associated with a UAS and found the course I wanted to do and went from there.'
>
> 'The fact that an URNU was located at Liverpool made me choose it over other (non-URNU) universities with similar entrance requirements.'

For others, it was one of a number of factors:

'I looked out for mentions of OTC units in prospectuses – at the time I did not realise that several universities were affiliated to one base. Eventually this did not majorly change my choice of applications, as the course I decided to apply for is very specialist.'
'Received a leaflet for UOTC at a UCAS fair; whilst it was a small factor, it did lead me to look at some universities in a slightly more positive light.'
'When left in clearing with weaker academic reasons on choosing a university, the reputation of EMUOTC was a factor in choosing a university in the East Midlands.'
'I made sure that all of my chosen universities were affiliated with a UAS so I [could] join a UAS, but beyond that actual selection of university preference was solely on the degrees on offer and not the individual UASs.'
'Typed in university air squadron in Google and UBAS came up first, Coventry was one uni on their list and so it became one of my potential choices and ended up going there.'
'Although my university education is first and foremost, my choice of university reflected my interests in joining Glasgow & Strathclyde URNU. My university career and URNU career enjoy nearly equal favourable status in prioritisation.'

This is a potentially significant finding, not least for universities working in a competitive undergraduate recruitment market.

Pre-university awareness of USUs is also differentiated by gender, and Table 3.3 shows pre-entry awareness of USUs amongst female survey respondents.

Over half of all female members of URNUs were not aware of the existence of the USUs before arriving at university, a lack of awareness repeated for the OTCs and UASs. In the OTCs 42% of women (compared with 27% of men) were not aware of the USUs. The proportion of women members of UASs using the existence of a unit as a factor in their choice of university was lower than for men, but still high. We discuss the wider issues raised by this question of differential awareness of USUs by gender in Chapter 7.

| Where you aware of USUs before arriving at university? | OTC | UAS | URNU |
| --- | --- | --- | --- |
| No | 42 | 38 | 55 |
| Yes, but it was NOT a factor in my choice of university | 46 | 40 | 37 |
| Yes, and it was a factor in my choice of university | 12 | 22 | 8 |

**Table 3.3:** Awareness of USUs prior to arriving at university amongst women, by percentage.

58  The Value of the University Armed Service Units

### 3.3.2. Finding out about the university armed service units

Survey respondents were asked about how they found out about the USU they eventually joined. The proportion from all three service units who received information directly from university careers services, Student Unions, a communication direct from a USU or via university or Student Union websites was minimal. Key sources of information are shown in Figure 3.11.

The Freshers' Fairs are evidently very significant as a mechanism by which students, on joining university, find out about the existence of the USUs. Freshers' Fairs appear to be particularly significant for the URNUs, which had the highest proportion of students unaware of the units prior to university. Freshers' Fairs are also slightly more significant for women than men: for the OTCs, 31% of female members identified Freshers' Fairs as initial sources of information, compared to 26% of male members. For the URNUs, it was the primary information source for 48% of women compared with 32% of men. For the UAS, it was the primary source of information for 30% of women and 18% of men.

The cadets (either single service or the combined cadet force) are also an important source of information and, we assume, encouragement to school-aged students to consider USU participation at university. We asked explicitly about membership of uniformed youth organisations whilst at school. Results showed that 42% of OTC, 48% of UAS and 31% of URNU members had previously been in the cadets; in comparison, across the sample of USU members, a quarter had been in the Brownies, Cubs, Scouts or Guides. Overall, sources of information under direct control of the armed forces or service units, that is the cadets, armed forces careers service, leafleting and USU websites, were primary

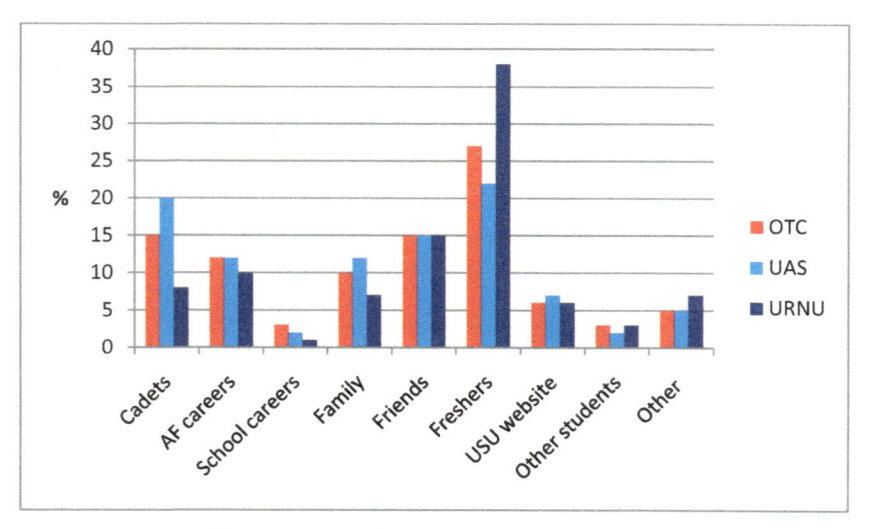

**Figure 3.11:** Significant sources of information about USUs, by percentage.

sources of information for 35% of OTC, 40% of UAS and 24% of URNU members. Sources direct from the university and from the Student Union, were negligible as sources of information.

Social networks, meaning friends, family and other students, were a source of information for just over a quarter of participants (28% of OTC, 29% of UAS and 25% of URNU members). We asked specifically about whether any relatives had been members of a USU, and 79% of OTC, 82% of UAS and 87% of URNU members said that they had no family connection. OTC members had the higher proportion of family connections, with 20% identifying a sibling, parent, grandparent or other close family member with USU membership.

We were also interested in whether the type of school attended was significant or influential in terms of finding out about USUs in the first place. For all USU members, the lowest proportion (20% of USU members) using Freshers' Fairs as their primary information source had attended an independent sector fee-paying school as a boarder. In contrast, 31% USU members who had attended a further education or sixth form college as a non-boarder identified Freshers' Fairs as their primary source of information, as did 25% of USU members who had attended state school as day pupils. We would suggest that Freshers' Fairs are more significant as a source of information for those attending state sector education.

Where respondents identified 'other' as an initial source of information, we asked for elaboration. Seemingly random browsing through websites was a significant here:

'While at school a few of us were looking at OTCs, researched it myself really. Leeds happened to have one, turns out a very good example of an OTC from my interaction with other South Yorkshire based units [...] and joined when I arrived at University.'

There were also chance encounters with individuals from the armed forces, or visits to schools by representatives from the armed forces, and even quite random encounters which turned out to be influential:

'Dancing at the Edinburgh Tattoo and meeting members of the OTC who were performing as pirates and fishermen and getting paid for it whereas I was not.'

### 3.3.3. *Motivations for joining a university armed service unit*

We were interested in student motivations for joining a USU, and asked respondents to identify factors motivating enlistment (students could select all that applied to them). Table 3.4 shows the patterns of choice across the three services and for the USUs as a whole, and Figure 3.12 presents this data graphically for ease of comparison.

60  The Value of the University Armed Service Units

| Motivation | OTC | UAS | URNU | All USUs |
|---|---|---|---|---|
| Adventurous training opportunities | 71 | 85 | 70 | 76 |
| Armed Forces or MoD bursary | 12 | 10 | 7 | 10 |
| For the challenge | 72 | 70 | 64 | 70 |
| CV enhancement | 59 | 57 | 58 | 58 |
| Flying opportunities | 1 | 84 | 13 | 33 |
| Interest in the military | 80 | 86 | 71 | 81 |
| Pay | 59 | 28 | 38 | 44 |
| Sailing/nautical skills | 6 | 9 | 59 | 15 |
| Shooting | 24 | 27 | 7 | 22 |
| Sport | 34 | 60 | 38 | 44 |
| Transferable skills | 57 | 71 | 63 | 63 |
| University course credits | <1 | 1 | <1 | <1 |
| Wanting to develop military skills | 55 | 52 | 42 | 51 |
| Other |  |  |  | 10 |

Table 3.4: Motivations for joining by service unit, by percentage.

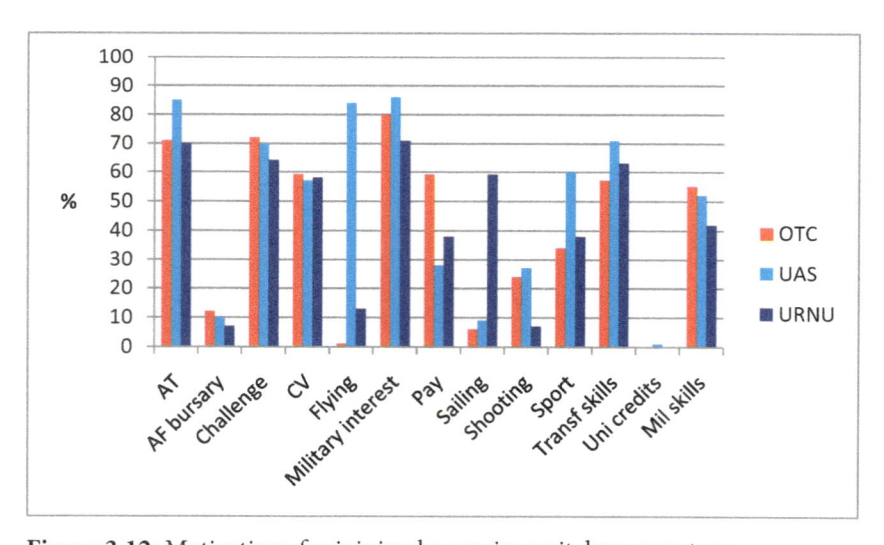

Figure 3.12: Motivations for joining by service unit, by percentage.

There are some very obvious differences in motivations between the units, with 84% of UAS members identifying 'flying opportunities', 59% of URNU members identifying 'sailing/nautical skills' and 24% of OTC and 27% of UAS members identifying 'shooting skills'. Overall, 'interest in the military' is the most commonly identified reason, with 81% of USU members selecting this, although note the difference between UAS and URNU members, with 86% and 71% respectively. Pay is a more commonly cited motivator for OTC (59%) than URNU (38%) or UAS (28%) members; for UAS members, the access to a flying opportunity (a scarce resource) is clearly more significant. There are differences too between the three services in terms of transferable skills, with a higher proportion of UAS members identifying transferable skills (71%) as a motivator than URNU (63%) or OTC (57%) members. Sport is more commonly identified as a motivator for UAS (60%) rather than OTC and URNU members.

If we compare motivations for joining not just across the three services, but between men and women in each service, we see a slightly different picture. Table 3.5 provides the data, and Figures 3.13, 3.14 and 3.15 show this information graphically for ease of comparison.

A higher proportion of men identify 'military interest' and 'military skills' as motivations for joining the OTC compared with women. A slightly higher proportion of women identify 'adventurous training' and 'for the challenge', 'sport'

| Motivation | OTC men | OTC women | UAS men | UAS women | URNU men | URNU women |
|---|---|---|---|---|---|---|
| Adventurous training opportunities | 70 | 74 | 86 | 85 | 72 | 67 |
| Armed Forces/MoD bursary | 15 | 6 | 11 | 9 | 7 | 4 |
| For the challenge | 70 | 72 | 68 | 73 | 58 | 74 |
| CV enhancement | 59 | 57 | 59 | 55 | 59 | 58 |
| Flying opportunities | 1 | 2 | 89 | 76 | 13 | 12 |
| Interest in the military | 85 | 69 | 91 | 76 | 83 | 54 |
| Pay | 63 | 50 | 32 | 22 | 40 | 35 |
| Sailing/nautical skills | 7 | 7 | 9 | 10 | 60 | 60 |
| Shooting | 27 | 17 | 31 | 21 | 10 | 4 |
| Sport | 30 | 44 | 59 | 62 | 38 | 39 |
| Transferable skills | 57 | 59 | 72 | 69 | 64 | 64 |
| Wanting to develop military skills | 63 | 35 | 60 | 37 | 50 | 31 |

**Table 3.5:** Motivations for joining a USU by service unit and gender, by percentage.

62  The Value of the University Armed Service Units

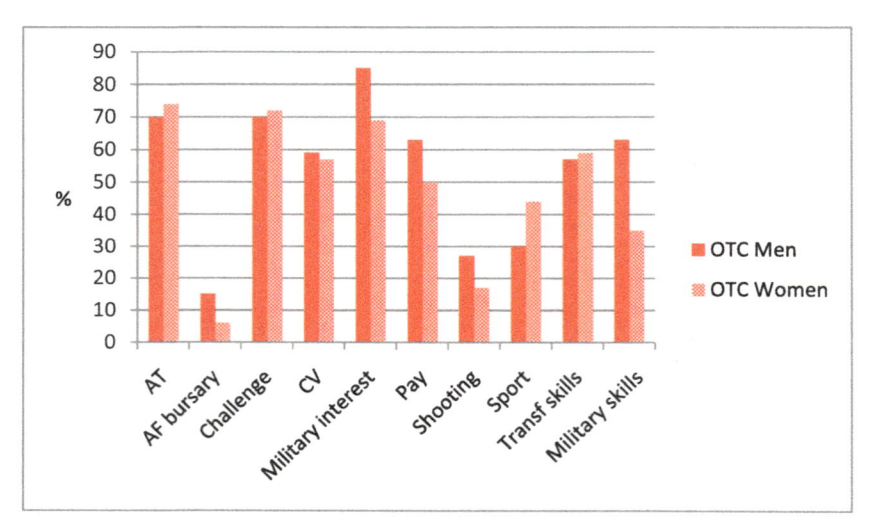

**Figure 3.13:** Motivations for joining OTC, by gender.

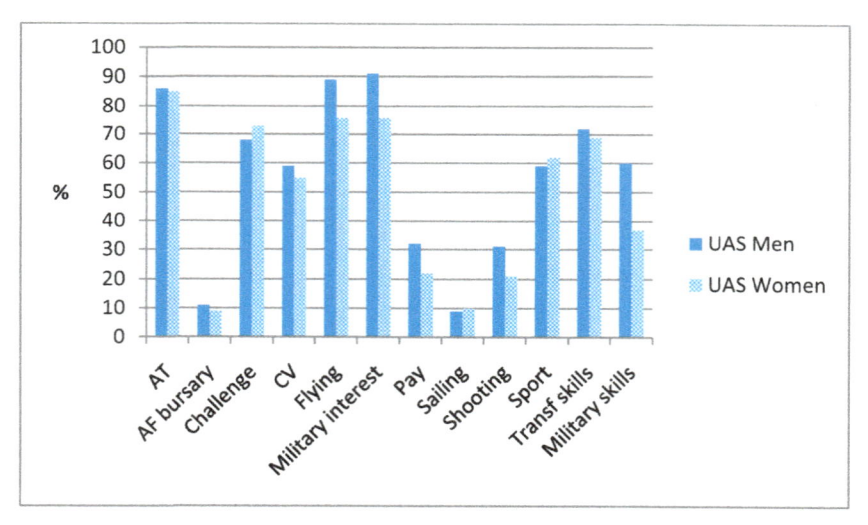

**Figure 3.14:** Motivations for joining UAS, by gender.

and 'transferable skills' than men as motivators for joining the OTC. In both the UAS and URNU, a higher proportion of women identify 'for the challenge' as a motivator for joining than men, and this is particularly marked in the URNU.

We also disaggregated motivations for joining by length of USU participation, but this exercise showed no clear patterns across the various cohorts of

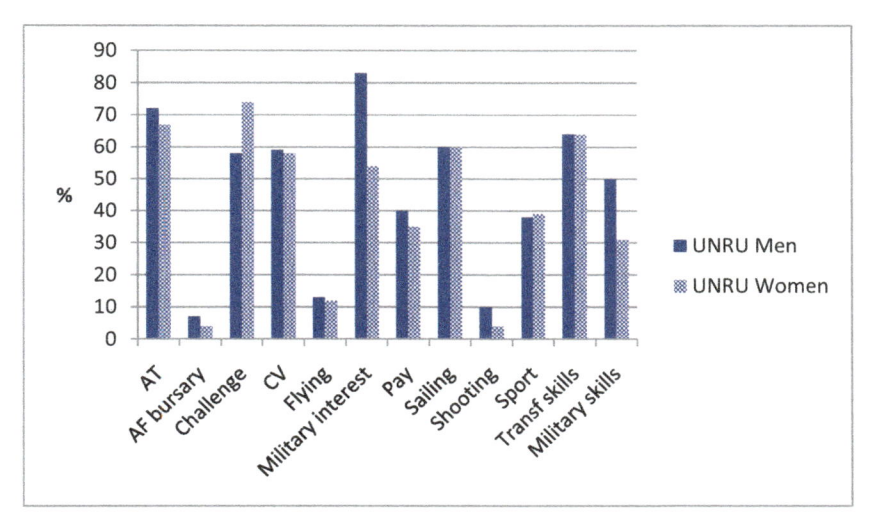

**Figure 3.15:** Motivations for joining URNU, by gender.

participants. For example, the proportions identifying adventurous training as a motivation remained fairly constant across different lengths of participation within each service unit.

## 3.4 University armed service units and skills development

One of the motivators for this research was to investigate the value of the USUs in terms of the skills development for students. As we indicated in the introductory chapter and above, this is an issue of interest in both the higher education sector and a motivation for students joining a unit.

Within universities, various schema exist to identify the nature of the graduate or transferable skills a university education might be expected to inculcate in students, beyond the subject-specific knowledge which their degree programme will have provided. In this research, we drew on the graduate skills framework developed at Newcastle University from 2010 onwards to devise a set of survey questions to establish both whether or not respondents considered their USU and their degree programmes to have helped them develop specific skills, and also to assess the extent to which students considered these skills to have been developed. Appendices 6 and 7 provide the data used to develop the graphics shown in the following figures, which compare student evaluations for each skill in turn. Note that the appendices list the skills in alphabetical order as they appeared in the original survey. In sections 3.4.1–3, we group skills together according to the categories used by the Newcastle graduate skills framework, and section 3.4.4 groups together an additional set of USU-specific skills included in the questions as part of the survey (and which are not included in the Newcastle University framework). For each skill, a Likert scale was used for respondents to evaluate the development of that particular skill, with respondents choosing between the categories 'not at all', 'some but not as much as I would like', 'about as much as I had anticipated', 'more than I had anticipated' and 'way beyond my expectations'. Respondents were also given the option 'not applicable', which we have excluded from the graphs.

In all the graphs that follow, we combine the data from the tables given in Appendices 6 and 7 to show, side by side according to each of the five points on the Likert scale, the proportion of students in each of the three service units making that assessment first (in plain colour shading) of their USU experience, and then (in stippled colour shading) of their university degree. The graphs which follow thus make it possible to see how students in each of the three units rate their skills development from both their USU and their degree programme experience.

### 3.4.1. Cognitive and intellectual skills

This set of skills comprises critical thinking (Figure 3.16), numeracy (Figure 3.17), literacy (Figure 3.18), information literacy (Figure 3.19) and synthesising information (Figure 3.20).

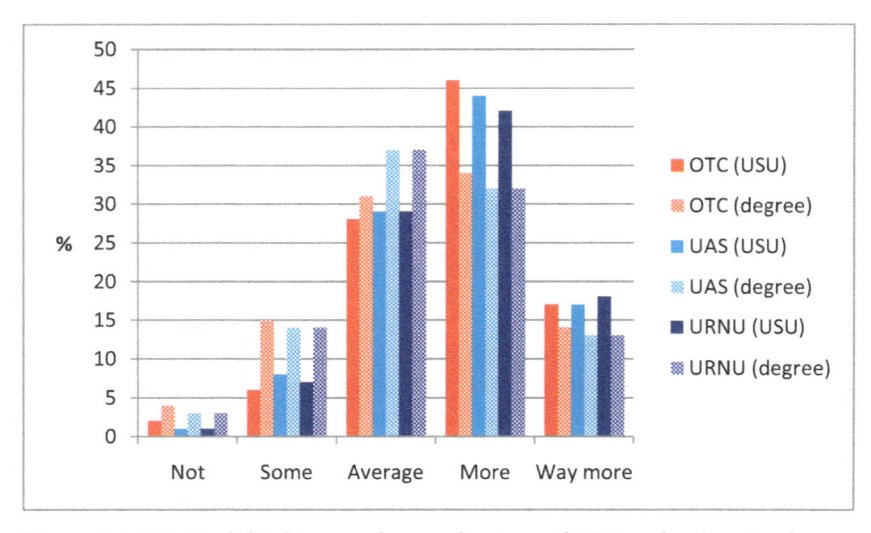

**Figure 3.16:** Critical thinking: student evaluations of USU and university degree.

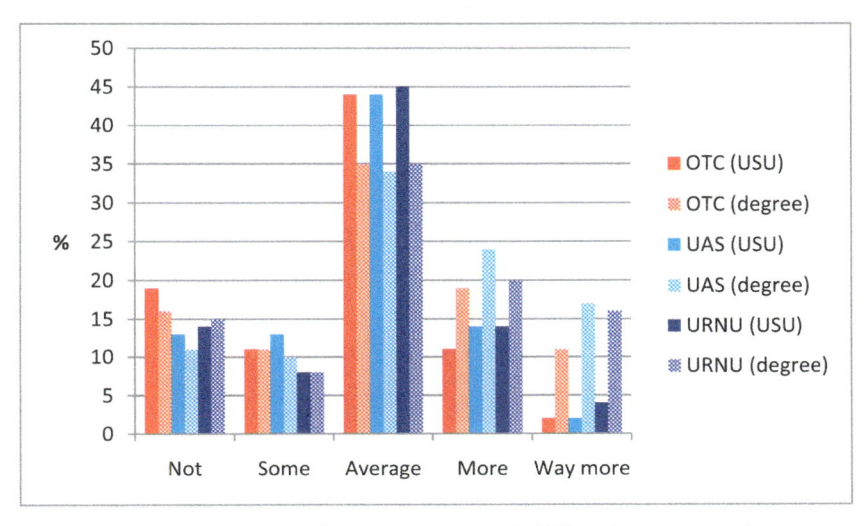

**Figure 3.17:** Numeracy: student evaluations of USU and university degree.

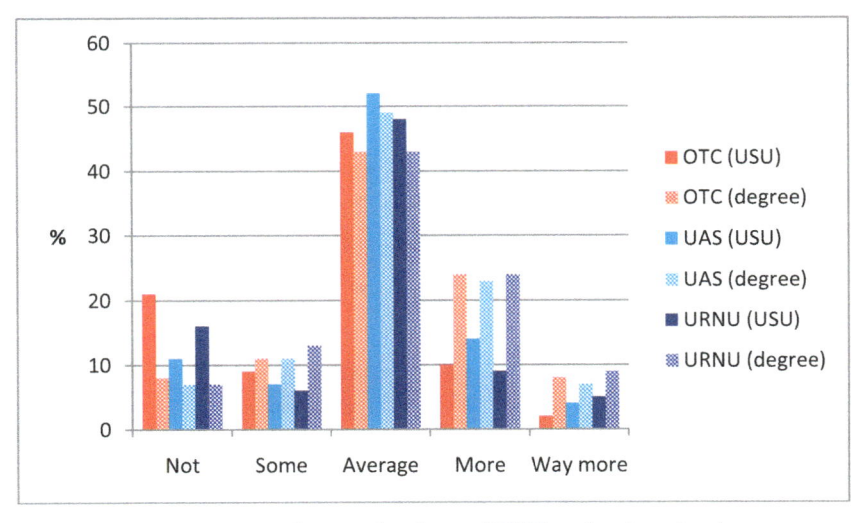

**Figure 3.18:** Literacy: student evaluations of USU and university degree.

The figures above show student evaluations (disaggregated by service unit) for their USU experience alongside their university experience. Student evaluations of cognitive and intellectual skills developed through degree programmes shows a broadly normal distribution. As might be expected, the skills in

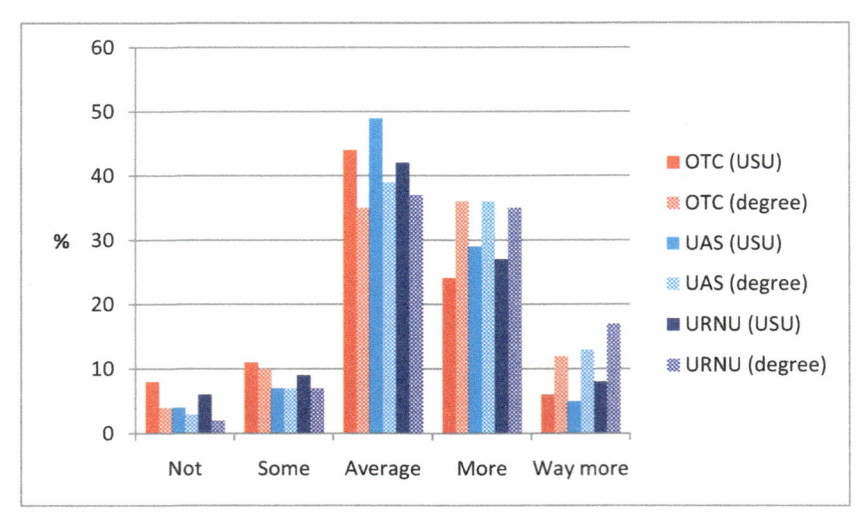

**Figure 3.19.** Information literacy: student evaluations of USU and university degree.

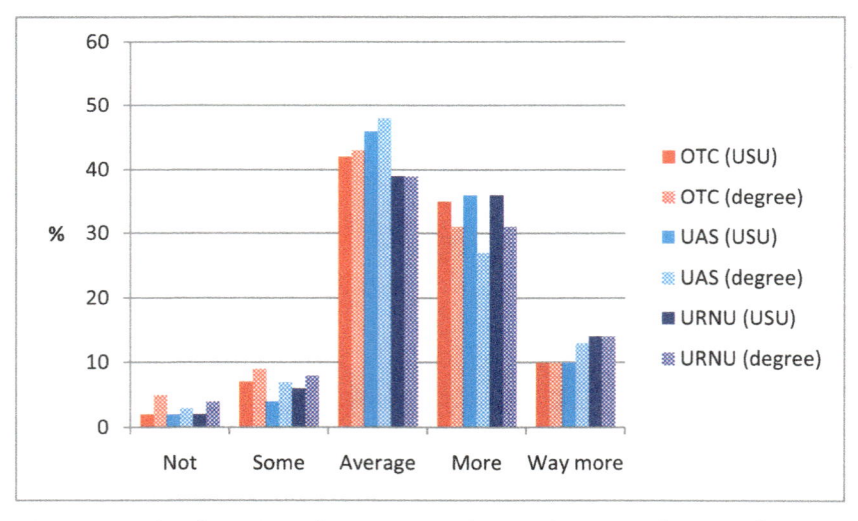

**Figure 3.20:** Synthesising information: student evaluations of USU and university degree.

numeracy, literacy, information literacy and synthesising information—skills which a tertiary-level education at university set out explicitly to develop—are evaluated as being developed 'more' and 'way more' at a higher rate by students through their university degrees than through their USU participation.

What is interesting here are the comparisons between evaluations for critical thinking between the USU experience and the university degree experience (Figure 3.16), which at the levels of 'more' and 'way more' for the USU experience, exceed those for the university degree. This suggests that USU participants both perceive that their USU experience helps them develop their critical thinking skills, and also that their level of expectation about the development of this skill in their USU activities exceeds that for their university education. Although, because of the quantitative questionnaire-based methodology we are unable to pinpoint precisely how and why students reach this conclusion, this is certainly an informative finding for those charged with skills development in both USU and university contexts.

### 3.4.2. Self-management skills

This set of skills comprises organisation and planning (Figure 3.21), project planning (Figure 3.22), decision-making (Figure 3.23), initiative (Figure 3.24), independence (Figure 3.25), adaptability (Figure 3.26), problem-solving (Figure 3.27), time management (Figure 3.28) and budgeting (Figure 3.29). Student evaluations of their USU experience and their university degree in developing these skills are shown in the following figures.

For self-management skills, student evaluations of the development of these skills through their university programme show a normal distribution, with the exception of budgeting. In comparison, student evaluations of the development

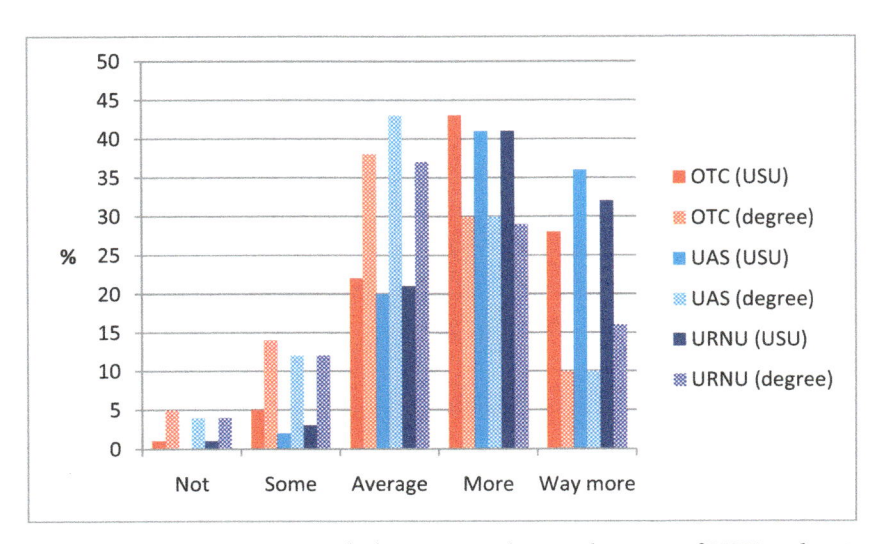

**Figure 3.21:** Organisation and planning: student evaluations of USU and university degree.

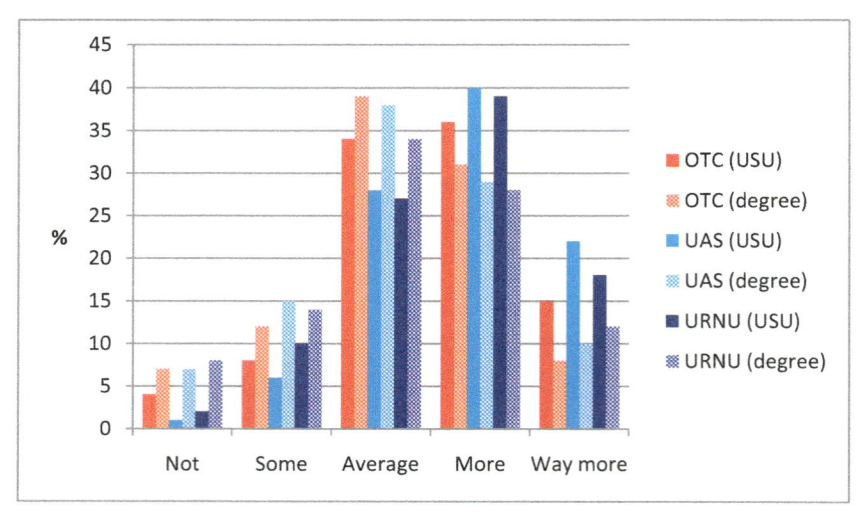

**Figure 3.22:** Project planning: student evaluations of USU and university degree.

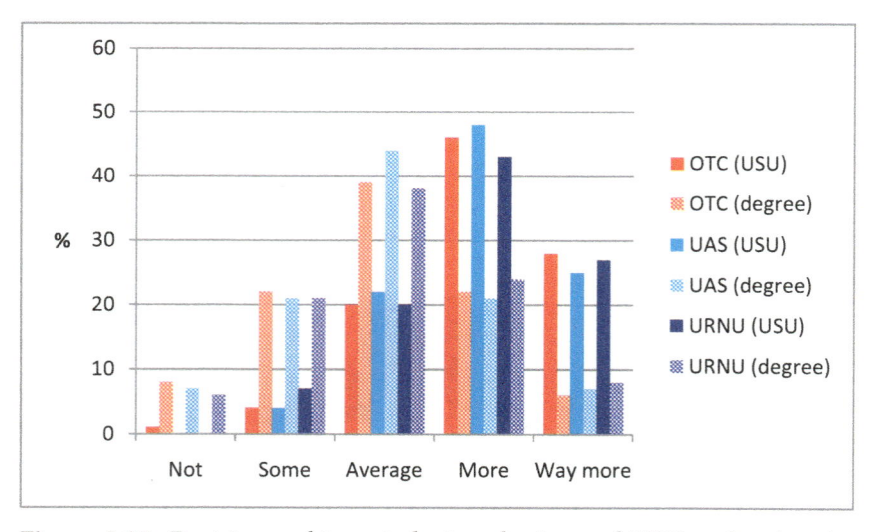

**Figure 3.23:** Decision-making: student evaluations of USU and university degree.

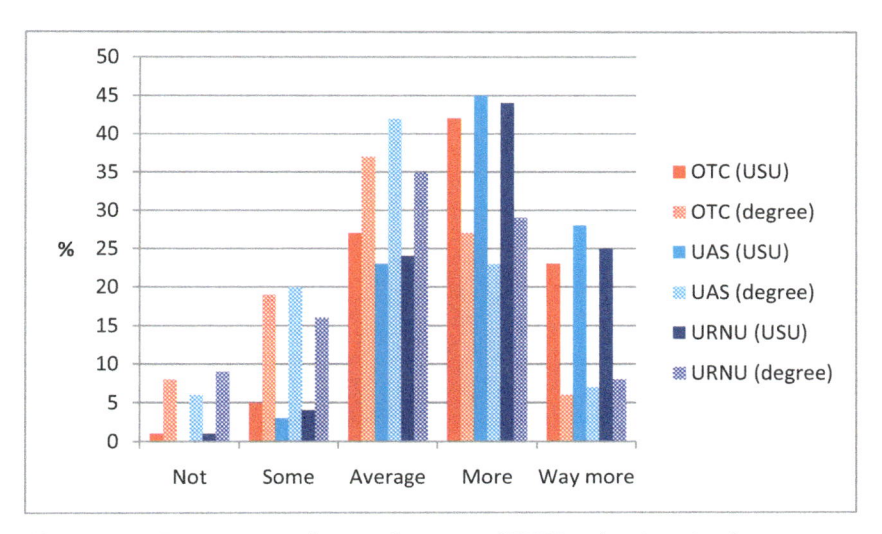

**Figure 3.24:** Initiative: student evaluations of USU and university degree.

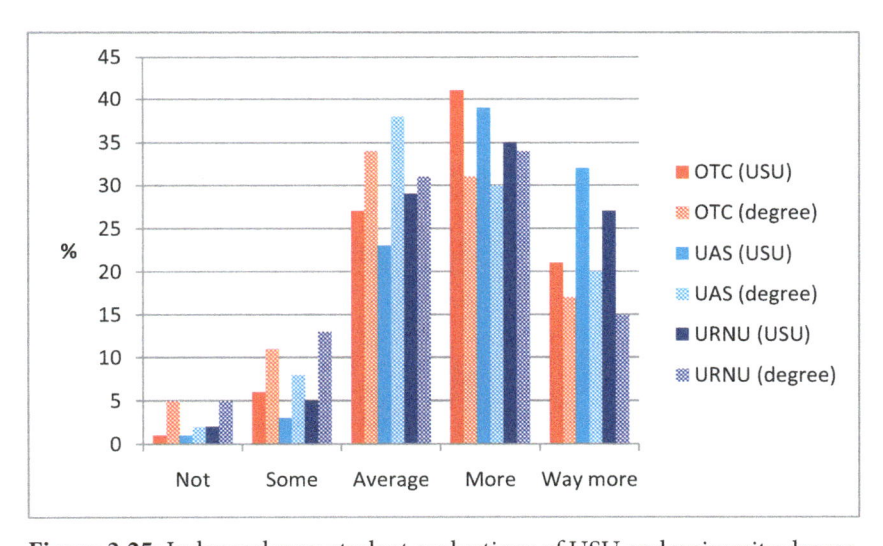

**Figure 3.25:** Independence: student evaluations of USU and university degree.

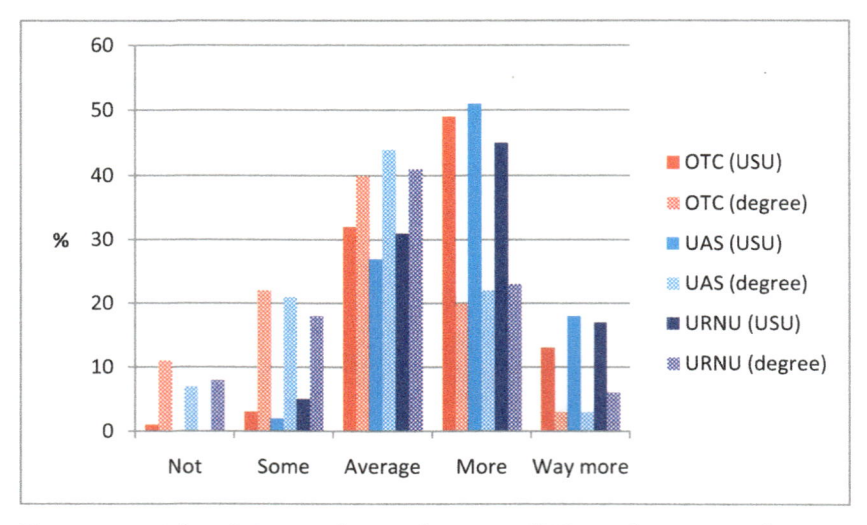

**Figure 3.26:** Adaptability: student evaluations of USU and university degree.

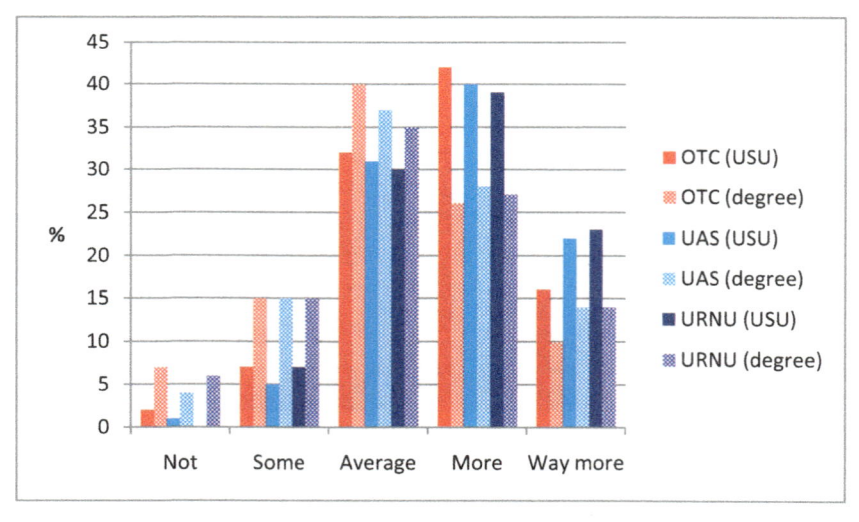

**Figure 3.27:** Problem-solving: student evaluations of USU and university degree.

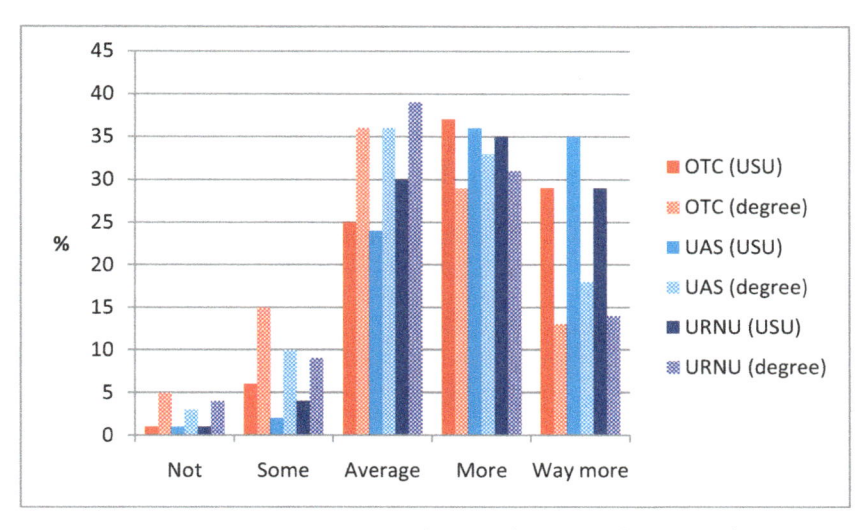

**Figure 3.28:** Time management: student evaluations of USU and university degree.

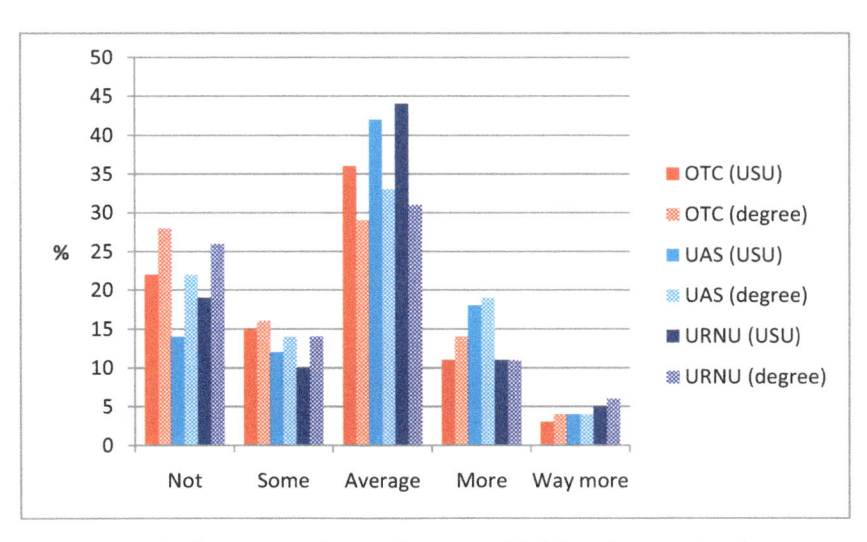

**Figure 3.29:** Budgeting: student evaluations of USU and university degree.

of self-management skills, with the exception of budgeting, show a markedly higher proportion considering that they had developed these skills 'more' and 'way more' through USU participation. From this, we suggest not only that students participating in USUs indicate that they are developing a range of self-management skills through this activity, but also that a significant proportion consider the level to which they have been able to do so to have exceeded their expectations quite considerably. Furthermore, this suggests that skills training at both university and USU levels are beyond participants' expectations, having not expected this as a focus of their activities, rather than any indication that this was necessary a good or bad thing. Once these activities become normalised as part of student expectations, we would expect a normal bell curve to reassert itself.

### 3.4.3. Interaction skills

This set of skills comprises communication skills (Figure 3.30), verbal interaction (Figure 3.31), presentation skills (Figure 3.32), leadership (Figure 3.33) and teamwork (Figure 3.34). Student evaluations of their USU experience and their university degree in developing these skills are shown in the following figures.

For the interaction skills of communication, verbal interaction, presentation and teamwork, student evaluations of the extent to which these have been developed through their university degree reflect a normal distribution. Of

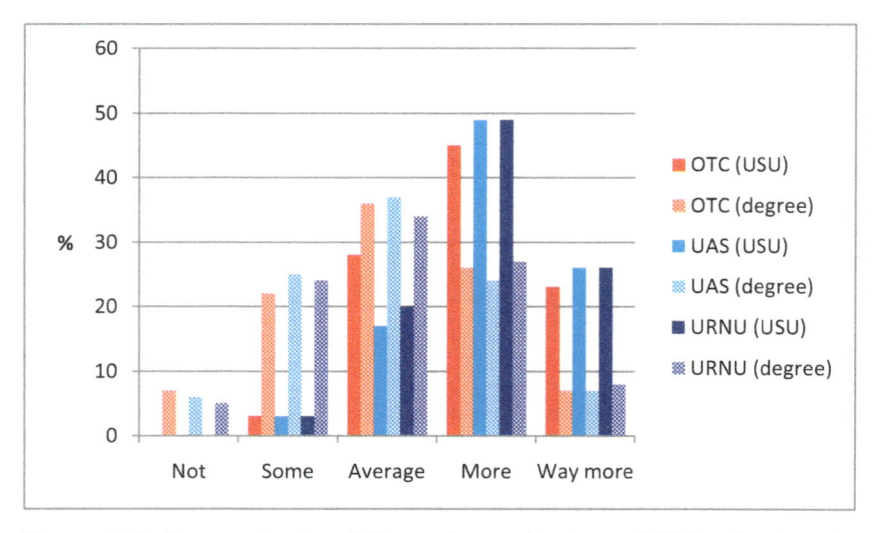

**Figure 3.30:** Communication skills: student evaluations of USU and university degree.

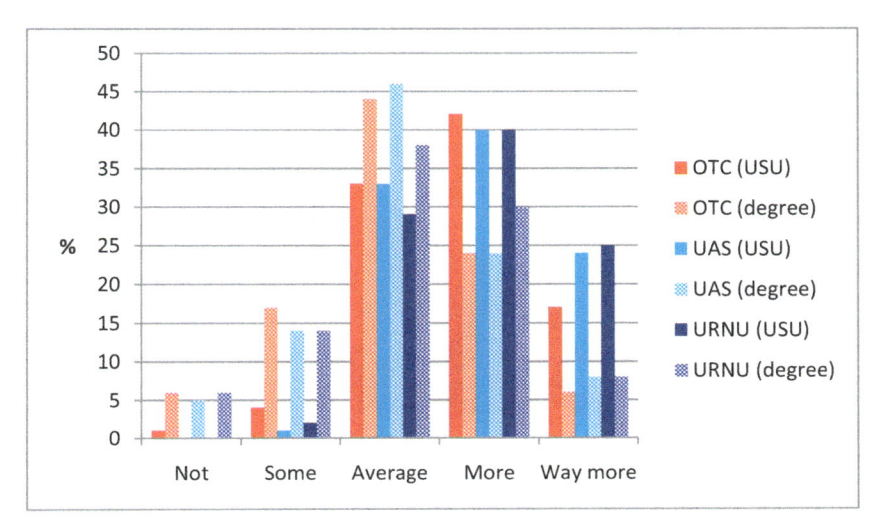

**Figure 3.31:** Verbal interaction: student evaluations of USU and university degree.

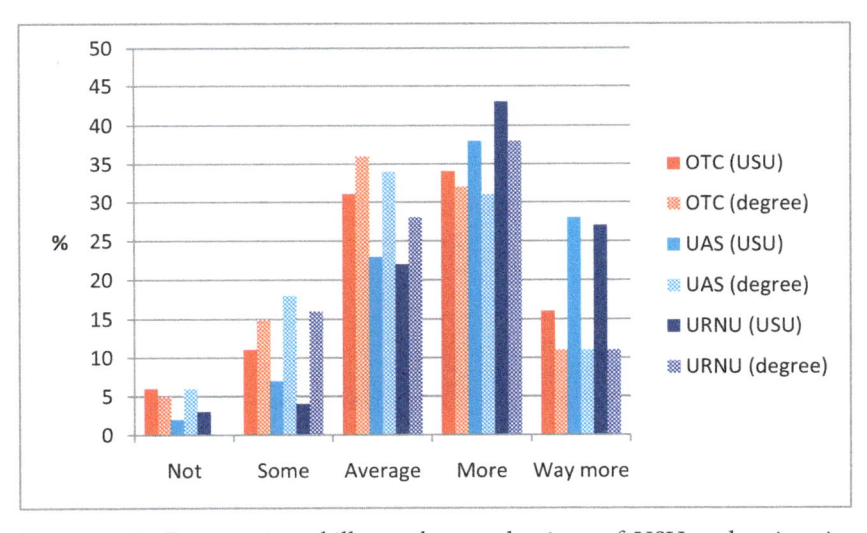

**Figure 3.32:** Presentation skills: student evaluations of USU and university degree.

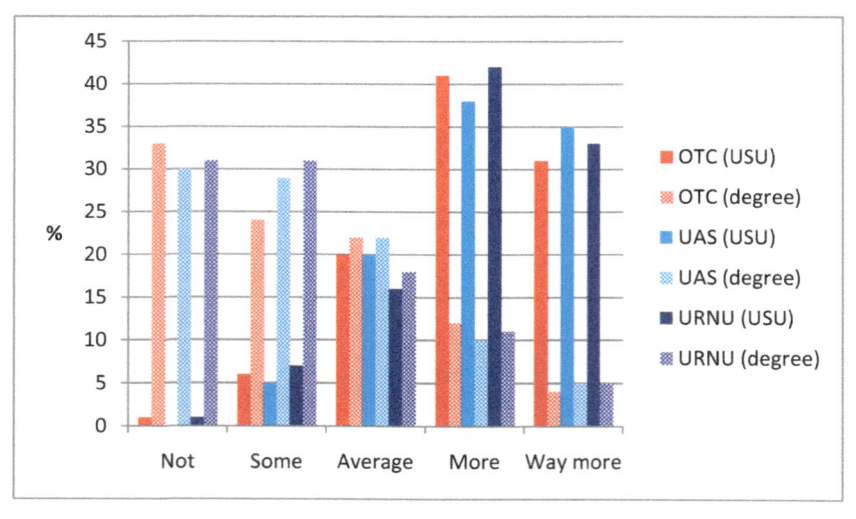

**Figure 3.33:** Leadership: student evaluations of USU and university degree.

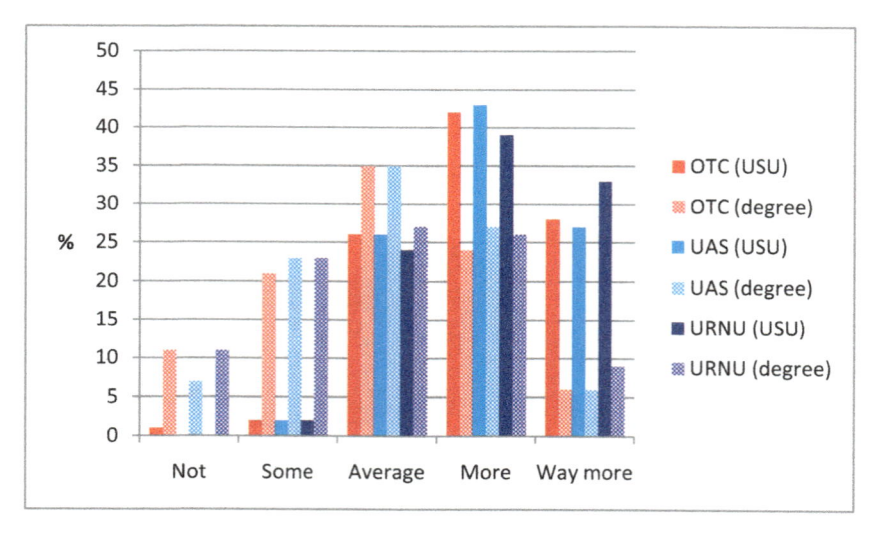

**Figure 3.34:** Teamwork: student evaluations of USU and university degree.

these skills, the exception is leadership, with higher proportions considering that they had had negligible or few opportunities for leadership development through their degree programmes. For all the interaction skills, student evaluations of the level of which their USU participation has helped them develop these skills show a marked skew to the right of each graph, indicating that a significant proportion consider that their USU experience has helped them both to develop these skills, and to do so to an extent which is more or considerably more than they had anticipated. Leadership is defined in the Newcastle skills framework as the ability to 'motivate and co-ordinate group members, taking responsibility for decisions and results'.[59] Although it is a graduate skill, it appears that a relatively small proportion consider their degree programmes to help them develop it. It is possible that in responding to this question, USU members are reflecting the influence of their USU training and the discourses through which it is framed during that training; note the emphasis on leadership highlighted in the mission statements for the units in Chapter 1. In other words, because students are both given training in leadership, and because those activities are explicitly flagged to students as contributing to their leadership skills, they are more likely to explicitly recognise it as a feature of their USU experience.

### 3.4.4. Other skills

We also included in the survey some questions about skills that are not included in the Newcastle University graduate skills framework. We were interested in knowledge of the armed forces (Figure 3.35), maturity (Figure 3.36), self-confidence (Figure 3.37) and social skills (Figure 3.38); a disparate set grouped here for convenience but speaking to rather different skill sets.

We would expect degree programme-derived knowledge of the armed forces to be low, and for expectations of the level to which the USU experience develops this knowledge to be both met and exceeded. For maturity, self-confidence and social skills, university participation again shows a normal distribution, and USU participation again appears to be both identified as responsible for generating this skill, and its development to a level that significantly exceeds expectations.

### 3.4.5. Skills development and gender

For some of the skills about which we asked our student respondents, there were noticeable differences between men and women in terms of the recognition of skills development and the level to which their expectations had been met or exceeded through USU participation. Figure 3.39 shows this data for self-confidence and Figure 3.40 for time management, disaggregated by gender with reference to USU participation.

---

[59] Details on the Newcastle University Graduate Skills Framework (2013) are available at: http://www.ncl.ac.uk/quilt/assets/documents/str-gsf-framework.pdf

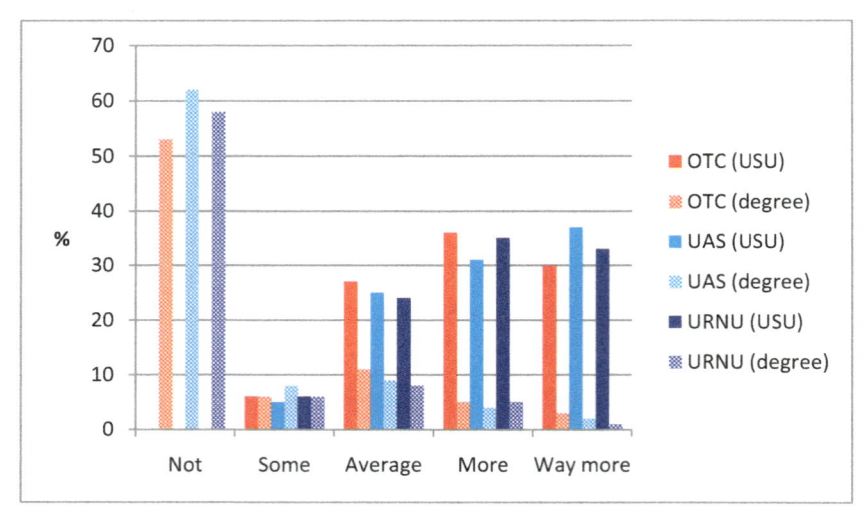

**Figure 3.35:** Knowledge of the armed forces: student evaluations of USU and university degree.

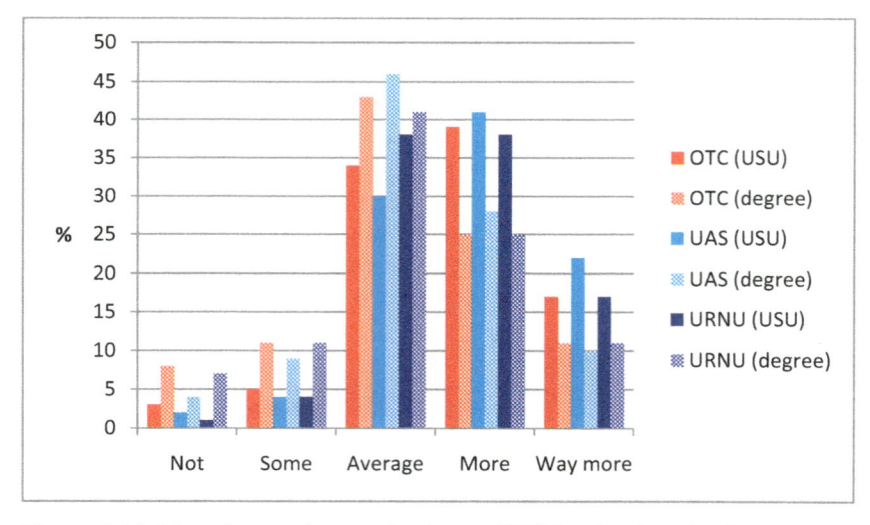

**Figure 3.36:** Maturity: student evaluations of USU and university degree.

Again, with a quantitative methodology, opportunities to explore with respondents the reasons for their evaluations are very limited, so there is no way of definitively explaining this gender difference. It may well be that the

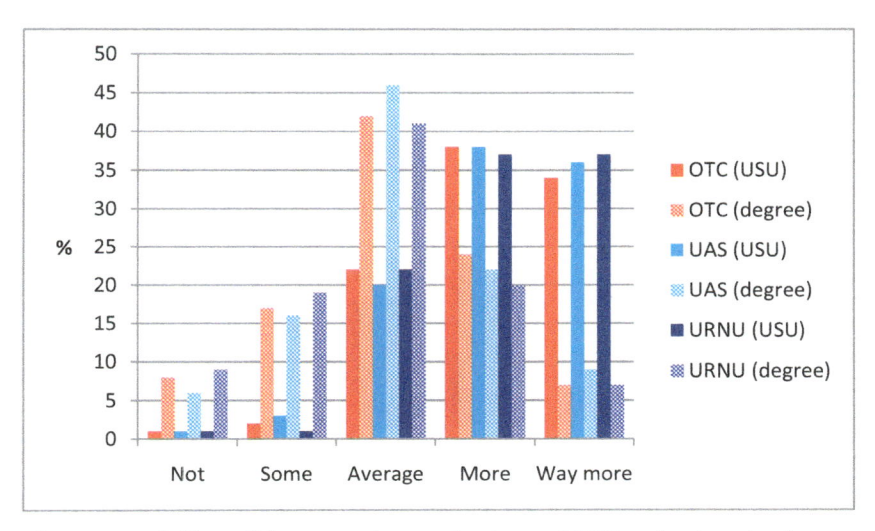

**Figure 3.37:** Self-confidence: student evaluations of USU and university degree.

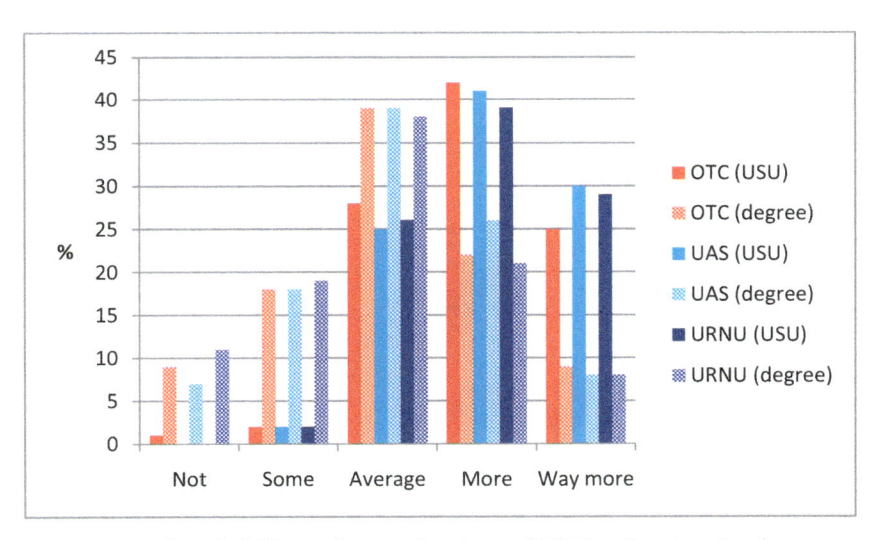

**Figure 3.38:** Social skills: student evaluations of USU and university degree.

female respondents to the survey were (for whatever reasons) more enthusiastic overall than the male. But what the data appears to suggest is that the expectations and anticipations about skills development for women in the service units exceeds that of men.

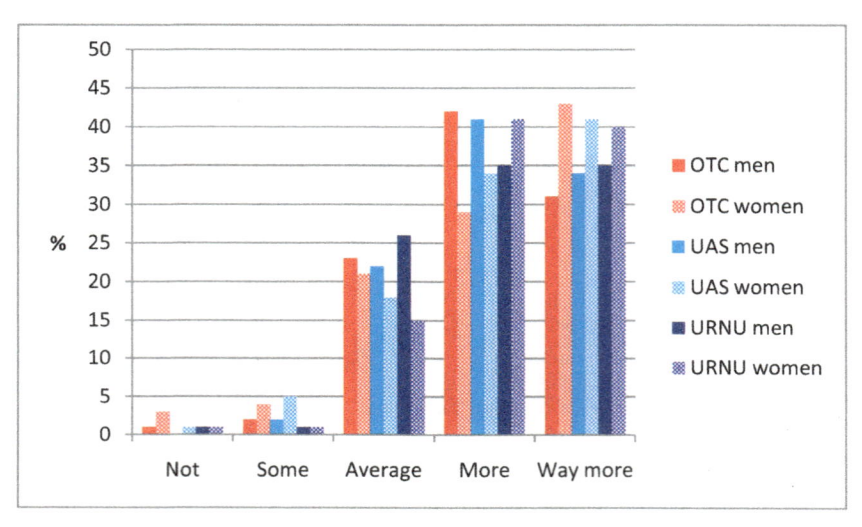

**Figure 3.39:** Self-confidence: assessments of USU skills development by gender.

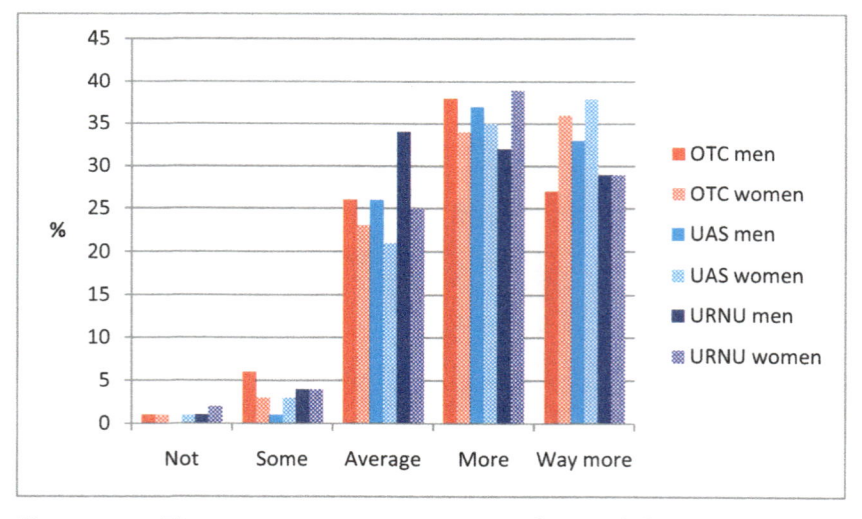

**Figure 3.40:** Time management: assessments of USU skills development by gender.

### 3.4.6. *Evaluating student skills development*

There are three contextualising points to make about the levels of skills development students perceive that they get through their USU experience and degree programmes, and the rates at which they evaluate them. The first is that we should remember that for the vast majority of students, their USU activities constitute a hobby outside the work of a university degree, work which is both intellectually demanding and often laborious. Although this kind of qualitative data capture cannot explore student understandings of the qualitative differences between their academic studies and their USU activities, it is likely that the former is seen as more mundane, even quite ordinary, compared with the latter which may be seen as more fun (and which certainly includes a considerable social element, evidenced from the qualitative comments in section 3.9 below). The second point, again not captured through this kind of methodology, is that it is possible that unit COs and others within USUs are extremely adept at communicating to students how and why particular activities that they undertake might provide them with skills development opportunities, and that this might happen to a greater extent than during the course of university studies. The third point is that the disaggregation of data above does not take into account the different degree subjects and qualifications being pursued by the cohort of students. It is highly likely that different subjects and qualifications include very different emphases in terms of skills training.

The final point, and this is significant, is that we asked students to engage with this fine-grained exploration of skills development only with reference to their USU experience and their degree programme experience. We did not ask student respondents to evaluate other activities using this same evaluation methodology, not least because of the range of possible activities and the difficulties of satisfactorily capturing such experiences in a reliable and comparative manner across this range. It follows that there will be a range of other activities that students undertake which also provide opportunities for graduate skills development.

We did, however, ask our respondents for a broad indication of whether the skills learned through their USU were also learnt from other activities. A total of 18% of respondents considered that they learned these skills nowhere else. Overall, 58% considered that USU-derived skills were also developed through their degree programme, 33% through university sports activities, 18% through a union club or society activity, 18% through charity or other voluntary work, 26% through paid employment and 3% through other activities. Figure 3.41 shows this data disaggregated by the three service units.

Students recognise to varying degrees the ways in which other activities beyond their USU experience inculcate many of the skills that they also recognise as receiving through their USU. We should be clear that we are not implying that the USU experience provides in some way a superior source for skills development for students.[60] Our conclusions are more nuanced than this, suggesting

---

[60] For a more detailed discussion of other activities undertaken by students and other young people, and the skills development opportunities which this then generates, see: **Baillie Smith, M.** and **Laurie, N.** (2011). International volunteering and development: global

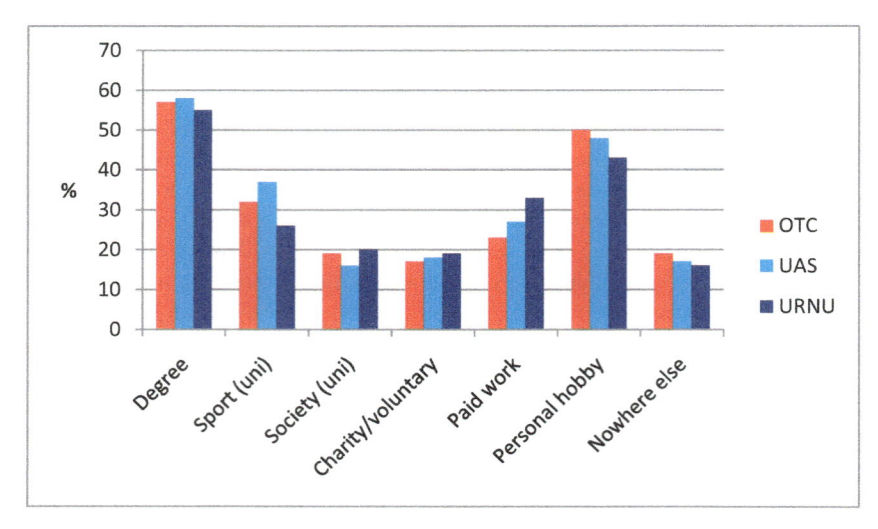

**Figure 3.41:** USU skills learned through other activities.

that the USU experience is one of many sources of skills, and that it provides a wide-ranging group of skills which students are adept at recognising. As we go on to explore in section 3.7 on seeking and gaining employment after graduation, and section 3.9 on overall assessment of the USU experience, it is the combination of skills and the applicability of those skills to the workplace which is seen as particularly significant by students.

## 3.5 Progression through university

We asked student participants whether being in a USU had helped them progress through their degree, and invited qualitative responses. This is a significant issue because of the time commitments USU participation incurs (something raised by both students and graduates), and the possibility that academic work might suffer because of USU commitments (something which commanding officers were keen to prevent). It is also significant because it had been suggested, anecdotally, by students to the research team prior to data collection that despite the challenges of competing commitments, participation in a USU

---

citizenship and neoliberal professionalization today. *Transactions of the Institute of British Geographers, 36*, 545–559; **Jones, A.** (2008). The rise of global work. *Transactions of the Institute of British Geographers, 33*, 12–26; **Holdsworth, C.** and **Quinn, J.** (2011). The epistemological challenge of higher education student volunteering: "reproductive" or "deconstructive" volunteering? *Antipode, 44* (2): 386–405; **Holdsworth, C. M.** and **Brewis, G.** (2014). Volunteering, choice and control: a case study of higher education student volunteering. *Journal of Youth Studies, 17* (2), 204–219.

had a positive knock-on effect on their attitude towards their academic studies. The beneficial knock-on effects of positive experiences in general beyond academic work is well recognised in universities teaching contexts, and so it was thought to be interesting to evaluate this.

Students were asked whether their USU participation had helped them progress through their degree programme. Overall, 53% of OTC, 61% of UAS and 59% of URNU members said that yes, it had. The higher positive assessment from UAS and URNU members may reflect the closer match between degree subject studied and its actual or potential application in military contexts (examples would be engineering or medical degrees). Figure 3.42 shows this data disaggregated by length of time in service unit.

Some caution needs to be exercised with regards to Figure 3.42, because those with more than three years in the unit constituted a very small number in the sample. The basic point suggested here is that student evaluation of the assistance USU participation brings to degree progression increases over time in the unit.

We also asked respondents to explain their answer. Ideas included the development of skills through USU activities which were transferable to academic contexts (time management was the most frequently cited), the positive effect of having an activity entirely different from academic studies, the pay, the benefits of the social life, the increased ambition and wider horizons that the USU experience inculcated in some students, and subject-specific assistance. The following quotations are illustrative:

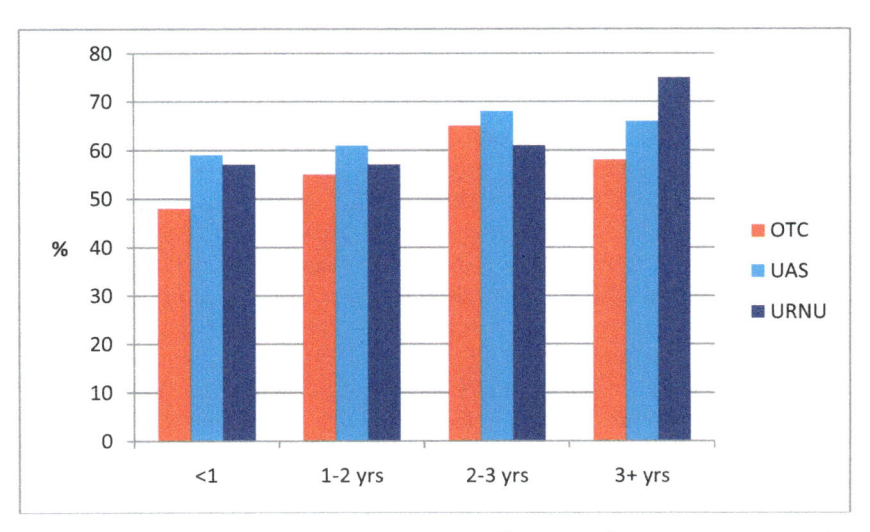

**Figure 3.42:** USU participation: positive effects on degree progression, by percentage.

'Having not found my degree programme as challenging as I expected, OTC doubled my enjoyment of university and introduced me to lots of people who don't want to sit on a sofa all weekend. Getting out of the work bubble has made enjoyment of the work I've been given slightly more enjoyable.'

'I cannot stand university, I would have left by now if it were not for this.'

'I don't exactly enjoy my degree. EUOTC could be the main reason why I haven't left University. It's taught me that having a degree is good no matter what it is, so I am now determined to finish it.'

'Given me a breathing space to occupy my mind outside of the lecture theatre, at times it has indeed proven to be another burden similar to having another course module to learn and succeed in (MOD2), however, for the most part it has proved nothing more than a positive experience with much needed financial support when things have been tight.'

'Motivates me to get out of bed and work hard. If I can get up at 6am in the freezing cold then I can get up at 7am to go to the library.'

We also asked respondents to the survey whether being in a USU had been detrimental to their progression through their degree. A total of 25% of OTC, 18% of UAS and 11% of URNU members said that it had been. In qualitative responses, prioritising of USU over academic work commitments was given as the explanation by virtually all respondents. Many also noted that this was a time management problem which they themselves had responsibility for and had failed to resolve adequately.

Respondents were also asked whether their USU activities could be used for credits towards their university degree. Overall, 72% said no, and an additional 23% said that they did not know. Amongst the 5% replying 'yes' (88 respondents in total), responses included workplace learning or skills development modules where USU experience could be used as a case study (and was accepted as an equivalent to any other paid employment). One student mentioned that their university (University of Glasgow) included on their final marks transcript their MOD1 and MOD2 awards, although this was not part of the credit structure for the degree itself. Students also mentioned other institutional schemes where USU experience could be included in an award (but again, not credit-bearing for degree purposes), such as: 'The Exeter Award', the 'ncl+ Award', the 'Plymouth Award', the Queen's University Belfast 'Degree Plus Award', the 'Bangor Employability Award', 'Sheffield Graduate Award' and the 'Ulster Edge Award'. The qualitative comments suggested that many students were uncertain about exactly what these awards constituted and how their USU experience might be used for accreditation. Qualitative comments also indicated student awareness of the utility of such awards for future job applications, alongside academic qualifications.

## 3.6 Career choices

The relationship between USUs and recruitment to the armed forces is a complex one. The three armed forces have, historically, had different understandings of the utility and advisability of using units for recruitment. As Chapter 1 indicated, at present two distinct UK armed forces recruitment issues have brought USUs into prominence. The first of these is the need for the armed forces to recruit the right people, of the right calibre, for available posts in a context where the armed forces, as a graduate employer (in this instance), is struggling to compete for applicants in a competitive graduate recruitment market. The second of these is the expansion of the Reserves under Future Forces 2020 and the utility of the USUs for direct Reserves recruitment and training, an issue applicable to the Army and influential in the development of the OTRs.

The survey asked respondents for their views about potential future armed forces participation, in terms of their pre-university aspirations and their current career plans.

### 3.6.1. Pre-university views on an armed forces career

We asked respondents to select which of seven different options best applied to them in the time *before* they arrived at university, with options outlining successively greater levels of proactivity and commitment towards determining the armed forces as a career path. Inevitably, we are reliant on respondents' abilities to accurately recall their activities and plans in the past, with the usual caveats that this brings in terms of reliability. That said, some clear patterns emerge, as shown in Table 3.6.

|  | OTC | UAS | URNU |
| --- | --- | --- | --- |
| I never considered joining the Armed Forces | 15 | 10 | 20 |
| I thought about joining the Armed forces, but took no positive action | 24 | 19 | 29 |
| I made inquiries about joining the Armed Forces, but took no further action | 24 | 29 | 22 |
| I attended a recruitment event run by an Armed Forces recruiting team, but took no further action | 12 | 12 | 7 |
| I applied for university sponsorship | 5 | 15 | 7 |
| I made a formal commitment prior to going to university to enter the Armed Forces on graduation | 10 | 3 | 3 |
| Other | 9 | 11 | 11 |

**Table 3.6:** Pre-university views on an armed forces career, by percentage.

The proportion who never considered joining the armed forces is small, with distinctions evident between the three service units. A total of 10% of UAS members had never considered joining, indicating that 90% of UAS members had entertained at least in some way the idea of joining prior to university. Conversely, one fifth of URNU members arrived at university without having considered the idea of an armed forces career. Across the three service units, over half of student members had thought about a career, made inquiries or attended an event (60% of OTC, 60% of UAS and 58% and URNU members).

The 'other' category (10% average across the three service units) provides some further insight into the range of decision-making processes, events, outcomes and circumstances which shaped students' motivations and plans prior to university. Qualitative explanations contained information about issues which had altered a previous decision to consider an armed forces career, including medical and fitness issues, the effects of defence restructuring and consequent removal of identified opportunities, failure to achieve a required set of qualifications or to get a place on a chosen programme (including at Welbeck, the Defence 6$^{th}$ Form College) and the realisation that a career in the armed forces was not after all what they wanted.

Given that a significant proportion of service unit members indicated that prior to university they entertained the idea of joining the armed forces, this suggests that the university service units are recruiting heavily amongst people who had already positively considered the idea of joining the armed forces (however vaguely). This is potentially a group receptive to the idea of military participation, although it should be evident that the decision-making process around an armed forces career is a complex one involving a confluence of individual abilities, circumstances and aspirations, and the availability of advice, opportunities and placements.

### 3.6.2. Student views on an armed forces career

We were interested in whether unit participants become interested in an armed forces career whilst serving in units. We asked survey respondents to select one of 10 different options outlining ways in which that interest or intentionality, or lack thereof, could be expressed (see Table 3.7).

Those who selected 'other' and gave qualitative commentary indicated uncertainty about their future options with the armed forces. Only seven (of 201 comments) indicated specific factors (medical, career or circumstantial) which prevented them being able to make this decision. The remainder indicated their uncertainty, indecision or their wish to keep their options open, or suggested that they had not considered an armed forces career as an option, as the following examples illustrate:

> 'I had thought about joining the armed forces but was not seriously considering it as I felt I had no idea what it'd be like and wouldn't want to

|  | OTC | UAS | URNU |
|---|---|---|---|
| I was intending to join the Regular armed forces prior to joining my USU, and still am. | 35 | 45 | 27 |
| I was intending to join the Reserve armed forces prior to joining my USU, and still am. | 5 | 2 | 2 |
| I was not intending to join the Regular or Reserve armed forces and still am not. | 8 | 7 | 13 |
| I was intending to join the Regular armed forces but am now intending to join the Reserve armed forces. | 10 | 6 | 6 |
| I was intending to join the Reserve armed forces but am now intending to join the Regular armed forces | 3 | 1 | 1 |
| I was intending to join the Regular armed forces but am no longer intending on joining any armed forces. | 3 | 5 | 5 |
| I was intending to join the Reserve armed forces but am no longer intending on joining any armed forces. | 1 | 0 | 2 |
| I was not intending to join the armed forces but now intend to join the Regular armed forces. | 9 | 13 | 12 |
| I was not intending to join the armed forces but now intend to join the Reserve armed forces. | 16 | 8 | 16 |
| Other (please specify) | 9 | 12 | 15 |

**Table 3.7:** Student views on an armed forces career, by percentage.

commit myself when I had no idea. I am now seriously considering joining the armed forces, although have not yet completely made up my mind.'

'I was not intending to join the armed forces, but am now considering joining the Reserve armed forces (part-time) or the regular armed forces. I think intend is too strong a verb for my current situation.'

'Intending is perhaps a too strong a word, I was indeed considering whether a career in the military would be for me and have used the OTC as an opportunity gain insight into what would be involved.'

'Before university I was interested in joining the RN but not fully convinced I could, after joining the URNU I know the areas I need to work on however I still haven't decided on whether I want to join the reserves or the regulars.'

Table 3.7 raises some significant points with regards to debates about USUs and armed forces recruitment. We can conclude, first, that there exists in the USUs a significant proportion who express an intention to join the regular armed forces upon graduation: crudely, a quarter of URNU, a third of OTC and nearly half of UAS members indicate this. There is therefore clearly an identifiable pool of potential armed forces recruits within the service units. The differences between service units reflect the higher proportion of UAS members considering RAF careers proactively prior to university (see Table 3.6) who are potentially using the UAS as a pathway to that career. It is clear that a much lower proportion arrive at university with the intention of joining the Navy. It is also clear that a proportion of students arrive in their units with no intention of joining the armed forces, but who subsequently change their minds (9% of OTC, 13% of UAS and 12% of URNU members). Second, a small proportion either had no intention of joining and still did not (8% of OTC, 7% of UAS and 13% of URNU members), or changed their minds and decided against joining the Regulars or Reserves after graduation (4% of OTC, 5% of UAS 7% of URNU members). Third, there is also a small proportion of students who had either intended to join the Regulars but are now looking to the Reserves (10% of OTC, 6% of UAS and 6% of URNU members), or had no intention prior to university of joining the armed forces, but now intend to join the Reserves (OTC of 16%, UAS of 8% and URNU of 16% members). Qualitative comments indicate that the Reserves features prominently amongst those still trying to decide on future involvement post-graduation with the armed forces. This point will be of interest to those with strategic responsibility for Reserves issues and recruitment. We return to the issues of USUs and armed forces recruitment in Chapter 7.

### 3.6.3. General impact on post-graduation career choices

As well as asking explicitly about intentions with regards to armed forces participation prior to and during university, we also asked student USU members whether joining a USU had impacted on their future career choices. A total of 67% of OTC, 73% of UAS and 65% of URNU members said that yes, it had. When this data was disaggregated by gender, 72% of female OTC participants said 'yes' (compared with 66% for male participants and 67% for OTC members overall). In the UAS and URNU, the proportion of women reporting that being in an USU had impacted on their career choices was lower than that of men (71% for women compared with 75% for men in the UAS; 63% for women compared with 66% for men in the URNU). We can speculate that the OTC experience may be more influential in shaping women's future career choices than the other two services, or that the broader range of degree subjects (and lower proportion studying vocational or applied subjects) in the OTC grants greater flexibility for OTC participants.

We asked respondents to explain their responses. Students mentioned how USU participation had opened up the idea of a military career, as the following examples illustrate:

> 'More interested in joining the armed forces.'
> 'I am now considering a career in the military, whereas before I knew little about the career opportunities.'

'Before joining URNU I had very little knowledge on the things they done during peace time and conflict, after being involved for a few months I have started to realise that there is plenty of opportunity for me in the Royal Navy. Having talked to visitors to our unit has given me a chance to gather knowledge on the skills and lifestyle in the armed forces.'

'I now consider choosing an Army career as I know there are so many opportunities for language students such as myself.'

'When I first joined I was 70% sure that I would not be joining the Armed Forces, however, now that I have been in WUOTC for around 10 months I am now around 60% sure that I WILL join the Armed Forces at some point after my degree is finished.'

'I didn't believe I would be able to cope with all the physical and mental demands of military lifestyle and therefore ruled out officer as a career choice - I now see that with determination it is actually a career I could pursue and am interested in.'

USU participation also consolidated existing aspirations to join the armed forces:

'When I came to university, I was considering a career in the military. Being in the UOTC has confirmed this for me.'

'It has widened my future career ideas, I have long had an interest in the military but didn't know the diverse range of jobs that were available until joining NUAS.'

'It has increased my desire to join the Air Force.'

'I'm joining the Army as I have realised that the forces are the place I really want to be. Always considered a military career but never seriously until I had been in the UAS for a while.'

'I've applied for the Officer selection board, I don't think I would have had the confidence to do this on my own.'

'Made me more determined to apply to join the regular army than before my time at university.'

Students identified how the experience enabled them to make an informed choice, giving a fuller insight into what such a career might provide:

'Before joining I was considering joining the Armed Forces. Having now been in the UAS for 4 years and been able to see the inner workings of forces life, I was able to make a more informed decision on whether or not I would want to join the Armed forces.'

'The exposure to the armed forces has helped me question whether or not a career within them would be a possibility. After much thought and looking at different aspects of potential military careers I arrived at a decision I would not have been able to make without experiencing the USU.'

'It has made me both more interested but also more wary of joining the armed forces. The activities and opportunities given to me have made me aware of the benefits of a career in the military, however it has also highlighted elements of the military that do not appeal.'

'It has given me insight into what life in the armed forces would be really like.'

Participation can confirm a suspicion that a military career would not be suitable for that individual, however much they might enjoy the USU experience:

'I joined UAS unsure if I would like to join the armed forces after my degree, but after several months I now know that whilst I have the utmost respect for the military, the lifestyle is not for me and I would prefer to do something related to my degree; although I have not ruled out reserve forces, i.e. TA.'

'I've emphatically ruled out any trifling consideration of joining the Army.'

'Whereas before I'd thought about joining the navy, but couldn't risk it as a career in case it wasn't for me. I now know that it's not for me. I'm more naturally suited to civilian roles.'

Participation can also raise awareness of a range of opportunities with the armed forces of which they had hitherto been unaware;- we have noted above the proportions (crudely, a quarter of URNU, a third of OTC and nearly half of UAS members) who were intent on a career in the armed forces whilst students. In identifying USU participation as impacting on future career choices, these students identified how the experience has expanded awareness of occupational choices available to them within an armed forces career:

'It's made me consider different branches in the military that I hadn't previously explored that may be more suited to my skills.'

'It has opened my eyes to the specifics of the job roles I strived for, and helped me understand the nature of the roles better. This caused me to consider a career in the Intelligence branch (something I would never have approached beforehand).'

'It has shown me the variety of military careers available alongside the pilot career I was considering.'

'I am currently at medical school and being in the UAS has made me consider a career in the forces post graduation in emergency medicine.'

'Knew I wanted to join armed forces and experiences through the OTC have helped me narrow down my choice of regiment/role. For example, talks from serving engineers or signals soldiers have been a great insight into the different roles within the army. The highlight being the visit by 21 SAS.'

'When I joined the UAS I was vaguely considering joining the RAF but my perception of the day to day job of an Engineering Officer did not appeal to me. Through my time in the UAS I have learnt more about the role of Junior Engineering Officers and am now seriously considering a career in engineering in the RAF.'

'I was fairly sure I wanted to join the navy after Uni but am now set on it. Though not in the same role: I was planning on joining as an engineering officer but am currently applying for warfare.'

Comments on career choice changes as a result of the USU experience revealed how participation can be significant in raising awareness opportunities with the Reserves, even if a full-time career was not considered feasible:

'I am still undecided between being a regular or TA medic but the OTC has me firmly convinced that the forces are a thing I would really like to be a part of in some capacity through my career.'

'Deciding between military and civilian life will be tough. Will probably end up in reserve forces.'

'It has encouraged me to join at least the reserve forces.'

'I was interested in the forces before joining, however I originally wanted to join the regular army but OTC has caused me to reconsider to joining the TA instead.'

'Yes - made me reconsider whether I wanted to join the RAF - very good insight into life in the forces and also into how we can be reservists and balance it with a civilian career. I am now considering joining as a pilot.'

'I originally wanted to be part of the RN, but now I would like to enter into civilian employment whilst keeping up my participation in the reserves.'

Participation also raises awareness of opportunities in sectors and occupations related to those encountered through involvement with the armed forces:

'Considering a career at sea. Navigation has been exciting and fun endeavour.'

'It has made me think that I am more capable than I thought, encouraging me to apply for a post-grad medicine course after my undergraduate degree.'

'I guess it's made me aim higher. My degree isn't very technical, but the skills I have gained in navigation etc have highlighted that I have skills in these areas. I will be doing nothing with the military though.'

> 'I will likely not join the armed forces after graduating but it has improved my graduate prospects in civilian areas and strengthened my interest in working in defence (e.g. for BAE Systems, Thales etc.)'

Participation raises students' awareness of what they might want to get out of a job when they graduate:

> 'I have never and still don't want to join the armed forces after graduation, however being in the OTC has shown me that I would not be able to cope with a desk or lab based job.'
> 'It has shown me that there is more out there than just sitting behind a desk.'
> 'It's confirmed that I'd ideally like a career in public service.'
> 'I now know I will not want to go into active service in the armed forces. However I also will be more able to support ex-service personal in work (I think!).'

It is also instrumental for many in developing personal awareness about their abilities, their confidence and the development of skills that they credit to USU participation:

> 'I feel that I can aim really high in graduate jobs and get the top positions as the UAS has given me a lot of confidence.'
> 'I believe it adds another string to my bow and adds weight to my CV when applying for new job roles, demonstrating that I am a team player with social skills and the drive to do things beyond my university degree.'
> 'As mentioned above, I now am aware that I am more capable than I previously realised. I now want to lead, and preferably in a sector or career that is dedicated to helping or defending the population, whereas I previously was never truly going to push myself.'

The significant observation here is about the positive value of the USU experience in developing, consolidating and confirming student perceptions about the possibility or otherwise of a military career. The experience offers a no-obligation mechanism for students to explore the option. This has long been suspected by those responsible for the USUs; what the survey data confirms is the range and nuance of student perceptions about career choices. This information may possibly be of use to recruitment strategies for the armed forces. It may also be useful for USU recruitment purposes, because it suggests the value of the service unit experience to students in helping them develop their thinking about career options in general, and not just around the armed forces.

## 3.7 Seeking and gaining employment after graduation

We were interested in exploring whether, and how, USU participants understood their USU experience in relation to their efforts to obtain employment after graduation. A total of 87% of OTC, 94% of UAS and 88% of UNRU members answered affirmatively when asked whether being in a USU would help them with getting a graduate job. About one third of the whole sample had already applied for a graduate job at the time of the survey. We elicited qualitative comments to explore this understanding of value in the labour market in more detail, and respondents had much to say (1,777 individuals provided comments). The most frequently cited reason why students thought being in a USU would help them get a graduate job was the transferable skills:

'Where do I start? The list of transferable skills goes on forever, and if an interviewer ever asks for an example of a situation that you have never even thought about, it won't take long to think of something you did on the UAS. The tick-list above [on the survey – see section 3.4 above] shows what skills the UAS has developed and I think most employers would value a person with just a couple of those skills, let alone the majority of them.'

The most commonly mentioned skills were leadership, time management, teamwork and presentation skills, and these were anticipated as useful on a CV or job application, or to discuss at interview:

'On a basic level, it gives us experiences that we can use to demonstrate our skills. "Have you ever worked in a team" - I not just worked with one, I lived with one.'
'The transferable skills with my time spent with the Air Squadron is second to none, I do not think there is anything quite like it to improve your personal skill set in such a short space of time at university.'
'The activities actually directly helped me get a year-long internship in Formula 1 Engineering, this was pretty much all we spoke about in my interview. In addition the communication skills gained in the Air Squadron helped me portray myself that much better.'

USU experience was thought to provide wider knowledge of the working world to which those transferable skills could then be applied:

'The structure within the armed forces of rank and hierarchy is not dissimilar to that of the world of health care, especially within emergency medicine and in the hospitals. The attitude of respecting your superiors, time management and being put into pressured situations are all transferable skills.'

'It already has done. Have gained a job in the oil industry based on experience and proven skills learnt from the URNU.'

'I am going into the field of civil engineering where leadership and team work are essential, and by being a part of the OTC I will have shown that I display these traits.'

The additional qualifications that USU participation could often lead to were valued as part of the package of skills the experience was understood to bring:

'It already has helped. I was awarded funding to do a PhD and in the interview they were impressed with the range of qualifications and experience that I had which has directly come from the OTC.'

'CMI qualification in management and leadership is beneficial and a lot of the qualities employers look for such as teamwork and leadership can be shown through experiences in the OTC.'

The students surveyed were very confident of their abilities to use their USU experience to confirm their skills and thus to demonstrate their employability:

'Even just for sake of saying "This one time on summer camp [...]" during an interview, would aid me in getting a job.'

'I have not had a single interview question that I would not be able to answer with an example of something that has happened to me during my time at the UAS.'

Given the competitive nature of the graduate labour market, it is unsurprising that students display this level of confidence; the USU experience suggests to students that they have additional qualities and experience beyond their academic qualification.

The military skills developed in the USU were, naturally, recognised as valuable to those seeking a military career following graduation, being seen as an 'obvious leg up into the military', 'sure to encourage a military selection board':

'The skills it has taught me will increase my chances of passing AOSB.'

'Hopefully being in the URNU will give me a better insight into the application process for joining the Royal Navy so I will be as prepared as possible, therefore potentially have a good chance of gaining the job I would like.'

'RAF selection looks favourably on having been a member of the UAS. The personal skills also aid the application and selection process.'

There was perceived value to gaining employment in the personal attributes and abilities the USUs were understood to inculcate. Increased self-confidence was frequently highlighted, which was stated by one member to have drastically improved their interview technique. Being in the unit was thought to show reliability, an ability to work hard, a proven ability at problem-solving and personal maturity:

> 'Better than a standard job - so many skills are developed such as team work, leadership, conflict resolution, that I think make you more employable. It brings up a lot of questions in an interview, from experience, and allows you to provide situations where you have coped with stress etc. Confidence in ability helps too.'
> 
> 'SUAS has made me a more attractive all-round candidate to potential employers as a result of my personal development.'
> 
> 'I have become much more assertive and career focused since joining the OTC. I also feel that the staff have been instrumental in making me more aware of my strengths and weaknesses, something that can only aid my career.'
> 
> 'I believe that the USU participation has helped me to develop knowledge skills and experience which surpass anything which is readily available from one club or society at university. My CV has been a struggle to fit onto just two pages, using the smallest viable font and the most concise written English. For that reason, I would say that the USU will most certainly be a positive focal point during any graduate job applications.'

In a highly competitive graduate labour market, this use of the USU experience was thought to make applicants stand out and give them a head-start over their peers:

> 'There are a lot of graduates every year, the USU experience can show employers that I am not like the average student; drinking, parties and the normal things students do in their free time. Instead I spent my time making new friends, improving most everyday skills in industry from writing skills, problem solving to teamwork and delegation skills.'
> 
> 'I am likely to get a 2:i, and the skills, which OTC demonstrates that I have, will help me (in addition to other extra-curricular activities) to stand out from the rest of the 2:i crowd.'

Students perceived that employers were looking for additional attributes and indications on a job application:

> 'Many employers look for outside activities from university.'
> 
> 'It has made me much more employable as companies like to see that you're not just about your degree but also about your extra curriculars as well, OTC has definitely made me massively more employable and is the only reason I got such a good graduate job.'

'It shows that we did something productive in our time at uni, rather than just drinking/clubbing etc.'

Students themselves have an understanding of what they think employer perceptions are, due to information from careers advisors, their degree programme and also very evidently, by USU training staff. Of those who had applied for a graduate position, a small proportion (3% overall) said they had sometimes omitted their USU experience from their CV or application; 97% had always mentioned it. USU members in Northern Ireland were sensitive to the security issue and were cautious about sharing information about their involvement on CVs (and, for one student, with family and friends).

Several students mentioned their concerns that by talking about their armed forces activities, an employer might consider them more committed to an armed forces career than the job for which they applied:

'I applied for a summer internship for a marketing firm and it seemed like they thought I was too involved with the armed forces so they did not want to invest their time and money in me. They did not specifically state this though. I subsequently omitted my USU experience from marketing applications (or at least downplayed it).'

Students were also asked about whether they were asked about USU experience in interviews, and individuals mentioned that they discussed this in response to questions about their competency for specific jobs or roles. Some employers were thought to be aware of the skills development aspect of the USU experience, as part of awareness of the armed forces brand:

'Whether being in a USU is relevant to my graduate job or not, I think the skills an employer believes I have gained from being in one will promote my chances of being employed.'

'The OTC is a respected institution that employers know provides you with valuable skills such as teamwork, communication, confidence and problem solving. Being a part of it shows that I am a balanced, sociable person that can add to the community of a business as well as its market value. I believe that in an employer's eyes it is a welcome addition to my CV.'

'Two of my close friends that have left the UOTC managed to walk into very good job positions at an oil company in Aberdeen solely on their involvement with the UOTC whilst at university. Many companies' values correspond closely to that of the British army and being an active member of the UOTC sets you apart from the rest as being that bit more mature and having the discipline and drive to settle into a hierarchical system such as the workplace that many other students don't have yet.'

'I have experience which very few people will have from their university years. Furthermore, the RN is recognised as a world class "employer" and therefore time spent with them will be taken far more seriously than say time with a standard university society.'

There was recognition, though, about the limits to employer understanding:

'The transferrable skills are excellent HOWEVER it requires people with a knowledge of the TA/UOTC to be in a position to hire those people with experience in the TA/UOTC.'

'This could be a yes/no, depending on my job and the sensitivity of such an organisation - in Northern Ireland does make this difficult to use on a CV.'

'[Being in a USU has helped] but not to a great extent since I don't think that most companies have a very good idea of what USUs are.'

'The transferable skills leant are highly valuable. I understand that some companies and organisations (i.e. Amnesty International) may not look at candidates with military experience so favourably. However the other opportunities made available to you career-wise through the OTC, are far more valuable than being overlooked by a minority of companies.'

In conclusion, student survey respondents were enthusiastic about the skills generated through their USU experience, with 90% overall considering that being in a USU would help them get a graduate-level job. Note that for many this is perceptual rather than proven. We also asked students whether being in a USU would help with getting promoted in a graduate job. The respondents were more cautious on this, with 69% of OTC, 74% of UAS and 67% of URNU members confirming that they thought it would, primarily on the grounds of the transferable skills they would bring to employment. The qualitative comments indicate greater caution here, both because of the lack of direct experience ('Having not been employed in a graduate job how could I possibly know?'), but also because of recognition that the experience of actually doing a job would be the primary factor.

### 3.8 Opinions about the armed forces

The survey asked students directly whether their experiences since joining a USU had affected their view of the British armed forces by being asked to select one of five basic statements which best described them. A tiny number (seven respondents) reported that their view remained unchanged and negative, and 1% reported their view had changed and was now negative. This is unsurprising; USU participation is not compulsory and if students do not like it (because, for example, of negative views of the armed forces), they will leave. A total of 77% overall reported their views as unchanged and positive, and 15% reported their views as changed and now positive. Of the 6% who selected 'other', we asked for further clarification; what emerges from these comments is the idea that participation in the USU provides a more nuanced view of the armed forces:

> 'Mixed. Changed with a more positive view on the regular army but with a more negative view on the Territorial Army.'
>
> 'Changed. Gained a lot of insight and definitely a positive view of the organisation as a whole, I have a lot of respect for what they do, but through the USU have actually been put off joining the military. So both positive and negative.'
>
> 'Changed and is now ambivalent. Before university, my view was positive, but increased exposure has made me sceptical about certain things: I still feel positively about the Forces on the whole, but I experienced a lack of morale in the Fleet that I found shockingly low.'
>
> 'Overall I am very positive about HM Armed Forces however having been to university and studied a social science I am now more acutely less favourable of current UK foreign policy. This is something not generally discussed in URNU but something I feel very strongly towards having developed my critical thinking skills at university.'
>
> 'Whilst I remain overwhelmingly positive, the OTC has shown me some of the flaws and failings in the Army, and has also (believe it or not) made me more open-minded regarding opposition to some of the Army's activities.'
>
> 'My opinion of the forces overall has not changed, but some of the people in positions of superiority have failed to meet my expectations.'
>
> 'I had mixed opinions of the Army when I first joined USU, I was very supportive of my brother so I had a positive opinion in the regard. However, I disagreed with the wars in Afghanistan and Iraq which painted the army in a bad light. Since joining the OTC I have come to understand and accept that the Army merely does what is told to do by the government so is not responsible for their decisions.'
>
> 'For the Armed Forces as a whole, it has made me realise that it is not nearly as professionally run as the civilian sector thinks at all and can be quite haphazard. At times the processes it uses to make decisions are overly bureaucratic, have a near dogmatic refusal to listen to common sense and are foolishly arbitrary. However my opinion of the Navy has greatly improved. Previously I thought it did nothing/ next to nothing. Now I know that is resolutely not the case.'

In conclusion, USU participants have a positive view of the armed forces. There is nothing particularly unsurprising about this: because participation is voluntary and because USUs are armed forces organisations, those who have or develop negative views of the armed forces on the basis of their participation to an extent where USU participation becomes untenable will leave. What is significant here is our suggestion that those who participate in the armed forces and who are thus exposed to the forces may feel better able to provide an informed explanation for their assessments, positive and negative, of the armed forces. This idea is explored further in Chapter 4, where we explore graduate views towards the armed forces.

## 3.9 Overall experiences of university armed service units

The survey asked students to give an overall assessment of their USU experience. Across the three service units, 90% rated their experience as 'mostly positive', 1% of OTC, 2% of UAS and 2% of URNU members rated the experience as 'mostly negative', and 9% of OTC, 9% of UAS and 8% of URNU members rated the experience as a 'mixture of positive and negative'. Qualitative responses (1,788 were provided) allowed students to explain their answer.

### 3.9.1. Positive aspects of the university armed service units experience

It is unsurprising that most students rate their experience as mostly positive: with the exception of the small numbers who are obliged for reasons of sponsorship to participate in a USU, participation is entirely voluntary. Those who feel they get something from their participation (which will be specific to each individual) that they feel is positive are, we suggest, likely to rate their overall experience as a positive one. Although quantifying responses (through post-survey coding) proved impossible because of the range and combination of responses and ways of expressing ideas, certain explanations stand out.

The USU experience is fun ('serious fun'), enjoyable and provides social opportunities to make friends, meet other people with shared interests and participate in the camaraderie of the unit. Comments include:

> 'Adding to my university experience through socialising, learning skills, gaining qualifications, supplementing student income and gaining perspective on the armed forces.'
> 'Excellent chance to meet people, encourages an active and organised lifestyle, informs about army life culture; and is a lot of fun.'
> 'Fantastic experience, meet new people and develop new skills, get out of the university bubble.'

The utility of the experience in providing new or different opportunities or opportunities not available elsewhere to undertake specific activities, was significant:

> 'Amazing opportunities which are not provided by any other society at university. Couldn't think of university without it.'

'Bristol UOTC is an amazing organisation, and has provided me with outstanding opportunities to gain an insight into an armed forces career, I have had the chance to participate in events and venues unimaginable to most of my course peers at university.'

The idea of the experience providing a challenge was also clear, in the sense of an individual facing and having to overcome challenges posed by new situations and experiences, in the sense of being pushed to achieve things, in the sense of understanding the value of a challenging situation (even if it had not been fun at the time) and in the sense of achievement this generated. Related to this were perceptions of the experience in enabling personal development, and students included comments about learning to take responsibility, and their increased self-confidence, self-knowledge and self-awareness:

'Any negative aspects e.g. punishments for own poor personal admin or PT in bad weather are all good for personal development and character. Apart from these I haven't had a bad experience in the OTC.'
'Enjoyably challenging - it has opened doors and showed me my potential.'

Getting physically fit, participating in sports and enjoying the practical activities and the military training were significant:

'I get paid to get fit, have fun and make great friends - what more could I want?'

A great number of responses mentioned the utility of the experience in terms of pay, the gaining of qualifications, the development of skills in leadership, teamwork, time management and other transferable skills, and echo the assessments of skills made by students in response to other questions in the survey. Respondents also discussed their increased knowledge, understanding and appreciation of the armed forces, including the utility of the experience in considering an armed forces career (which included a perceived advantage in officer selection).

In a separate question, students were asked whether they would recommend joining a USU to other students. A total of 94% of OTC, 96% of UAS and 98% of URNU members said that they would.

### 3.9.2. Negative aspects of the university armed service units experience

The negative issues raised primarily concerned local organisational issues around unit administration and management, bureaucracy, lack of communication and the time spent waiting for things to start. A small number mentioned the time commitment unit participation required, including travel time to units. There were a small number of comments about the specifics of the organisation and delivery of the training syllabus associated with the change in one unit to an OTR. Note that the survey coincided with a time of change in this unit:

> 'Enjoyed my time, but often it seems that my unit cannot decide whether it wants to be a TA unit or a youth club and often strikes the wrong balance. It can be frustrating as certain individuals and sub units appear more valued than others.'

A small number of comments were critical of the attitudes of other students, including relating to excessive drinking and the social attitudes of students from different educational institutions within a unit. A small number also mentioned casual sexism within units, evident through derogatory comments towards women.

In conclusion, the survey showed that students overall have a positive attitude towards their experience. We suggest that this reflects the assessments students make of the value of what they as individuals get from their participation (whatever that might be for a particular individual). It is also possible that those who are more inclined towards a positive view of the USUs would have been more inclined to complete a survey on their experience; participation bias is extremely difficult to control for in a survey of this nature. Yet the point remains, in responses to the range of questions asked, that those who completed the survey provided an assessment was overwhelmingly positive.

## 3.10 Conclusions: the value of the university armed service units for participating students

The key findings from the survey of students participating in the USUs are as follows.

In terms of the types of students participating in USUs, we would suggest that unit participants are not representative of the UK student body, or even of the Home (that is, UK domiciled) student population. Participating students are more likely to attend a Russell Group university, are more likely to have attended an independent sector school, are more likely to be male and are more likely to be studying particular subjects at university than suggested by national student average figures.

In terms of joining a USU, there is diversity across the three service units in terms of levels of awareness of the existence of USUs prior to arrival at university, and for UAS participants in particular, the availability of a UAS may be a factor in choice of university. Women appear to have lower levels of awareness of USUs prior to university. Freshers' Fairs were a significant source of initial information about the units for 29% of USU participants overall, and are a more important source of information for women compared to men, and for students arriving from state schools than the independent sector. Motivations for joining are a combination of military-specific interests, sporting and adventurous training opportunities, transferable skills suitable for CVs and pay. There are slight differences between men and women in terms of motivations for joining.

In terms of the skills that USU participation helps develop, specifically transferable skills of value to subsequent employment, the USU experience is seen as both providing skills development opportunities across a range of skills, and to an extent that very often exceeds expectations. Assessments of the level that expectations have been exceeded through degree programmes is higher for most cognitive/intellectual skills than for USU participation with the exception of critical thinking, but for communications and interactional skills, expectations are exceeded to a higher degree through USU participation than through degree programmes. There are gender and service unit differences across student assessments of skills development. USU participation is seen as helping positively with degree programme progression by 58% of USU members.

In terms of careers in the armed forces, a significant proportion had considered a future military career prior to arriving at university. The USU experience appears to be important in shaping student views both with regards to a career in the armed forces, and with regards to potential participation in the Reserves. The experience is also influential in shaping student understanding about wider career options beyond the armed forces.

In terms of employability, 90% of USU participants thought that being in a USU would help them with getting a job. The transferability of the skills developed through USU participation was seen as the most significant factor in this regard.

In terms of opinions about and perceptions of the armed forces, 92% overall stated that they had positive opinions about the armed forces, with 15% of these identifying their views as having changed to a positive assessment as a result of their USU experience. Finally, 90% of students rated their USU experience as mostly positive.

CHAPTER 4

# Graduate Evaluations of the University Armed Service Units Experience

Annually, around 2,000 students with experience of the OTC, UAS or URNU leave university and enter paid employment. We can assume, if we extrapolate from the evidence presented in Chapter 3, that having maintained a relationship with their unit for a significant period of time during their studies, these individuals recognised at the time a value to their USU participation. The question which then follows is whether, and in what ways, that experience is understood as having value after graduation. In this chapter, we explore four quite distinct ways in which graduates perceive there to have been value in their USU experience. We consider what they say about value, specifically in the workplace and around their employability, we assess the idea that USU graduates might be 'defence-minded' for life and how that might be understood and seen as manifest by graduates, we consider how individuals assessed their own value to the USUs and the armed forces, and we explore the wide-ranging perceptions of the graduates about the value of the USUs.

## 4.1 The sample of graduates

Chapter 2 outlined the methodology used for this part of the study, which involved semi-structured interviews with individuals across a range of ages and experiences of USUs. The schedule of interview questions is given in Appendix 2. All direct quotations included in this chapter are taken from transcripts of those interviews.

---

**How to cite this book chapter:**
Woodward, R, Jenkings, K N and Williams, A J. 2015. *The Value of the University Armed Service Units*. Pp. 101–138. London: Ubiquity Press. DOI: http://dx.doi.org/10.5334/baq.d. License: CC-BY 4.0.

### 4.1.1. Demographic features of the sample

We interviewed 54 individuals (38 men and 16 women). The gender ratio roughly matched that of the current student cohort, but did not necessarily reflect that in place at the time when interviewees were members of their USU. Indeed, two women talked of their novelty as women in units that had previously been closed to women, or had not had women participants until they themselves had joined.

We did not ask interviewees for their age directly, because it was the period of their past participation which was more significant. We did however, establish from interviewees' narratives sufficient information to allocate each individual, very crudely, to an age cohort, as follows:

- Two interviewees (3% of the sample) started university between 1953 and 1962, and were assumed to be in their 70s at the point of interview.
- Three interviewees (5% of the sample) started university between 1963 and 1972, and were assumed to be in their 60s at the point of interview.
- Four interviewees (7% of the sample) started university between 1973 and 1982, and were assumed to be in their 50s at the point of interview.
- Five interviewees (10% of the sample) started university between 1983 and 1992, and were assumed to be in their 40s at the point of interview.
- 22 interviewees (40% of the sample) started university between 1993 and 2002, and were assumed to be in their 30s at the point of interview.
- 18 interviewees (33% of the sample) started university between 2003 and 2012, and were assumed to be in their 20s at the point of interview.

Three quarters of the sample were therefore discussing a USU experience in the previous 20 years, and the remainder had an experience further back in time. This was useful in order to generate data (from more recent graduates) which spoke to contemporary issues and concerns, whilst providing data (from older graduates) through which we could assess continuity and change. By interviewing graduates across a range of age cohorts, we were able to put together a picture of the changing ways in which the USU experience might (or might not) impact in different ways at different points in working lives.

Our graduate interviewees were a highly educated group. In terms of undergraduate or first degrees, 3 had medical or dental degrees, 18 had degrees in science subjects, 17 had degrees in social science subjects (of which 7 had law degrees and 7 had geography degrees), 10 had degrees in arts and humanities subjects and 6 had degrees in vocational applied sciences or applied social sciences. In addition, around 15 had a postgraduate qualification of some kind, either academic (Masters or PhD qualification) or a professional qualification for competency to practice (for example, in law or accountancy).

### 4.1.2. University and university armed service units experience

The universities represented by our interviewees ranged across the higher education sector, and included established institutions including the ancient universities, the red brick universities established for the purposes of civic education in the 19th century, the plate glass institutions reflecting the impact of the Robbins reforms of the 1960s, and the new universities, former polytechnics and technical training institutions granted university status and degree-awarding powers from 1992 onwards. Interviewees were not sampled according to the type of university they attended, but we are pleased that the final sample reflected institutions across the diversity of the establishments and mission groups in the sector.

The vast majority of interviewees were USU participants whilst taking their undergraduate degree, with some continuing whilst undertaking postgraduate study. Four interviewees had non-standard participation patterns: two had had a year abroad as part of their degree programme (and discussed their efforts to maintain unit participation whilst away), one Commonwealth student had participated for a single year as a visiting student to a UK university whilst on his degree programme and one individual had participated as a student whilst at sixth form college rather than at a university.

The broad aim with the sample was for a proportional balance across the three service units. Allocating an individual to a service unit was complicated by the fact that some individuals had participated in more than one unit (for example, a period of time in the OTC, followed by participation in an URNU). The final sample comprised 24 former OTC participants, 13 UAS participants and 17 URNU participants, when allocated according to the first unit each individual joined. There was, therefore, a slight bias in the sample towards URNU, which is the smallest of the three USUs. Overall, the aim was to capture the views and experiences of former members from across the three services rather than compare experiences between services. We were reliant on individuals coming forward for interview, and did not set out to interview individuals with experience in a particular geographical area. In terms of geographical spread, there was a slight bias in the sample towards graduates from USUs in Eastern Scotland (Dundee, Stirling), Newcastle, Manchester, Liverpool, the East Midlands, Oxford, Cambridge and London. We did not interview anyone with USU experience from the South West (except for one from the University of the West of England) or Wales. The effects of this on the research findings are negligible as it is unlikely (given that units are centrally directed) that individual units have processes, structures or practices which are hugely at variance with each other, and the continuous rotation of COs and training staff through units produces a commonality of experience across units. Although some individuals identified some units as having specific strengths, this was interpreted as a reflection of the loyalty and affection which units generate amongst their former members, even years after graduation.

### 4.1.3. Patterns of employment

All the graduates interviewed were either in professional employment (including individuals on maternity and parental leave), ran their own business or had retired from professional employment, with the exception of one interviewee who was starting his first job shortly after the interview, having very recently graduated. We use the terms 'professional' and 'graduate' employment interchangeably in this book, to indicate employment which requires, at least at entry point, education to tertiary level, whilst noting the difficulties of defining these terms (something which professional careers advisors recognise).[61]

The majority of our interviewees worked (or had worked) in the private sector (for example, business services, the legal profession, the financial sector, engineering, aviation, media and logistics) and a much smaller proportion in public sector employment (for example, the National Health Service, the civil service, policing and higher education). Sampling was not structured by sector of employment or by employment status; it is therefore merely an effect of the sampling strategy outlined above that the majority were working in professional occupations in the private sector. The career pathways of our interviewees were completely diverse, and defy any attempt at categorisation; there is diversity in the sample in terms of use of degree, strategies for determining career pathways, availability of opportunities and influence of lifestyle factors in careers. What is evident through comparisons between individual interviews across the dataset are the effects on graduate employment of shifts across the decades in terms of labour market elasticity and structure, with the demise of full employment, the rise of a tighter and more competitive graduate labour market in the 1980s and again in the post-2008 financial crisis period, the emergence of portfolio careers, of self-employment and of a small business economy around consumer, health and producer services. We can also identify the expansion and consolidation of employment rights for parents, particularly women taking maternity leave, and the expansion of employment opportunities for women into sectors where they had had a minimal presence in previous decades.

### 4.1.4. University armed service units awareness

Given the age range of our interviewees and thus the effect of generational change, and given the range of universities which they attended and thus the very different sets of circumstances potentially shaping decisions to join a USU,

---

[61] **Office for National Statistics.** (2013). *Graduates in the UK Labour Market.* London: Office for National Statistics. Further details are available from the Association of Graduate Careers Advisory Services: http://www.agcas.org.uk/articles/746--non-graduate%20jobs-data-an-AGCAS-perspective

it is virtually impossible to be definitive on patterns of pre-university awareness about USUs amongst our sample. Broadly, our respondents appeared to mirror the experiences of current students (see 3.3. above, on joining a USU), with a proportion finding out through Freshers' Fairs ('walking around the Freshers' Fair with some friends and the guy quite literally grabbed me and [...] said "we have a ship if you want to join us"'), some joining following advice from armed forces careers advisors, or following experience in the cadets (when asked directly, just under half said that they had been in the cadets at school), or advised by friends or family who had been members. Given that people were being asked to recall something that might at the time have seemed very incidental, and which may have happened long ago, it is hard to be definitive on this point, but it would suggest that both Freshers' Fairs and cadets' experiences are significant. Over half had no family connection with the armed forces beyond grandparents.

### 4.1.5. Participation in the Reserves

We intentionally sampled for interview those who had not pursued a full-time career (of any duration) with the UK armed forces. This is because one of our key research questions concerned the value of the USU experience in the civilian workplace. We made this explicit in our call for research participants. We did not, however, explicitly exclude those who had served as reservists. A number of interviewees came forward who had previous or current experience with the Reserves (across the three armed forces). We decided to include them in the sample for two reasons. First, we were interested in the transferability of skills from military training to civilian employment contexts, and recognised that this process is not unique to the USUs but features as a factor for those working as, and employing, reservists. Second, whilst the interviews were being planned and then conducted, the Government announced the first of a series of interventions under the Future Forces 2020 programme, designed to reduce the number of full-time Regular members of the armed forces and increase the proportion of reservists, particularly in the British Army.

A total of 22 respondents had had, or maintained at the time of the interview, a relationship with the Reserves following their USU experience, and six of the sample had had a relationship of some kind with the Reserves whilst a student. Where this was the case, some additional questions were asked about this experience. We have identified an effect of this in our sample; it could be argued that the sample included over-representation from those who had had additional socialisation into the armed forces further to their USU experience. It would, however, be virtually impossible to quantify the extent to which the sample was skewed because of this (bearing in mind, for example, that some interviewees were discussing Reserves participation up to 40 years previously, under an armed forces structure and organisation which was very different to the present). However, despite the possibility of over-representation amongst those with greater armed forces experience, in our view this was balanced by the additional insights which these individuals were able to bring to the research. In being able to compare and contrast their USU and Reserves experiences, we were able to tease out during interview something of the specificity of each and commonality of both. Furthermore, given that at the time of writing the expansion of the Reserves remains a pressing policy issue, and given that much of our analysis suggests findings which might usefully inform ongoing debates about mechanisms for the expansion of the Reserves and the role of the USUs in that, we consider the possible over-sampling of reservists to be a strength rather than a weakness of the data. Indeed, a few interviewees who had not been in the Reserves were considering the possibility of joining as their living and working patterns opened up the opportunity to do so.

## 4.2 The value of university armed service units experience in the workplace

In this section, we assess the value or otherwise of the USU experience in the workplace. Note that the research was exploring the question of value beyond that outlined by the USUs. The focus on workplace achievement is not explicitly stated as part of the USU's missions, which are more broadly framed (see Chapter 1). As we have seen in Chapter 3, contemporary student USU participants see the experience as potentially extremely valuable in applying for and performing a graduate-level job, and this idea has to have foundation in something concrete for it to have the tenacity that it does. We were interested, then, in whether it is indeed the case that the USU experience has a value in the workplace, and one way to evaluate this was to talk to graduates themselves, who were working and who had been through a recruitment process (often many times over the course of a career).

We speculated that there were two primary ways in which the value of the USU experience to the workplace was manifest. It could be evident as individual, personal benefits which graduates with USU experience identify as accruing to them on that basis, which could then have value in the workplace, either directly or indirectly through transferable skills. It could also be evident in benefits for employers in the execution of employment tasks, which could be enhanced through the skills and training which individuals receive through the USU (for example, through knowledge of defence-related practices or terminologies). We were also interested in how value in the workplace might vary with time across an individual's engagement with the labour market from the point of application onwards. In this section we consider the utility in the job application process, and in the performance of a graduate job.

### 4.2.1. Applying for a job

We were interested in exploring with graduates the use or otherwise that they made of their USU experience when applying for a job (note that we were focused on the application process, rather than on the decision to pursue a job in a particular sector on the basis of the USU experience). This seemed significant because of the emphasis current students placed on the utility of the USU experience to the job application process (see section 3.7 above).

The interviews explored how the graduate's USU experience was framed within an application. Graduates mentioned their pride in their association with the units, and also the profile and kudos associated with the British armed forces as a brand. But more specifically, particularly for more recent graduates, 'it gives you demonstrable qualities' which make an application or CV stand out. The USU experience can be used prominently to complement or act in lieu of work experience (that is, civilian paid employment):

> 'My CV maybe has less work experience on it, but because of that I actually have a greater focus on my OTC experience [...] the second thing on my CV [...] is actually NUOTC.'

Interviewees, particularly more recent graduates, appeared to view their USU experience primarily as a demonstration of aptitude for work, rather than as part of their education. The experience was thought to show an individual as having been motivated to something requiring commitment, and to have managed to do this successfully whilst also studying for a university degree. Having USU experience on a CV was believed to make an application stand out, even if the recruiter knew little about what participation involved.

The USU experience was particularly prominent for those applying for their first jobs. A recent graduate working in the media industry said:

> '[...] my time in the University Air Squadron was the main emphasis of every single job application [...] when I was applying for this internship [...] that I am on at the moment, the very fact that I was in the university air squadron, and I've been told this from my boss while I have been here, did stand me out from the applications [...] in interviews, every single question they had I could relate it back to being in an air squadron.'

The experience provides examples about which to speak. There may be differences of emphasis because CVs and applications are tailored to specific jobs:

> '[...] the ones which I focused my university air squadron elements on and really emphasised, were the ones that had a direct military connection.'

'When I was going for different roles within marketing I made more emphasis on my English degree, my writing and my analytical skills, and when I was going for more managerial things I [emphasised at university] captaining certain sports and the managerial stuff with the URNU.'

Other graduates discussed how elements of a USU experience would be drawn on to fit an application; one discussed emphasising 'all this crazy stuff like flying and climbing and all that adventure training stuff' for job applications in broadcast journalism, and the more managerial and organisational skills were emphasised in applications for more desk-based jobs.

We were interested in what, exactly, the USU experience was used to demonstrate, where it was used on an application. Graduates talked primarily about transferable skills:

'The skills you do pick up [...] skills that industry itself will find useful [...] leadership skills, organisation skills, time management skills [...] it gives you demonstrable qualities that when an employer picks up a list of CVs from graduates, those that actually have degrees and experience that are relevant – [it] makes them stand out.'

This idea of having an edge, standing out, being somehow distinctive, is central to the narratives of younger graduates, reflecting the competitive graduate recruitment market, and applicant strategies presumably suggested by careers advisers (and indeed university educators and USU staff) to focus on the transferability of skills. But some skills have particular purchase when understood as originating in a military context. Evidence of leadership ability was frequently cited, along with the use of the USU experience to demonstrate time management (meeting demanding educational and military training commitments), resource allocation and use, and motivation. Reference to generic transferable skills developed in the USU figured in graduates' recollections of their applications. However, there was little sense that graduates thought that their USU experience somehow spoke for itself. The key lay in being able to articulate how and why a particular skill or experience in a USU context might apply in the workplace:

'It might seem strange to try and sell yourself in the book publishing world by using my experience in the military but I actually did that. I knew I was willing to work hard at all hours for not a huge amount of money, I knew I could work as a team [...] I was trying to get into quite a creative role, which is very difficult to get into.'

Graduates also discussed how they might refer specifically to the USU's military context and thus to military-specific knowledge in emphasising their skills. Distinct in the group of graduates were those with UAS experience who had then proceeded to careers related to aviation, and those with URNU experience who were able to draw on sea-faring experience for maritime roles (including an applicant drawing on URNU experience for a job with a shipping law firm, 'I had basic knowledge of ship handling, which was more than most trainee lawyers had'). Again, the knack in using this in job applications was to demonstrate the applicability of military-context skills to a civilian workplace, rather than just assume it:

> 'I talked a lot about leadership in the Royal Navy, in the Royal Navy Unit and on the ship, in deployments'.

One mentioned his ability to understand hierarchies and command structures and to then communicate that as a skill, because:

> '[…] when you've had that military training, you think: "right, the bigger picture – how does my role here actually affect my bosses job, or the person under me?"'

Another talked about how he deliberately drew parallels between his responsibilities in an URNU and analogous civilian business tasks:

> '[I was] kit officer, I had to buy, design and sell merchandise for the unit, which was a self-defined role, I could do as little or as much as I wanted, but it basically amounted to running a small business for a year, which I thought looked very good on my CV. PR and recruitment: I helped with recruiting new students in my final year […]'

Placing emphasis in a job application was not, however, a universal activity. Four issues emerged here in the graduate interviews. The first was a caution in overplaying this one experience:

> 'I certainly don't remember it being at the top of my list.'
> 'I don't want to overplay it, partly because you want to show you've got breadth.'
> 'I'd try not to just use URNU experience because it would be too limited.'
> 'I didn't list them as a job – however, I did list them in my interests – I felt that having those on there would make my application stand out.'

The second concerned time: as might be expected, the significance of USU participation and related activities on a CV diminishes as applicants progress through their careers accumulating more specific experience of greater relevance to a job application at that particular career stage. 'I had lots of other things to talk about', noted one. 'It's one line – whereas it used to be three paragraphs' reflected another. There was a marked difference between older graduates ('I don't think it even gets a mention on my CV now – but you're talking 15 years ago') and more recent graduates ('for each of the examples we had to give [in the application], a lot of experience [...] came from the URNU').

The third issue shaping the use of USU experience in job applications was graduate perceptions of the likely reception by a potential employer to the idea of a USU itself, and USU experience. This was explained in a number of ways; one graduate working in Northern Ireland had left it off his CV for personal security reasons, not wanting direct visible association with the British Army. The palatability of military association was identified in other contexts:

> 'It wasn't trendy when I came out of university to say very much that would be considered right wing – I shut up about it a bit – it was a one-liner [...]'
> 'I dropped it after an unpleasant interview experience.'

Another (more recent) graduate chose deliberately to portray her UAS involvement as an additional interest rather than work experience when applying for jobs in a sector which she felt was antipathetic to the idea of military activities and institutions:

> '[...] the [jobs] which maybe had an environmental focus or shied away from defence or military, I didn't emphasise what I had done. I used it more as a – this was one of my hobbies [...] Different amounts of emphasis depending on the connection that the organisations had to the military.'

An older graduate with UAS flying experience, and who listed this and shooting as hobbies on her CV felt that she had been chastised for these activities in several interviews (perhaps a reflection of that time period). Clearly, graduates had to consider a recruiter's receptivity to the idea of a USU on a CV, and our interviews produced accounts of very different strategies:

> 'If it was a big blue-chip organisation type thing I might have [emphasised it more], you know, the bigger firms, and the more I could determine that they were very supportive, I would emphasise it. But I would always mention it.'

Conversely:

> 'I would leave the OTC out much more for certain applications. I was very conscious of distancing myself from them because their immediate understanding of the OTC is [names a university with reputation for privileged students] based [...] and I wanted to really distance myself from that because I didn't want to be tarred with the same brush.'

A fourth issue was the concern that recruiters would not necessarily 'have the experience of the military to be able to translate it or understand it', 'A lot of people didn't understand it really [...] the recruitment agents just didn't understand'. Furthermore, recruiters may have heard of certain USUs but not others. Placing emphasis on the USU experience also depends, then, on the idea having purchase in the graduate recruitment market. This is an issue in an international labour market, and USU experience needs to be nuanced accordingly:

> 'If it was a British [company] like HSBC or something like that then I assumed that they would know more about the Territorial Army and then OTC being a part of it, whereas if they were a French bank then I'm not sure if I even put it down at all.'

The reaction from international or foreign-owned companies could vary, with those based or run from the USA considered to have a generally more positive reception to the idea of military participation. Companies in other national contexts were thought to have neutral or negative perceptions of the military experience and its connection to the workplace.

In conclusion, a key determinant in shaping the use of USU experience in a job application was the career that a graduate went in to. Those pursuing military-related careers were clearly able to use the USU military skills experience to sell themselves in an application. The transferable skills element appears to have been more important for people looking for professional careers where the types of leadership and other skills practiced in the armed forces are looked on favourably. Where graduates did not use their USU experience in applications, or downplayed it, this was either a strategic choice (for employers perceived not to understand or value military experience), or a reflection of graduate perception of their USU experience in job application terms, either because it was one of a range of university experiences which developed similar skills, or because they wanted to identify their skills as separate from, rather than bound to, a military environment. For example, an individual might want to emphasise management skills but not suggest that they had a military management style, or that they had leadership skills but not suggest that they could only exercise these in a military manner.

### 4.2.2. Being interviewed for a job

Graduates were asked whether they could recall how their USU experience was discussed at job interviews. Those who said that interviewers had expressed an interest noted that it had appeared to have been viewed favourably, either as a talking point or as something that might indicate specific skills (for example, aviation-related skills) or knowledge (for example, defence-sector related skills), or as something that might spark curiosity or interest in the interviewer.

In some cases, explaining the transferability of USU-derived skills to an employment context was made relatively easy when interviewers indicated that they had military experience themselves (and this was more common amongst our older interviewees, reflecting the wider armed forces knowledge base which National Service had produced in civilian society). Some reported that interviewers were very focused on USU experience because of a lack of familiarity with the organisation. As with job applications, graduates commented that the relationship between a USU experience and the requirements of a job had to be proven when explored at interview:

> 'What I'd always find was people were like "oh that's interesting, but how does it relate to [the] job?"'

But as with job applications, there were particular interviews and jobs which were assessed by the interviewee as requiring emphasis on USU-derived skills rather than the military context in which they had been acquired. USU experience could be interpreted by interviewers as an indication of maturity or indicative of life experience. For example, one graduate mentioned an interview for a job with a magazine, where 'they were very keen on my OTC experience. I suppose 'man of the world', a bit more, you know, than otherwise […]'. In some workplace cultures:

> 'It was always looked [on] more favourably – that's possibly a function of working for white middle class professionals, probably purely male professionals as well, in many cases and certainly at the recruiting level.'

As with applications, there were perceptions that some organisations would be less than sympathetic to a military background. There may also be wider social attitudes towards the armed forces to consider, beyond specific workplace or economic sector responses, which were felt to shape responses to a military background.

More commonly mentioned was an experience where it was clear interviewers had no comprehension of what the USUs were. They were simply not very well known:

> 'I think that probably Duke of Edinburgh [award scheme] will get a tick, you know, University Officer Training Corps, not too sure'.

There were indications in interviews of uncertainty about what the USU experience might bring. Examples were given of interviewers rejecting answers to competency questions based on an OTC experience on the grounds that 'that's not really what we're looking for'. When interest was shown, this was sometimes indicative of a low knowledge base:

> 'They would say "oh, well I see you have been a member of the RAF reserves for the past three years, how on earth did you do that at Uni?",

and it does show that they don't really know much about University Air Squadrons, but they were intrigued [...]'

Ultimately, graduates understood that it was an interviewee's responsibility to explain the relevance, 'because generally most people don't really understand what the Army do', so the challenge lay in being able to explain the transferability of the experience. However, in doing so interviewees then had the opportunity to discuss their skills and to focus on aspects of their USU experience which they judged interviewers to be interested in.

There was also an issue around misunderstanding what previous USU experience might mean for future career aspirations. One graduate mentioned how discussion of USU experience had to be undertaken cautiously in case this past experience was taken as indicative of a future military obligation. Another spoke of his sense of interviewers trying to gauge whether he was actually more interested in an armed forces career:

> 'They would look at my CV and say "oh we noticed you'd done this military leadership training, why haven't you gone on to being a full-time army?".'

This issue was also raised as a potential problem in qualitative responses to the student survey (see Chapter 3) when students were asked about their prospective or actual use of USU experience in job applications.

In conclusion, it is clear that in using USU experience in the job interview process, graduates have to feel their way, reading an employer and interview panel to work out whether or not they should discuss their USU experience, and if so, how to do so. USU experience, and the transferable skills that it might develop in students which are then of use in the civilian graduate labour market, is not a solution in itself to getting a job. Rather, relevance has to be proven.

It was also clear that lack of awareness of the armed forces amongst employers, and lack of awareness and knowledge of the USUs, is quite fundamental in shaping the context where USU skills and experience can (or cannot) be discussed. This is not an issue unique to USU graduates: the work of explaining the relevance and transferability of skills derived from a military context is undertaken frequently by the thousands who seek civilian employment after leaving the armed forces, or who seek to combine their work in the Reserves with civilian employment.[62] What we would emphasise here, on the basis of evidence from graduate interviews, is that the knowledge base about USUs amongst employers is low. We return to this point in Chapter 7.

---

[62] The armed forces, primarily through SaBRE (Support for Britain's Reservists and Employers), are increasingly having to explore mechanisms whereby the transferability of skills from military to civilian life can be used in employment contexts.

### 4.2.3. University armed service units experience in the workplace

Some interviewees noted explicitly that they did not discuss their USU experience at work because, for example, 'URNU was not a particularly major part of my life at university', or because, 'I try and separate my personal and professional lives'. Not discussing an experience is of course not the same as not using the experience, and those working in international contexts were unlikely to mention their USU experiences with colleagues or clients because it could be meaningless in those contexts. Nevertheless, we were interested in whether, if at all, a USU experience has continued relevance in the workplace as former USU graduates proceed through their working lives.

USU experience might be appropriate in dealing with ex-military colleagues in terms of understanding how they work:

> 'I have a newish colleague, ex-Army, there's a bit of rapport, and I know he'll do what he says he'll do'.

This point is interesting because of the ways in which certain personality traits become labelled 'military', when they might equally originate in a completely different formative experience.

USU experience might also be raised occasionally in conversations with colleagues with a USU or armed forces background, or if it was known that the individual was in the Reserves. Those working in occupations where some understanding of specific armed forces roles was relevant suggested that they might share something of their USU background where this was appropriate. This came up in discussions with, for example, an engineer who worked for a commercial airline and interacted from time to time with flight crews who had military backgrounds. Interviewees who worked in the police service (which at various points in time has recruited strongly from former armed forces personnel) also discussed sharing their USU experience with colleagues. Sharing with colleagues was dependent on context.

In workplace social interactions, military-derived language or terminology could be used, or slang:

> 'Things like saying 'Roger' instead of 'I understand' is quite standard, which people find funny [...] we sort of do it in a tongue-in-cheek way.'

A former UAS graduate similarly observed that it came up in rapport with her colleagues because she now worked primarily with British Army personnel in her (civilian) job, but it was only done that way because 'it was just university air squadron, it's not real life – they don't see that as credible, which is fair enough'. Being known as a former USU member might bring tangential knowledge ('in the land of the blind, the one-eyed man is king'). One interviewee talked of the diverse reactions she had experienced from people finding out about her OTC participation, from expressions of interest to incomprehension 'because they think tax payers' money is being paid – we got wages to go and have fun in a field with a gun and then join the army'. It might be used as a conversation starter, or just as a quirky bit of self-revelation:

> 'I'm old enough to be their [i.e. younger colleagues'] mother [...] and I made some comment about diving, and they said 'is there anything else you've done?' and I just said, you know, I used to have a pilot's licence [...]'

There were generational effects: one of our older interviewees observed that in the 1950s and 1960s military service was mentioned because of the number of people who had National Service or Second World War backgrounds and ended up in the legal profession. A former UAS member who graduated in the 1980s said she rarely mentioned it because 'I don't need to make myself sound interesting any more'. A former UAS member who graduated in 2010 said she mentioned it all the time. Past USU experience might also be used by workplace colleagues to explain a personal characteristic: an ex-URNU member working in advertising found that he 'can end up presenting in naval command mode', something noted by colleagues. An ex-OTC member recalled how colleagues had recognised it. On one occasion, it had come up in conversation after a busy work event when they were relaxing over drinks, and the interviewee had been seen to be taking command, having an idea about self-discipline in a public/client context, and getting on with a job that had needed to be done.

Rather than deliberately sharing information about a USU background, in some employment contexts an understanding of specific language or communications protocols derived from that background was thought to be more useful. Individuals also mentioned their ability to identify symbolic markers (for example, a regimental tie, cufflinks and the wearing of a poppy) and to use this ability as a conversation starter or in the development of rapport in work-related situations.

We asked graduates whether they discussed their USU participation with clients encountered in workplace contexts. Graduates were less likely to do so, but recognised that their USU background could be judiciously used to develop rapport or as an ice-breaker where it was known or suspected that the client in question had a military background. But as with workplace discussions with colleagues, graduates were cautious in discussing their past military experience, indicating awareness that it might be seen as having possible negative connotations and consequences in the eyes of others.

In conclusion, graduates suggested that the continued relevance of USU experience is dependent on context. This context includes interactions with close colleagues, with more distant colleagues or individuals encountered for a brief period in organisational contexts, and with clients. In the workplace, the ability to stand out as an individual can be useful, and to an extent it seems that having USU experience may allow former members to do so. In part, this reflects the fact that the individuals concerned may not have been anticipated to have had military experience at that age, or in that occupation.

It was interesting to observe how, in our interviews, certain characteristics were labelled as 'military' (being a team worker, being organised and being self-disciplined), despite the obvious fact that such characteristics are by no means the sole preserve of individuals with a military background. This is notable because it indicates a broader point about how the conditioning received in a USU functions by identifying specific characteristics as military, and how that association continues on into the workplace.

## 4.3  Defence-minded for life?

A long-standing and very significant rationale for the existence of the USUs, and their maintenance through the defence budget, is the idea that the USUs develop 'defence-mindedness'—an understanding of and attitude towards defence and the armed forces which is broadly positive—which graduates then take with them into civilian life. An often-repeated idea from senior military personnel is the notion that the USUs are influential on people who later go on to achieve prominent positions in business as 'captains of industry' or in public life. We were interested, then, in assessing the continued validity of this idea.

### 4.3.1.  Attitudes towards the armed forces

One of the objectives of the graduate interviews was to explore quite explicitly graduate attitudes towards the armed forces. A set of very nuanced ideas emerged from the interviews about how, exactly, those attitudes are framed and how those individuals might or might not be influential in promoting those ideas. It is also worth pointing out the diversity of the graduate labour market: the idea of training a very small elite who proceed in due course into roles with power and authority taking with them and disseminating a positive view of the armed forces may still have an element of truth, but it was notable from the interview data that a much wider set of ideas and experiences are taken into working lives, including the use of the USU experience to develop informed critiques of defence and military matters. Although one (older) interviewee had indeed been a true captain of industry in his career, a much larger proportion of the sample were younger, were not in particularly dominant positions in their sector and were speaking of the diffusion of ideas in very diverse employment contexts.

We asked quite explicitly whether being in a USU had given the interviewee a positive or negative regard for the armed forces. No-one said that their views were negative and just over one third said their views were positive, providing no further elaboration. A further one third said their views were positive and provided an explanation or further elaboration on this, with the most common explanation being that they felt they had some kind of understanding of what the armed forces as an organisation, and what individual personnel actually do. Respect for either named individuals, or for what individuals do, was a common theme. Graduates were also asked whether they thought their positive views were representative of other former members. Generally they did, with the caveat that positive views were held by those who had participated in their units for a period of time, and who had not left after a shorter period of experience (on which they could not comment).

There were individuals who felt that their positive view came with some kind of qualification. These were primarily to do with the culture and organisation (or otherwise) of the armed forces as an institution, with working practices cited as having negative effects, including issues such as perceptions of mismanagement. Those who said that their views were both positive and negative (who were a small number) were critical (again) of the organization and management that they had encountered in their USU.

We can infer from this that the USUs tend to instil individuals who have participated in the units with a positive regard for the armed forces. What is useful to note is the sense from interviewees that theirs was an informed view, developed on the basis of experience. In addition, a number took the trouble to point out and to qualify their statements by noting that the USU experience was something quite specific, and did not equate directly with the experience of regular personnel, particularly deployed personnel.

We also asked our graduate interviewees whether they thought they had been influential to others in terms of their positive or negative view of the armed forces. Responses here tended to be quite cautious, with very few describing themselves as vocal advocates of the armed forces. The majority of interviewees suggested that they were actually quite cautious in the ways in they might draw on their USU experience to be influential to others, suggesting that they were not setting out to change minds or influence opinion, but rather that they felt able to give a qualified view of the armed forces in contexts where the question arose and they thought it appropriate to give a view.

In conclusion, graduates tended to be positively well disposed to the UK armed forces and recognised the advocacy function that they might be able to perform for the armed forces because of their USU experience, but were cautious about the extent to which they felt they could claim expertise about defence or military matters. There was a sense from some of how little power they might have, as individuals, to shape the opinions and views of others (even if they wanted to). The strongest sense we gained from responses to this question was the idea that it was with family members and younger people that interviewees felt they had greatest sense of direct influence on the attitudes of others towards the armed forces. This might be evident in encouragement to family members or younger people to consider joining a USU, or to consider a career in the armed forces. Although there may be instances of direct, visible and pronounced influence of benefit to the armed forces from former members now in powerful positions in civilian life, the research found very little evidence that this was a common experience across the cohort. The key conclusion is that USUs graduates are influential in terms of their positive views of the armed forces in individual and quite personal ways.

### 4.3.2. Taking account of the university armed service unit experience as a civilian recruiter

We were interested in the practical application of defence-mindedness inculcated through the USU experience. One of the ways in which we hypothesised that this might be manifest was through the ability of former USU members to understand the value or otherwise of the USU experience in their capacity as recruiters in the civilian labour market. We have already noted that there was some management of the USU experience in some contexts in the job application and interview process, and this included awareness of the lack of knowledge among recruiters about what the USUs provided. We were interested in the flip-side of that, where recruiters might have experience of USUs and how that might affect their decision-making. Ultimately, recruiters will almost always recruit according to the match between a job specification and an applicant's competency for the role (and equalities legislation and human resources practices ensure this). We were therefore not expecting unfair advantage to be manifest. Rather, we were interested in how pre-existing USU knowledge might be handled by recruiters, given what we have observed about graduates' negotiations of their USU experience in their own job-hunting practices. About one third of our graduate interviewees had personal experience of recruiting in the civilian labour market or for social organisations, so spoke from direct experience. We did not restrict questioning to just USU experience, so we have also included comments made about the recruitment of former armed forces personnel.

Former unit participants who, as we have already indicated, tended to have a fairly positive view of their own experience, were ready to show an interest in someone with a background which they could recognise. USU or armed forces experience was not the only activity where this was pertinent, but it was significant:

> 'I've done a lot of recruiting in my career, a lot of interviewing, a lot of recruiting graduates as well, and I'm always interested in anyone who's been in the OTC [...] or Territorials, that's a very positive interest. I'm not saying I would give them preference but its certainly a big influencing factor – the fact that someone at the university has got off their rear end to go and do something, I think that gives me a good indication of the sort of person that might be.'

> 'I've always looked favourably on people who've had a military background, and the reason for that is, generally speaking, they tend to be hardworking, they tend to be diligent, what they perhaps lack in some cases in imagination they make up with good strategy.'

The individual quoted above noted how she had 'seeded' people with military backgrounds into teams, not specifically because of some kind of trained ability for teamwork, but because in her view good teams needed different types of people– and as a type, those with military backgrounds had recognisable roles and thus a positive effect on their team. An individual who recruited volunteers for a youth organisation made a similar observation about his experience in recruiting someone who, despite personal differences, he felt he could understand in terms of how this individual worked, because of the individual's military background and our interviewee's experience with the URNU.

An individual who ran his own software company commented that he would be more inclined to look favourably at a CV showing USU experience, because having established a person's technical ability to do the job in question, there was a very significant question of whether the potential employee would fit with the team. Getting them to talk about their military background at interview was a useful way of providing someone with the opportunity to demonstrate their attributes: 'actually it's a question of "are we going to get on? Is the team going to work well together?"'.

The idea that certain skills or abilities might be associated with a military background was evident:

> 'When I joined [the police] there was a large tranche of NCOs [...] you do tend to find they make really good policemen – there must be something in certain aspects of people from the military fits in well with it. [...] it's a discipline job.'

One interviewee talked of the 'phenomenal' abilities she had encountered in ex-forces personnel in terms of logistics and project management, areas she saw the Army as excelling in anyway. Another with a career in higher education administration found ex-service personnel 'business-like, efficient looking, and they tended to know stuff'. An interviewee saw former forces personnel as 'more organized, calmer'. An assumption about abilities for teamwork was also noted.

Although this was seen in some circumstances as advantageous, there were cautions and caveats. The individual quoted directly above also noted that in his profession, air traffic control, he was aware that although former RAF members were seen 'in a certain favourable light [...] they often don't transition well to the role'. An interviewee with a long career in the public sector, including in defence-related activities, drew distinctions between ex-military personnel on the basis of rank. He said he had developed a view later in his career dealing with very senior military personnel which 'unfortunately wasn't very positive'. Military personnel constantly moved jobs, roles were often narrow and:

> '[...] it's a different way of working in civilian life – I think you behave as if you are there forever [...], that you would expect to see the consequences of your decision, one had the sense with the military that [...] there wasn't the sort of holistic responsibility that I expected of managers.'

Deference and an expectation of working in a hierarchical culture meant that there were adaptation issues, as was the (in)ability of senior officers in civilian roles to develop concepts and innovate at a strategic level. However, there was the opinion that their ability to manage real time changing situations was well developed.

In conclusion, there was nothing from our interviewees to suggest that former armed forces personnel or people with a USU background receive an unfair advantage, but in some contexts that background could be advantageous.

## 4.4 Considering a career in the armed forces

None of the graduates we interviewed had pursued a military career. With a cohort of the diversity that we had, there were inevitably a wide range of structural labour market factors and recruitment contexts shaping career choices and the question of military participation (and for a couple of our interviewees, this was not optional as they had been required to do National Service). Beyond this, we were interested in whether these individuals had at one point intended to join the armed forces, and the reasons why they did not. It is worth reiterating that the sample contained successful, educated people who would be attractive recruits for the armed forces, so we were mindful of the potential utility of the graduate responses we received.

### 4.4.1. 'Try before you buy'

Roughly one third of our graduate interviewees said that they had entertained the idea, at some point prior to or during university, of entering the armed forces. This figure corresponds with that in section 3.6.2 above showing student intentions with regards to an armed forces career. This included those with childhood aspirations (fighter pilot is a common one), and those who had given the idea no consideration at all until participating in a USU at university. Of these, a small number proceeded with applications to commission into the Army, RAF or Royal Navy, but either failed to meet the required standards or decided to follow another career path. A number of comments were made to suggest that during their time in a USU, the armed forces had been far less proactive about using it for recruitment than was perceived to be the case at present. The remainder determined through their USU experience that a full-time career in the armed forces was not for them, and for a variety of reasons. This seems a highly significant beneficial effect of the way that USUs are organised and structured, around voluntary participation: the value of the USU experience, for many people and for the armed forces as organisations, was felt to be that they provide a space for potentially interested recruits to the armed forces to determine whether or not a career in the armed forces is actually right for them, and if so, in what capacity or role. In the words of one interviewee, USUs provide the opportunity to 'try before you buy'. In a number of cases, individuals who had intended to proceed to officer training before joining their unit but ultimately did not, were thoughtful about the benefits of the USU: by joining a unit and deciding not to pursue a military career, they did not then become either dropouts or rejects from an officer training programme, or disgruntled or ineffective officers once commissioned.

When reflecting back on their personal contribution to the units, there was a sense from many interviewees that by participating, both they and the armed forces had the opportunity to establish whether or not that individual had the potential for a career in those forces. A good example of this came from an individual who, by his own measure, had been highly motivated to join the RAF on graduation, and indeed had been in receipt of a bursary whilst a student in recognition that this was going to be his likely post-graduation destination. Yet he said that he had found himself getting more and more frustrated with the RAF whilst in the unit, and in turn, that the RAF through his UAS participation had had the opportunity to vet him, and in the process had found that he was not right for the organisation. Another noted that he had suggested to people (who were not in an OTC) who were keen to join the Army to try the OTC first, saying that he had been 'sort of the opposite of a recruiting officer to people who say they'll join the Army. I say "go along to the OTC and see if it's actually going to turn out how you think"'. One interviewee likened the unit experience to a two or three year job interview, an opportunity for screening applicants.

Although ultimately these graduates decided not to join, what we consider significant in reviewing the interview data is the idea that one of the greatest benefits of the USUs is the opportunity it provides for carefully considering a pre-university intention to join the armed forces. By being able to 'try before you buy', these individuals could experience military life without having to commit, and were able to use that opportunity to enable a decision to be made with huge potential consequences for subsequent careers. The value of the USUs, then, may well include unit abilities to shape recruitment by dissuasion (again, echoing the comments of current students in section 3.6.2. above).

### 4.4.2. Push and pull factors and career choices

The remainder of interviewees provided a range of explanations as to why they had not pursued a military career, ranging from lack of interest, medical issues, personal circumstances and family commitments, to the availability of more attractive alternatives. In exploring why a group of people who overwhelmingly indicated that they had enjoyed their USU experience had determined that a full-time career in the armed forces was not for them, explanations can be categorised as 'pull' factors (the attractions of a civilian career and life) and 'push' factors (features of the armed forces and a military life which dissuaded individuals from a military career).

Pull factors were quite straightforward: individuals wanted a career in a particular sector, or to pursue an occupation where opportunities were limited in the armed forces, or to use their degree more directly. Interviewees, who as we have noted were all highly educated, and largely a dynamic and high-achieving group (judging by their maintenance of professional careers), had higher aspirations than a career in the armed forces was perceived by them to afford. A number explained that their younger selves had been ambitious, and more ambitious than a career in the armed forces could accommodate. It seems that the very thing that is celebrated as a quality required in USU participants, that dynamism, get-up-and-go, the urge to achieve and to do something different, is also the thing that pulls many away from a career in the armed forces. Whether this is perceptual or actual seems beside the point; the fact is that the armed forces were seen by many as offering limited career opportunities to bright graduates.

The push factors, things that actively deterred USU participants from considering an armed forces career, were more complex. A small number cited medical reasons, that is, they would not have passed the required medical tests for commissioning into the armed forces (or at least for the specialism they were interested in). The remainder cited perceptual issues, and the following were cited either singly or in combination.

The lifestyle demanded of a career in the armed forces, including the perceived impact of that lifestyle on later family life, was key. The articulation of reasons against joining on the grounds of lifestyle were about potential, perceived future aspirations. There were those who cited issues such as the lack of appeal of barracks life, of being told where to live and/or of continued personal mobility. One talked of wanting to live in a particular geographical area. Another wanted the option of not going to war, if required. Then there were those who cited lifestyle in terms of aspirations towards family life. This was expressed in terms of wanting to have children and to get married within the context of a civilian home life, a perception that a military lifestyle was incompatible with family life, and a perception that the mobility required of a military career would potentially have a detrimental impact on a spouse. With graduates whose partners had also been in units, the idea of them both being in the armed forces was seen as impractical in terms of being able to spend sufficient time together because of demands (in the case of the Royal Navy) to be away at sea, or because of the demands of a period of deployment. We would note at this point that these ideas are not specific to graduates; the point, however, is that it may be during USU participation that these ideas become consolidated.

Graduates also talked of their own limits, of using their self-awareness as a factor determining their decision not to pursue a full-time military career. Examples included wanting variety in a job, and perceiving (in this case) a job in the RAF as restricting choices, keeping that person doing one particular thing. Individuals noted their levels (and lack of) of self-confidence and maturity at the time. One spoke of not having the requisite intelligence ('I would have found it hard to keep up with the syllabus'), and another noted that other people were better suited to such a career.

The culture and class structure of the armed forces was mentioned by a small number. One individual perceived that his failure to pass through the (Army) Regular Commission Board was class-based: he felt that he had been treated differently because of his class background and noted how bitter he had felt at the time. Another mentioned his perception of male chauvinism prevalent in the service to which he had applied, which he found distasteful ('I didn't like what came out of Sandhurst'), and felt he would have found living and working with such people intolerable. For others, it was simply not wanting the military discipline, authority, the command structure or to be working in such a structured hierarchical environment.

There were also the limitations of an armed forces career, particularly at various points when the armed forces were contracting and opportunities were seen as limited. Three women also mentioned that restrictions on the employment of women in place at that time had meant that there were no desirable jobs open to them, or in one case, an instance where her corps of choice (the Royal Engineers) had only just started taking women, and she did not want to have to deal with what she perceived as the challenges that would follow by being in the first cohort of women in that corps.

For the interviewees who had Reserves experience, there were useful insights in responses to the question as to why that individual had chosen not to pursue a full-time career in the armed forces. For example, whereas the lifestyle associated with full-time participation was perceived as unattractive, the ability to combine paid civilian employment with Reserves participation, and thus take a further step having participated in the USU, was significant. One interviewee, for example, noted how attractive the Reserves had been as an option as a good break from his daily working life, though he felt that doing it full-time 'would ruin my hobby'. Another noted how he had joined the Reserves in preference to the Regulars because he wanted a home life. Also mentioned were ideas about being able to keep a distinction between a civilian occupation and a Reservist role; an interviewee discussed how he enjoyed the hands-on aspect of his work in the Territorial Army (TA) in contrast to his desk-based civilian job.

In conclusion, there was a diverse set of reasons why the graduate interviewees had not pursued armed forces careers, around push and pull factors. It should also be noted that a number talked about how the decision ultimately was quite circumstantial, with the arrival of a job offer from a civilian employer at a specific point in time being the determining factor, although the choice between a military and civilian career option had been a close-run thing. There was also a sense from a number of interviewees of an element of chance, with the idea of joining the armed forces fading away as the person ended up pursuing something else, rather than the individual making a deliberate decision not to join. Generational differences were also evident, with people graduating in the 1990s quite possibly facing a different labour market than those in the later 2000s. What was evident, overall, was that reasons for not joining can work in combination. People make choices that are rational at the time. Some people do not have a single reason that they can articulate. We were also aware whilst interviewing that the explanations that people give for past choices and decisions may change over time, with the benefits of hindsight.

## 4.5 The value of the individual to their university armed service unit and the armed forces

The schedule used to interview graduates who had participated in the units as students focused primarily on the detail of the value of the USU experience to that individual. However, we also asked individuals what value they, as individuals, might have brought to the armed forces or the USUs. This was an interesting question to ask because it provoked considerable thought on the part of interviewees. The responses, however, could be categorised quite clearly. We have not attempted to quantify these and many individuals made several points in response to this question. The purpose of the analysis here, given the qualitative nature of the material, is to provide a sense of the range of ideas forthcoming in response to this question, because they suggest some additional issues pertaining to questions about the overall value of the USUs.

### 4.5.1. *Tangible benefits to the armed forces*

In responding to a question about their value to the armed forces as individuals, there was a good sense from interviewees that the investment of defence resources in them whilst they were USU participants could reap tangible rewards for the armed forces further down the line. Those rewards might be incidental, and when expressed as single examples may seem very modest. Cumulatively, though, they point to a return on the investment.

The practical effects of the knowledge that individuals gained about the armed forces, and about individual services and their functions, was cited as a range of small examples indicative of a broader process of practical assistance. Examples included: providing a civil servant with experience which helped her deal with military colleagues in her job to the advantage of those colleagues through her understanding of rank, manner and organisational culture; a logistics manager working in air transportation using his UAS experience to assist with outsourced elements of the Army supply chain; a marketing manager working in public relations and using their USU experience in developing a customer relationship management strategy for an armed forces account; a police officer alert to the specific issues that might affect veterans encountered in the course of his duties (including, for example, knowing that a claim of status as a veteran could be very readily tested by asking an individual for their service number, something this individual understood was never forgotten) and another member of the police service able to use knowledge to assist with local military ceremonial events. Included amongst the practical benefits to the armed forces were instances of assistance to USUs. Examples included: an air traffic controller able to facilitate his local UAS's flying training by management of landing slots and airfield use costs; an individual with accountancy qualifications able to assist with business processes for his local OTC unit and a former UAS member now working on a voluntary basis as a flying instructor for the Royal Auxiliary Air Force:

> 'I've put back a thousand-odd hours of flying instruction and I got 100 hours out of them as a University Air Squadron member – I've now given an order of magnitude more than that back to the next generation of Air Cadets. I'm doing that on a volunteer basis because it feels worthwhile, I owe them some debt and because I enjoy it, I want to pass on some of that enthusiasm to other people. So in my case I suspect that's the most tangible benefit.'

There was also benefit in the simple fact that the service units comprise a body of people, in uniform, to be deployed for assistive tasks, such as playing the enemy for military training exercises or able to (quite literally) fly the flag for the armed forces. In the words of one former URNU member:

> 'They got my hands for free, or at very low cost. We went around the coast flying the flag. It would have been very difficult for the military to have been able to pay for a patrol boat to go round and do those particular public relations jobs we did without having cheap student labour driving them.'

Another URNU member noted that:

> 'I manned a P2000 going round British waters showing the flag to parts of the UK that don't see a grey-hulled warship. It's difficult to justify paying full-time naval personnel to do that kind of exercise when the Navy is otherwise overstretched. We would open the ship to the public [...] beat the drum for the Navy. [...] I remind my fellow [professionals in a maritime-based occupation] that the only reason they can safely go around the world taking measurements is that there's a Navy there to protect you from all sorts of things – the fact that there's piracy still going on these days means that you need the Navy and without it you couldn't have a nice slow-moving research vessel safely pottering around the place to do the business. For my own community's point of view, I don't mind trying to remind people of that very important fact.'

In conclusion, with the exception of one former UAS member who had gone on to work at a very high level in defence procurement, our sample of interviewees did not really match the anecdotal figure of the captain of industry, using his or her authority at a senior level to influence either the business of a company or employees in that business in ways that would be beneficial in some way for the armed forces. Rather, the evidence collected showed individual acts, sometimes incidental, sometimes occasional and sometimes more day-to-day, which in turn could 'repay the favour' of an initial investment in an individual. This is significant because it suggests nuance and unpredictability to the benefits accrued to the armed forces (and the defence community more broadly). Investment in individuals through the USUs is, in a sense, a leap of faith on the part of the armed forces. That this investment continues reflects a tacit understanding of this within defence, based on decades of experience.

#### 4.5.2. Intangible benefits to the armed forces

We noted above how the USU experience had given participants a generally positive attitude towards the armed forces, and have also noted how that attitude might translate into practical activities. What was also evident in talking to former participants about the value of individuals to the units was the role they might play as advocates for the armed forces.

This advocacy might be evident in a variety of different situations at different times. Examples included: support given (in time and money) for armed forces charities, encouragement individuals might be able to give to younger people about the benefits of an armed forces career, being involved in public remembrance events or being able to include consideration of the armed forces in public educational events. The idea of being an ambassador for the armed forces was often mentioned:

> 'I can point out the value and professionalism of the armed forces.'
> 'They've got a positive advocate, someone with an appreciation for what we are trying to do and why.'
> 'I'm able to correct people's misconceptions about the military and what they do.'

A few individuals made the point that precisely because they did not think they were perceived as military types, or according in some way with a cultural stereotype of what the armed forces represent, that this was of value:

> 'I can go out and promote what the armed forces do, with my peer group, friends. I'm a Guardian-reading, go-on-strike fire-fighter – I'm on the other side of what a lot of people are, I can see the benefit of

having an armed forces system. I'm not right-wing, I have a liberal point of view, which can be beneficial.'

In conclusion, the mechanisms for the translation of positive attitudes toward the armed forces through advocacy or ambassadorship were often low-key, incidental, seemingly prosaic and were mechanisms used with friends or family, or in occasional encounters. Again, the captain of industry model seems a little outdated for this mode of communication, but the substance of what interviewees said is significant because it speaks to the intangible (often non-quantifiable) benefits of the existence of the units.

A further point to note here is (again) the caution expressed by graduates about the extent to which they could claim expertise and thus incur influence on the basis of their USU experience. There was considerable awareness of the inadvisability of over-claiming experience, expertise and thus influence.

### 4.5.3. *Socialising the armed forces*

A small number of interviewees raised the very interesting issue of the extent to which the USUs serve to 'socialise' the armed forces, specifically the Regular forces. We use the term socialise to refer to activities and attitudes which work to connect the armed forces to a set of wider civilian cultural practices.[63]

In terms of what they might have brought to their units as individuals, some interviewees made the point of stressing what they as students brought which was distinctive. One, a mature student at university and thus the oldest officer cadet in her OTC, thought that she had demonstrated through her presence and her contribution a valuable point for the unit's command and training team that it was indeed possible to recruit mature students, and that units could get something quite specific from them in terms of an individual with some life experience, which she considered to be helpful for the younger students in the unit. Another (a graduate from a plate glass university founded in the late 1960s) thought that the inclusion of people like her who did not come from ancient or high-profile, long-established institutions gave the OTC an understanding of the different backgrounds that officers could come from, in addition to the way in which the unit experience provided an opportunity for people from less prestigious educational backgrounds to prove themselves. Another talked about how, with a group of people like herself who knew that they did not want a military career, they:

---

[63] This idea resonates with observations within military sociology, that military forces in many ways operate according to distinct cultural codes and practices which reflect their specificity and social distinctiveness as a group holding state-legitimized authority to execute lethal violence.

'[...] kept it real for them. Not everybody is obsessed with three letter abbreviations and doing everything military style, we kept it so it didn't become a recruitment facility, kept it as a university club with a bit more purpose.]

For the officers and Other Ranks in charge of her unit, 'it was interesting for them, we were a bunch of students, had that headiness'. An URNU member observed that for Royal Navy members with organisational responsibility:

'[...] it's an interesting posting for them, working with a bunch of students who don't follow orders, are always questioning, being fairly irritating – I hope it was positive for those guys, certainly different from what they did previously and did afterwards, hopefully it gave them some benefit.'

Another noted how her UAS brought life to the officers' mess at the facility where they trained, that it was refreshing for the military to have 'young blood'. An OTC graduate spoke of how:

'[...] we used to get interesting Sergeant Majors who thought they'd come to the posting for a couple of years off, but they wanted to stay, they really enjoyed working with the students, it was a learning experience for them, working with us.'

So whilst those in charge of the units might have 'had days where they queried why they accepted the post' because of student rowdiness from time to time in the mess bar, it also made for an interesting posting. Students 'annoy the living daylights out of Sergeant Majors and Sergeants everywhere'. Yet it was notable how so many former USU members spoke of their COs and training staff with warmth and respect.

We would not want to overstate the case about the socialising effect of the units on the wider armed forces. This would appear to be an incidental consequence. However, there is a wider point to be made here about the value of this, given the context for the contemporary British armed forces where debate continues about the level of connection between civil society and the military; this connection is, of course, a two-way street, an idea often missing from commentary about the issue.

### 4.5.4. Recruitment to the Reserves

A visible, material and distinct benefit to the armed forces, in the view of former USU members, was their post-graduation involvement with the Reserve forces. As noted above, a considerable proportion of the sample had some kind of relationship with the Reserves, and for the majority this developed after graduation. This was a clear and direct value to the armed forces of an individual's participation in a unit:

> 'They benefitted considerably – they had a very competent TA officer, very energetic, enthusiastic, conscientious.'
>
> 'They got a Reserves officer for 15 – 20 years. I didn't break anything expensive [...] I think they got their money's worth out of those three years.'
>
> 'They got 12 years of service, involved in officer training with other officers, conducted operations, kept continuity in the regiment as senior reserve officer, helped with corporate memory of the regiment, helping with [a high profile international sporting event] with communication support, they certainly got their pound of flesh.'
>
> 'As an individual their investment in me was tremendously well spent, in terms of national budgets. Much better than attacking Iraq. It's not a simple question. They got my technical abilities – working intelligence in the TA, I could fire a 25 lb gun. They got my academic abilities in geography, surveying, linguistics, photographic interpretation [...].'
>
> 'They got 20-odd years of me in the TA as a communications manager in [regiment], making a contribution during the floods in Cumbria [...] the firemen's strike, helping with the G8 summit in Northern Ireland. I've given something back, and bring on individuals from the next generation.'

What was illuminating in the interviews were the number of critical comments made about the proactivity or otherwise of either the parent services or the units themselves in encouraging individuals, at the time of graduation, to think seriously about a future with the Reserves. These comments reflect recruitment practices at the time in which individuals were getting ready to leave university, and so varied over time. What was evident and notable were individuals' regrets, looking back, that they had not taken further steps towards the Reserves. Two significant points emerged from this discussion. The first was that graduates themselves noted that in the two to three years post-graduation, during which they were busy with new jobs, possibly involving additional training, possibly involving relocation, and also new relationships and activities, the sheer busyness of their lives made it easy to lose sight of the Reserves as a possible activity. Once they had undergone the transition from student to worker (a process that takes time), a number reflected that it would have been at that point (rather than immediately on graduation) that they would have been most receptive to the idea of Reserves participation. The second point to emerge in discussions followed from this: graduates reflected that the armed forces themselves could have been far more proactive in keeping in touch with their alumni specifically because of their potential receptivity to the idea of Reserves participation. We return to this point in Chapter 7.

### 4.5.5. Sustaining the university armed service units as organisations

Evident in the comments of interviewees both in response to a direct question about their value as individuals to the armed forces, and in responses to other questions about their activities in their unit, was the idea that the units are, in certain respects, quite self-sustaining. A large proportion of respondents talked about how enthusiastic they were as student participants. This enthusiasm is not an insignificant issue for the units, of course: unit participation for the majority is voluntary rather than necessary, and a unit which does not provide an experience about which people can be enthusiastic will of course struggle to maintain its numbers.

But more significantly, it was evident how this enthusiasm was seen by participants to translate into practical activities and input. Examples include: organising a rugby tour for the unit squad to the Czech republic, helping organise a UAS squadron as acting pilot officer, organising social events ('some damn good socials!'), bringing on younger students through mentoring and support, organising adventurous training, helping with recruitment, assisting with the organisation of unit attendance at public events and assisting with publicity ('they got a fantastic website'). We have already noted how the USU experience provides for many people an evidence base for claiming competency in particular skills in the job application process. Some of these skills, particularly organisational, recruitment, managerial and business-related skills, may have been noted by individuals primarily for the edge that it might have given them in the labour market; there was also a strong sense that the flow of value or benefit in the USUs was not one way in favour of students, but that students were in a good position to give something back to the organisation through their work with the units.

In conclusion, whilst we did not set out to provide a cost-benefit analysis of the value-for-money of the USUs, one of the benefits to units that was apparent (at least in terms of graduate explanations) was the value of the labour expended by student participants in the organisation of activities of the unit. It is these activities which are the prime draw of the USU experience. Some of these activities require trained, experienced staff to facilitate them. But a lot of them do not, particularly sporting and some adventurous training and social activities. We suggest that the units are more self-sustaining than they are often perceived to be. They may require funding from the defence budget in order to exist and function, but in many ways that investment is very well targeted at meeting quite specific costs; student labour may not be entirely free (because participants are paid), but the value of that labour can be very high in terms of contributions to the unit.

## 4.6 Graduate perceptions of the value of the university armed service units

At the start and conclusion of each interview with USU graduates we asked them a very broad question, which they could answer in any way they chose, about what they thought the value of the USUs is, was or could be. Many of these ideas were then rehearsed in the body of the interview, and are evident in the sections above. They bear possible repetition here because in collating them, a very distinct picture emerges about who benefits from the USU investment, and how exactly that might be defined.

### 4.6.1. *The personal value and individual benefit of university armed service units participation*

The dominant response of graduates to the question about value was to emphasise value to themselves as individuals. This personal or individual value was manifest in multiple ways.

The USU experience was seen as valuable in individual terms because of the opportunity and structure it provided for the development of capabilities of the self and of personal attributes. These included self-discipline, perseverance, facing and overcoming challenges, resilience, determination, drive, self-confidence, self-awareness, self-knowledge, an ability to work under pressure, self-respect, independence and initiative. Some of these personal qualities were recognised as having reach beyond individual benefit, and included: being able to act with responsibility and being willing to take on responsibilities, respect for others, the ability to undertake collaborative work, the ability to consider issues from different perspectives and a sense of moral and social responsibility and commitment (the idea of putting oneself out for the benefit of others).

Specific skills and abilities were also a value of USU participation. These included leadership, teamwork, communications, problem-solving, making presentations, time management, liaison and organisational skills. The correspondence between this list, and the list of graduate-level skills discussed in Chapter 3 is evident. Some practical skills were mentioned, such as driving and catering for larger numbers, but primarily in terms of skills it was the transferable skills which were of benefit.

The development of personal attributes and transferable skills in turn had value in leading to paid employment. Graduates highlighted how attributes and skills contributed to their CV, and how the USU experience might be understood as bringing something a bit different, lending distinction to a CV. The experience was thought to help in performing a job and encouraging a positive attitude at work, notably in developing an attitude of getting on with things. It was viewed as instrumental in raising aspirations and giving individuals such as young students an awareness of the possibilities they could entertain in terms of their personal career goals. More practically, it provided an insight into the working world and into different kinds of jobs and occupations, and gave students an experience both of managing and of being managed in the workplace.

In terms of non-military activities, the USUs provided opportunities for improving physical fitness and for engagement in sports. Otherwise quite expensive leisure activities, such as skiing, were made affordable. Activities unavailable either in civilian life or through other student societies were of individual benefit, including opportunities for travel both within and beyond the UK.

The knowledge and understanding that individuals gained of the armed forces on the basis of their USU experience was of individual value because it gave individuals the ability to get what they wanted out of the experience. The armed forces were organisations which nurtured skills, talent and potential, and this was part of the way in which the experience of USU participation developed positive views of the armed forces. This was coupled with education and increased awareness of armed forces roles, responsibilities, organisation, function and structure. The unit experience encouraged people to keep up with current affairs, and could be influential on an individual's political views.

The USUs offered a very valuable opportunity for individuals to assess whether an armed forces career was the right choice for them. Participants could experiment with the idea of joining in order to assess their 'fit' or otherwise with the armed forces, and the units offered a safe and controlled environment in which to develop that decision, including having units act as a safe place in which to make mistakes. The units provided an opportunity for potential recruits to identify a suitable career path within the armed forces. The units also provided exposure to different types of people within the armed forces themselves, such as NCOs, and a socialisation experience within the armed forces prior to joining.

The social life offered by the units was identified as important. Ideas articulated by our interviewees included meeting new people and mixing with a range of other people, including different types of people that an individual would not otherwise have an opportunity to engage with, such as those beyond an individual's degree programme cohort; the units broke down the insularity of degree programmes. Interviewees mentioned camaraderie, the familial relationships within units and the ways that units generated tolerance for other people. Units enabled students to develop a sense of identity whilst at university, particularly during the first stages of the first year, whereby they gave students a feeling of being part of a group and provided a support network whilst at university. Participation was fun, 'like glorified Scouts […] but with beer' in the words of an interviewee, and although there was caution about seeing the units as just a type of social club, there was clearly fun to be had.

Unit participation was valued because for many it gave a sense of purpose whilst at university, grounding them, giving them a sense of a reality beyond what one respondent termed 'the university bubble', keeping students on track with their studies and providing a structure to the university experience. The experience was seen as prompting students to put greater effort into their academic studies because of the unit emphasis on teamwork, leadership and time management, and some observed that the skills learnt through their unit experience were transferable to the skills required to succeed in an academic programme.

The income received through unit participation was a value. The USU experience may be more fun that bar work and brought the rewards similar to a part-time job in terms of remuneration:

'The money influenced me slightly because I was paid, I couldn't have afforded to do it if I didn't get paid.'

There were a small number of critical comments about the social mix at the units, with the dominance of people educated in the private (fee-paying) sector being noted. That said, a number of women mentioned the benefits of unit participation that they felt they had received as women. Being able to engage in adventurous training opportunities was significant. One respondent made a very interesting observation about how, as a woman in the OTC, it was one of the first places that she had seen real gender equality, which she'd found surprising and 'eye-opening' given the Army context. She commented on how it had been 'amazing' to see team members work as team members if one was struggling. This idea had stayed with her:

'I've never yet been in a role or a job where men and women [have had] an equal playing field. So it was really interesting to see and I think that's really stayed with me.'

In conclusion we would emphasise that the USUs are not the only student activities where these individual benefits can be accrued. Our respondents attributed these individual benefits to their USU experience in response to questions about that specific experience, and we did not explore other student activities and their benefits during the interviews (and there would certainly be room for a comparative study on this). The key point here is that for our graduate interviewees, a key aspect of the value of USUs is the personal and individual benefits that participation brings.

### 4.6.2. *The value of the university armed service units for the armed forces*

Although not mentioned with the same high frequency as the individual benefits identified above, interviewees articulated a number of different reasons why the USUs had value specifically for the armed forces. Again, we have made no effort to quantify responses here, but rather show the range of ideas articulated across the sample.

Just as there were individual benefits in terms of understanding the armed forces, the armed forces themselves were perceived by graduates to draw value from the units as vehicles for enhancing knowledge, and many of the responses mirror those above. The recruiting function the units served for the armed forces was key here, as the armed forces were seen as having a tacit or implicit opportunity to assess whether individuals had a potential future with them, and could provide contacts for individuals with specific branches within the armed forces. The units were an opportunity for the armed forces to encourage people who had not previously considered an armed forces career, and provided a good introduction to the Reserves, generating good officers (although this comment was also made with the caveat that there had been scope for greater proactivity by the armed forces in encouraging recruitment to the Reserves in the past). The armed forces could 'weed people out' of the recruitment pool. The armed forces also benefitted through the utility of unit participants being influential on others either joining a USU or the armed forces. The units were increasingly significant for recruitment of trained officers for the Reserves, with one interviewee who was a Reservist noting that his regiment relied on the OTC for direct entry officers to his regiment because of difficulties in recruiting.

The armed forces were thought to benefit through the increased public understanding that USUs generated in people who would not go on to join, and through the generated empathy, affinity for and insight into the armed forces. The units gave individuals a fuller picture of the armed forces beyond a 'glossy public image', a fuller understanding of military roles in political and international situations, and an understanding of both day-to-day activities and the more theoretical or abstract roles. At a time of contraction of the armed forces, this was thought to be important. Insights developed into the organisation were valuable, and the broader understanding units helped develop of the armed forces was significant because members might become influential in later life. The units also provided opportunities for cross-national and cross-cultural understanding of other national forces. There were also practical benefits in terms of the availability of additional personnel (unit participants) for emergency response activities, and were thought to enhance the capacity of the Reserves. The question was raised, however, about how quantifiable these benefits might be.

The value to the armed forces was also evident because units might have generated sympathetic employers with a positive attitude towards the armed forces. They may have enhanced the public visibility of the armed forces in general, and in university contexts, and stopped the armed forces becoming too insular through student engagement with those forces and enabled networking between the military and civilian worlds.

A very small number of respondents talked about their perceptions, as students, of how sometimes the units were viewed by personnel from the Regular armed forces in a negative light. One noted how this might reflect an atmosphere of concern about wider issues affecting the armed forces, particularly redundancies and budget cuts.

### 4.6.3. *The wider social value of the university armed service units*

Although far less frequently identified as a value of the USUs, the units were thought to bring wider social benefits beyond the value to individuals and the armed forces. The idea was articulated (rather similar to the idea of the value of a university education) that employers, and thus the wider economy, benefitted by having individuals with an enhanced set of skills and experience. Having educated, successful and knowledgeable people in the workplace was a societal advantage. As one respondent noted, he had spent 12 years working in transport infrastructure 'taking half the people' in a major city 'to work and then home again'. He judged the air squadron to have been instrumental in setting him on a path which led to that job, and creating someone contributing to society.

The USUs, it was thought, 'produced better citizens' and brought social benefits through the units' inculcation of a sense of discipline in individuals, rather like National Service had. More broadly, the units enabled the bonding of the military into civilian social life.

Universities were thought to benefit by producing 'better graduates', and the link between education and the military was thought to be useful, with student participants bringing qualities, ideas and experiences back to their respective universities.

The units were mentioned as enabling social mobility, although this might be era-contingent. What was significant here were the opportunities the units could provide to students, particularly those educated in the state sector or from backgrounds of modest means, to participate in extracurricular activities otherwise not available to them. Similarly, the units provided access opportunities for women to activities that might otherwise be less available to them; an example was cited of the UAS training women pilots before the RAF.

In conclusion, although the wider social benefits of the USUs may be identified, this was not a primary source of value of the units in the experience of graduates.

## 4.7 Conclusions: the value of the university armed service units to graduates

The sample of graduates interviewed for this element of the research was a diverse one in terms of interviewee age, educational background, career and work experience, and USU participation. This reflected the aim of the sampling strategy to generate data on a wide range of experiences. The point of qualitative methods, such as those used for exploring the question of USU value amongst graduates, was not to seek representativeness in the sample, but rather to explore the diversity of experiences in order to enhance understanding of the role of USU experience through post-university life. This diversity of experience is reflected in the responses, although certain key findings emerged.

In terms of the value of the USU experience to graduates in the workplace, there is utility in the citing of that experience in job applications and throughout the process of getting a job. However, this utility has to be proven by the individual and cannot be assumed, not least because of the absence of knowledge about the USUs amongst many employers. The potential attitudes of prospective employers to military experience also has to be carefully negotiated. The utility of the USU experience may be useful in the workplace, often in quite modest ways, and there is evidence of utility and value to the armed forces as a consequence of the presence of individuals in the civilian labour force with USU experience. It is notable that the significance of USU experience in job applications is greatest in the first two to three years following graduation, giving graduates a set of experiences and evidence of skills that are beneficial in the job application process, but which are superseded as careers progress with the development of civilian workplace experience.

In terms of the USU experience generating defence-mindedness amongst a group who go on to pursue civilian careers, and this is the great majority of USU graduates, the USU experience develops and instils a positive attitude towards the armed forces. However, graduates are cautious about claiming any specific expertise on the basis of their experience. They may be modestly influential to others in terms of family members and younger people with regards to transmission of attitudes and endorsement of the USU experience. This positive attitude is reflected in attitudes towards the employment of others with an armed forces background, within the parameters of equitable practice.

In terms of the utility of the USU experience in shaping attitudes towards a career in the armed forces, there was strong endorsement of the idea that the USUs serve a positive role in establishing, for both potential recruits and for the armed forces, the suitability or otherwise of an individual for such a career. The graduates, on the basis of their USU experience, had illuminating points to make about exactly why they had chosen not to pursue an armed forces career, emphasising both factors which had pushed them away from those career pathways and factors which had pulled them away towards other career options. This was despite a significant proportion (about one third) noting that they had entertained the idea of an armed forces career whilst in their USU.

In terms of the value of individuals to their units, points where made which were illustrative of the function of the units. There may be tangible benefits to both the USUs and to the armed forces in terms of things which individuals may be able to contribute, or an individual's utility may be manifest in more intangible ways through their advocacy of units and the armed forces. The USUs were thought by some to be a mechanism for the socialising of the armed forces. Individual returns on the investment in them through the units could be evidenced through those individuals' activities in the Reserves. The point was also made about the value of student labour in sustaining the activities of USUs.

In terms of the overall value of the USUs from the perspective of graduates, this was to a significant extent thought to be manifest in individual benefits.

These benefits were in the form of the USU experience providing opportunities for self-development, the development of transferable skills, enhanced understanding of the armed forces, information to inform a decision on whether an armed forces career was appropriate for that individual, the experience of a good social life, the provision of an experience in addition to academic study whilst at university and of course, the benefits of being paid whilst a student. There was also thought to be value to the armed forces, again in terms of establishing the suitability of USU participants for careers in the armed forces, whether Regular or Reserves, in terms of enhancing wider public understanding and visibility of the armed forces, and the wider social value which might follow from the existence in civilian society of individuals with the skills and attitudes developed within the USUs.

A key conclusion from the interviews with graduates with USU experience is the idea of the range of components which contributed to the value of the units. The units are not reducible to one single thing, but have value to individuals and the armed forces in a range of different ways.

Looking beyond the empirical data to consider the context, we have a number of additional observations. The first concerns the availability of the opportunity to participate in a USU. As we discussed in Chapter 1, although restricted to a smaller academic elite in the past, a university education in the present is not an unusual experience for young people in the 18–24-year-old age group, and particularly not for those from middle and higher income backgrounds. Degree-level education has become normalised, routine, expected and unexceptional. The USU experience stands out in contrast, and was perceived by graduates to have substantial individual benefit. As we have noted, the numbers participating in the units are small as a proportion of the overall UK student population, and smaller as a proportion than in the past, and thus the USU experience remains distinctive. A number of graduates discussed ideas around the expansion of the units, either in terms of the size of individual units or the total number of units, being of the view that the value of the experience could and should be available to a wider number of students. It was not within the remit of the research to adjudicate on questions about the expansion or contraction of the USUs; this is properly a matter for the Ministry of Defence and the three armed forces themselves, in the context of wider debates about defence structures and strategies. The point remains, however, that for graduates with unit experience, there was a strong sense that the experience should be more widely available.

The second point concerns the necessity of considering value-for-money, whilst recognising the non-financial benefits of the units within a context of public sector austerity where state expenditure is being slashed. The USUs represent a financial investment through the defence budget. The intention of the research was explicitly not to provide a cost-benefit analysis using economic methodologies to establish this, but rather to explore using a sociological approach as to whether or not the USUs have value, and if so, to whom. That said, the question of value-for-money was raised by a number of graduate interviewees. The financial contexts shaping USUs come not only from defence budgets, but from the current student funding system. As one interviewee noted, his generation got paid, and did not pay tuition fees, so 'we could really commit'. He reckoned that the pay provided payback in recruitment and 'it's got to be cheaper than careers offices', 'people end up as advocates so it's worth paying for'.

A significant proportion of our interviewees were curious about the overall purpose of the research, and whether it had been initiated or would be used as the basis for cost-cutting measures. One interviewee put it most succinctly when he said:

> 'I see it in my day job, accountants can't see the benefit of investing time and energy in people, but hopefully, somebody somewhere, buried in one of the MOD offices or Land Command, the Army, actually says no, save the OTCs. Hopefully your research will show the benefits and show them that. For me it was life-changing. I just couldn't imagine it not being part of my life, and I'd be sorry to hear if that kind of opportunity was taken away from anyone else.'

CHAPTER 5

# The Value of the University Armed Service Units to the Armed Forces

In this chapter, we draw on interviews conducted with unit COs to explore the value of the USUs to the armed forces, from the perspective of those charged with unit leadership and management. The interview schedule used for these interviews is provided in Appendix 3. Note that in this chapter, we focus on those parts of the interviews which discussed the question of value in terms of the USU-university relationship. The interviews with COs also included a large number of questions about the value of the USU experience to student participants. We have not included analysis of responses to those questions here, because there was nothing in CO responses which diverged from the accounts given by students and graduates and detailed in full in Chapters 3 and 4. Unit COs were asked questions in interviews about the value of the USUs to students with no prior knowledge of the results of the student survey or the graduate interviews, and it is notable therefore that COs discussed exactly the same points as were raised in the survey and graduate interviews. We do not elaborate on these points here, but would emphasise that omission here is not indicative of lack of understanding and awareness amongst COs but rather of a desire to avoid repetition. The correspondence between student, graduate and CO views on value was striking.

## 5.1 The commanding officers

A total of 15 commanding officers were interviewed for this research, five each from the OTC, UAS and URNU, in five different geographical locations around

**How to cite this book chapter:**
Woodward, R, Jenkings, K N and Williams, A J. 2015. *The Value of the University Armed Service Units*. Pp. 139–154. London: Ubiquity Press. DOI: http://dx.doi.org/10.5334/baq.e. License: CC-BY 4.0.

the UK. The sampling strategy was not determined by a need for representativeness across the 46 units, but rather by a need to explore the experience of command in different localities, and to capture something of the differences and similarities between service units in locations which engage with universities of very different types. Further information on the methodology used to define the sample and conduct the interviews is given in Chapter 2.

### 5.1.1. Postings and experience

OTC and URNU COs stated that their postings were of two and half years' duration, with the UAS postings rather shorter (up to two years). We interviewed COs whose period in command to date ranged from two months to just over three years. One CO had had a previous appointment to a USU before the present one, and one had experience as a commissioned officer and staff member whilst at university (rather than as a student member of a USU). All the OTC COs had attended a university, and of these five, three had been OTC members. Two UAS COs had been to university, and one had UAS experience. Four of the five URNU COs had graduated from university (and the fifth had left his degree programme in his first year to join the Royal Navy). Four of the URNU COs had no prior experience of the URNU, and one had had a reserve place in an UNRU in his final year of study once he had been selected to join the Royal Navy on graduation. Two of the COs were women and 13 were men.

The 15 COs had, between them, tremendously varied careers in their respective armed forces to date. Two of the OTC COs were reservists so had combined civilian careers with work in the British Army (including operational deployments). All the UAS COs were qualified flying instructors with jet or other pilot experience. All the URNU COs were navigation qualified.

All three parent services had pre-requisites for CO selection. For the OTC, the CO post is classed as a command tour. All five COs interviewed had slightly different understandings of both the Army's rationale for selecting them to that post, and their own rationale for wanting to take up the command (and note that all were familiar with the OTC themselves prior to their posting). One of the Reserves members had expressed an interest in the post, both because he was familiar with the OTC and because he was a reservist and thus in civilian employment with limited personal mobility. One CO considered that his previous Army career in a range of varied and significant roles meant that he was considered to bring something quite specific to the role ('you want someone who has done something'). Two COs had personal connections with the cities (and in one case, the local university) to which they were posted. Two of the COs noted how keen they had been to take up the CO post, one because 'I knew I would have a really good time, because you're dealing with young people who are enthusiastic', the other because under a previous post he'd been so impressed by the junior officers under his command ('they changed my view very much of the educated youth of today') and how 'phenomenally good' many of them were. The UAS COs cited their enthusiasm for their flying instructor roles. One cited parental responsibilities which were seen as compatible with the posting. Two talked of the appeal of the post because of the autonomy and responsibility they would have and the challenge of this (and one talked of turning down what was seen as a more prestigious posting as a squadron flight commander to take up the UAS posting). One mentioned how another RAF colleague had urged him to take up a UAS command post were one to become available, because it was deemed both challenging and enjoyable. The URNU COs all mentioned how the post, because it was a command post requiring command qualification to take charge of the P2000 ships, was a good career move. Two mentioned explicitly how hard they had worked to get that command, and one spoke of what a privilege it was to be in command of an URNU.

Three issues emerged during the interviews regarding CO placements. The first was a question about the length of the CO posting. The time period accorded with standard lengths of time for postings within each of the three armed forces, but the question was raised about whether, given the nature of the CO role and the significance of relationship-building in that role within the host universities and the wider locality (particularly with business), the two and half year average posting was sufficient. The second issue was RAF-specific and concerned the lack of sufficient numbers of suitably qualified applicants for the CO role, given that it required a flying instructor qualification (something felt to be essential in the role) and the relative lack of qualified applicants. The third issue was URNU-specific and related to a shift initiated in 2014 by which URNU command was de-linked to P2000 command. Previously, URNU commanders had had responsibility both for the unit and for the ship. The Royal Navy instigated a change splitting this role between two posts. All the URNU commanders indicated that they saw this as a positive development, not least because it expanded the range of command opportunities within the Royal Navy, and also because it would enable other specialist areas in the Royal Navy to become involved with URNU (and not just those who were qualified to command a Royal Navy vessel).

### 5.1.2. *Commanding Officer remits*

It was clear talking to the COs that their remits encompassed formally defined responsibilities, but also that individuals had the opportunity should they wish to undertake a variety of additional activities; the remit was therefore often much 'broader than people realise'.

COs had responsibility to deliver a training syllabus, determined centrally by, respectively, Royal Military Academy Sandhurst (for the OTC), RAF College Cranwell (for the UAS) and Britannia Royal Naval College (for the UNRU). COs had command of staff working under them in their unit in the delivery of that training, which included military-specific and other (for example, adventurous training) activities. Their responsibilities included oversight of training for that staff, who comprised both Regular and Reserves personnel in many cases. The COs were adamant that the priority for students was to complete their education and graduate with a degree, and that this was the fundamental context to their delivery of the training syllabus and management of the unit.

For the OTC and UAS, although not for the URNU, there was a far greater emphasis on the potential use of the USU as a mechanism for recruitment. This included providing practical assistance with applications (for example, writing reports on students applying for selection with the Regular and Reserve armed forces), and a more general process of gauging the interest of potential applicants in an armed forces career and offering guidance where appropriate. COs could assist with the management of an application to join the armed forces, and there was awareness that this might also involve engagement with parents. Although the URNU places far less emphasis on recruitment as a core part of its mission, the assistance URNU COs could provide to students considering Royal Navy participation was of course recognised.

Unit COs recognised that they were ambassadors for the armed forces in terms of wider civilian engagement. They might be influential on individuals who would go on to achieve positions of leadership and responsibility in later life (where having a positive attitude towards the armed forces might, in due course but in unpredictable ways, be positive for the armed forces). They could also be significant within universities by showing the presence of the armed forces. This was primarily through channels facilitated by the MEC, but not exclusively.

A key point made by some COs was that they had considerable capacity for autonomy in determining how best to work to achieve the requirements of the job ('mission command', as an OTC CO put it). They could use their own judgement to determine how exactly specific parts of the unit remit would be delivered (within an established framework). This had been noted as one of the attractions of the job. Having the capacity to do this was also felt to be beneficial; for example, one CO talked of how significant he thought wider public engagement activities were for his unit, despite not being explicitly stipulated in his remit, and another gave an example of engagement in university debates on defence issues as evidence for wider engagement.

## 5.2 The university armed service units and the universities

COs had many, very interesting things to say about the military-university relationship, significant both for the specific details provided enabling a picture to be built up about how that relationship functions, and also for the wider issues this picture then raises for the question about the value of the USUs underpinning this book. It was clear that the military-university relationship went a considerable way beyond the simple fact that students registered at one or more universities will also attend an OTC, UAS or URNU in the region and work under the command of that CO.

### 5.2.1. *University armed service units and their catchment universities*

All the USUs draw students from more than one university, and one CO in the sample had a particularly large catchment from a federal university. It was clear that the specificities of each university, in terms of institutional origins, its positioning in the national market for undergraduates under the fees regime and more internationally in the global higher education system, the types and range of degree programmes on offer, a university's research reputation, its current or past patterns of UK student recruitment (nationally or locally) and a university's physical location in relation to the unit (thus shaping the ease of student engagement) were all factors shaping the military-university relationship. Also mentioned were universities' existing links and past traditions of engagement either with military forces or one of the branches of the UK armed forces within the locality, which might be influential on the USU-university relationship. For example, one university located in a city with centuries of marine industrial involvement seemed determined to maintain strong and visible links with its local URNU. Universities were perceived as exhibiting a range of views along a continuum from support to antipathy towards the armed forces. However, on probing it was clear that it was Student Unions which were the issue rather than the institutions themselves (and we consider this issue in more detail in section 5.2.3. below).

All the COs had much to say about the differences between the universities within their catchment area, which translated into often quite marked differential levels of recruitment from different institutions. It was partly a question of geographical proximity and distance, reflecting historic patterns of USU basing and the considerable longevity of some units, particularly amongst the OTCs. This meant that it was, quite simply, much easier for some students to attend weekly drill nights than others, depending on their place of education. Some units provided assistance with transport in recognition of the challenges of distance (particularly for UAS members). Differential levels of recruitment also reflected the nature of the universities in a catchment: as a rule, the more established, research-intensive Russell Group universities had greater levels of involvement, and although that dominance was receding it was still notable. A number of COs talked at length about why certain recruitment patterns persisted, and what they as COs could and could not do to shape these. We encountered no comments which suggested that the students in certain universities were somehow seen by COs as unsuitable or unsuited to USU participation; indeed, the point was made that it was students in the newer or smaller specialist universities who potentially had the most to gain from USU participation, in terms of the individual benefits and value-added of the experience. This was thought to be a reflection of the socioeconomic background of students attending these institutions, in turn reflecting the fact that these students may not have had access to particular opportunities, for example to adventurous training, which students from more advantaged backgrounds (and attending Russell Group universities) may have had in their pre-university lives.

All the COs reported that although there were differential levels of recruitment to their unit from the various universities in their catchment, the mixing of students from different institutions was beneficial both to the students and to the unit. Some commented that differences between the students, on the basis of university attended, were discernible; for example, a URNU CO noted that he could see differences within the unit between the students from a very prestigious academic institution, a 1960s plate glass university, and a small, new post-1992 institution. The point was not that some students were 'better' than others, but rather that the range and thus mix of student abilities and aptitudes was beneficial both to the unit in operational terms, and socially for the students themselves.

### 5.2.2. University armed service units and the Military Education Committees

There are currently 20 Military Education Committees (see Chapter 1), and they are often part of the formal governance structure of universities, a reflection of the Haldane reforms which established the OTC units in 1908. All the COs attended MEC meetings, which are held two to four times per year, and to which COs provide a report on unit activities.

A range of opinions were expressed about the utility of the MECs for the units, and for the COs. MECs were recognised as a mechanism for USU-university contact, and some COs considered how useful MEC members had been in helping them work their way round and understand a university's systems and practices. Other COs had more critical views on what MECs could provide. Much seemed to depend on the make-up of the MEC. COs noted the significance of the role of the MEC Chair, and the utility of the relationships they were able to cultivate with that individual if he or she had a position of significant influence or responsibility within a university, or had high-level contacts across several universities in a locality. Some COs reported that they had been proactive on arriving in post in developing a relationship with that individual, and they valued the line of communication with the university which that relationship could potentially open up. A number of COs had also developed relationships with academic registrars or equivalent (who may or may not be members of an MEC), because of the significance of the registrar's role with responsibility for student experience.

What was less clear to some COs was the value added by the MECs beyond this. Units are run autonomously from MECs, so MECs had no active input into the units. Although they were conduits for communication with the universities within a USU catchment, much depended on the position of an individual representative within their university, for example, whether they were appointed to the MEC because they had administrative authority, or because of a more general interest in military matters. Where MEC members had administrative responsibility at senior level, this was far more effective than those involved with an MEC solely on the basis of past educational or military experience, or just interest in military affairs. Whilst it was recognised that individual members often brought educational and military experience with them, there were questions as to whether this was the right kind of expertise needed. One CO talked very explicitly about what he needed from his MEC: he needed to feel that the university was taking an interest in the USU, and needed an MEC which could help him in terms of opening up opportunities for the unit to show the university what it was and what it could do. An example was given of OTC involvement in a week-long series of events run by one university around innovative learning, where the OTC was able to provide some events with a leadership focus. The CO concerned felt that this had been a valuable event, not just for the student participants (who by definition were not OTC members) but also for the wider visibility of the unit.

There were questions too about the purpose in the present of a committee established under a very different set of educational and military circumstances, which had differing levels of involvement from participating universities dealing with a broad range of issues across the three service units (and some also include DTOEES representation where a DTUS squadron is present). One unit had established a Liaison Committee to meet its own needs for university liaison, which included one representative from each of the 10 universities in its catchment. The advantage of this was that this group could focus entirely on issues specific to that unit, and that unit's engagement with students in a range of universities in the catchment area.

The relationships which COs reported with university Vice Chancellors varied markedly. Some COs saw their Vice Chancellors as largely uninterested in the work of the units, and some had managed to meet with these individuals directly. The point was made that in the context of large organisations such as universities, USUs are quite small and potentially quite ephemeral to the daily and more strategic business of running a university.

### 5.2.3. *Relationships with student organisations*

COs reported a range of experiences in their relationships with student organisations, primarily Student Unions. Student Unions exist independently of universities, and are not subject to strategic steer from Vice Chancellors, academic registrars, MECs or individual academics. The relationship with Student Unions is significant for USUs because of the need for units to recruit from the student body, particularly at Freshers' Fairs and similar events hosted by Student Unions to enable students (particularly on arrival at university) to join various clubs and societies. Some Student Unions were antagonistic towards the idea of USU involvement at Freshers' Fairs, and COs perceived this as being driven by a (mis)understanding of the role of the units in recruitment to the armed forces to the exclusion of other opportunities that the units offered students. In some cases, this meant that USUs were denied the opportunity to have a stall in the central Freshers' Fair location.[64] One CO reported that one of his Student Unions had not wanted students and personnel in uniform on the stand, but were happy to host a stand staffed by individuals wearing polo shirts with the unit logo.

COs also raised the question of charges to USUs for participation at Freshers' Fairs. Student Unions can charge organisations for having a stall at an event. Some COs reported that they had been charged a corporate or business rate rather than student society rates, which they thought was unfortunate, given that their mission was focused on student development rather than commercial enterprise. The question was also raised about pressure from headquarters, in view of charges, for units to prioritise representation (particularly if they were being charged corporate rates) at Freshers' Fairs in universities which traditionally had higher rates of USU participation, as a cost-saving measure. In the view of some COs this was misguided because in their experience this might mean differential access to USU participation.

Some COs were quite explicit in identifying certain universities as having a long-standing anti-militarist politics, such that they did not want to see USUs on campus. Student Unions in the newer universities were often identified as more likely to hold this view, although it was often hard, in conversation, to conclude the reasons for this, as many of the newer universities had far less experience with the units and it was unclear whether it was a question of lack of interest, lack of knowledge or explicit resistance to the idea of the units. This was thought to be ironic because, in the opinion of one CO, students attending a new university in his catchment had the most to gain (the most value added) from the USU experience in terms of their skills development and increased employability. We should also emphasise that the issue of antagonism from Student Unions was not universal, and some COs reported no issues at all.

Questions were also raised about how, exactly, engagement with the wider student body could and should be pursued by COs. One CO noted that he

---

[64] From an alternative source (and not from an interview), we were told an anecdote laden with irony about the consequences of Freshers' Fair organisation. In one university where the Student Union had resisted the presence of the USUs at the Fair, the organisation of the event had been outsourced to a private sector events planning company. This company had in turn responded positively to a request by a local Reserves unit for a stall at the Fair for Reserves recruitment purposes. So Student Union resistance to the USU on the grounds that, in its view, it was a recruiting organisation for the military, had come to nothing.

had deliberately sought out a meeting with the new Student Union President-Elect in one of his universities, on the grounds that he thought his role should include engagement with representatives from across the university, including the Student Union, and that personal contact was the best mechanism to achieve this. As with COs themselves, the regular rotation of Student Union presidents and officers was also an issue in relationship building and maintenance. There appeared to be quite a short window of opportunity for COs to make contact with incoming union officers, and this compounded the issue that unions might change over a period of time with regards to their acceptance or otherwise of USU recruitment stalls at Freshers' Fairs. COs were very aware of how they might be perceived on campus. Another CO discussed an event which had been held for students at one of his catchment universities which, in his view, had ended up portraying the armed forces in a very traditionalist way ('if you had never come across the Army before it might have looked all a bit Ruritanian and quite bizarre') and which had not, in his view, given students a more appropriate view of what the Army, via the USUs, could offer them. COs were also aware that, for the OTC with an increased emphasis in its mission on recruitment to the Regular and Reserve forces, that the 'pitch' units made could easily get caught up in the fallout from current affairs. COs were also very aware of the need for dialogue with student organisations; one CO, for example, questioned why Student Unions were not represented on his local MEC as he could see value in having a student presence at these meetings.[65]

### 5.2.4. *Informal university armed service unit-university relationships*

The military-university connection also worked in highly informal ways. COs gave examples of being approached by colleagues within the armed forces needing information on a particular topic, which was provided by academics within a CO's university, of being approached to engage in defence debates, and of being asked to assist with the delivery of training packages run through a university business school to a third party. Much seems to depend on the ability (because of competing time commitments) of a CO to undertake such liaison activities, not least undertaking the basic groundwork required to establish and maintain relationships with individuals in an institution. Because universities are often very complex organisations in institutional terms, the development of personal links was thought to be key. It was also recognised that this took time.

---

[65] This echoes practice adopted in many universities (seen by many as an example of good or best practice), of including student representation at the Boards of Study or equivalent which oversee the management and strategic direction of degree programmes.

There was also an issue of perception amongst university staff of what, exactly, the units were for. COs recognised how difficult it was to communicate this message to a large number of staff, particularly around the skills training, employability and personal development work that USUs saw themselves as conducting.

## 5.3 The value of the university armed service units to universities

We asked COs for their observations about the value that universities get from their association with a USU. A number of them commented that they were not necessarily the best people to ask (and indeed, we asked this question directly to university representatives – see Chapter 6). All the COs emphasised that there had to be value to universities through the skills, personal development and thus employability of students as graduates. A number of COs were able to provide anecdotes about the effect of unit participation on particular students, in terms of their increased confidence and abilities, and extrapolated from that that there had to be benefit to the universities in terms of the quality of the graduates, who would then become ambassadors for a particular university in later life. One university contributing small numbers was thought to benefit greatly because of the opportunity the unit provided for participation to be accredited as part of the public service-related degree programme. The obvious point, which a number of COs also made, was that the numbers of students who could use the USU experience in this way was actually tiny, relative to the number of students graduating each year from a UK university. Indeed, the proportion was getting smaller over time as units maintained their size and universities (and the higher education sector) expanded. Furthermore, the experience was not open to all students, either because of the nationality qualification (so apart from Commonwealth students, international students were not eligible to join) or the medical and fitness requirements.

COs raised other points about value, from the influence that USU members might have on the attitude of their student peers. Two COs talked of the kudos two of their respective catchment universities were thought to achieve through association with the units (one a UAS in a prestigious university, the other a URNU in a maritime city). Another talked of the public relations work done by the UNRU ships when sailing away from their home ports but visibly representing a particular city or region and its universities. Yet there was significant discussion about whether, in fact, universities understood the units, an honesty about whether in fact the universities did get anything out of the relationship and the fact that the relationship and thus value to universities was subject to change over time. One CO in particular was adamant that his main recruiting university could do much more to promote his unit, for example by featuring it as a recruitment factor for the university in its prospectus and other promotional literature. Another talked about his suspicions that one of his catchment universities (again, a significant source of recruits to his unit) had at best a lack of interest, or more specifically an antipathy towards having visible links with a military organisation. One CO was very frank in his assessment that the higher education sector probably gained relatively little, directly, through the relationship with the USUs. We return to this question in Chapter 6.

Also noted by COs was the value to individual academic researchers in universities of having on hand an identifiable contact within the armed forces who could assist with questions about military issues arising from academic research. We, as authors of this book, recognise this absolutely, having on a great many occasions drawn on our local COs for points of information both about USUs and about wider military issues. We are also aware of other colleagues doing the same, from disciplines as disparate as engineering, food marketing, archaeology and fine art. Several COs mentioned how they had similarly been approached by academics in their catchment universities, and indicated how willing they had been to provide assistance and contacts.

## 5.4 The value added to university armed service units and the armed forces from the university relationship

COs were asked about the value which they thought their USUs gained from the association with universities. Having access to students to participate in the unit was the obvious answer, and these may be high-calibre individuals which the unit would benefit from having, and who might potentially be interested in a career in the British armed forces. But this was also a provocative question because it then raised the issue of what specifically the value might be in a demonstrable link to universities. The units, in other words, could recruit students freely, without needing a relationship to the universities from which students were drawn. A number of COs noted the benefits that accrued for the units through the relationships they were able to foster and engage with via MECs, but this was not universal. The units in some cases recognised that there was value to be had from association with a particular university, if that institution were a prestigious one. One CO also mentioned access to university estate resources (for example, their sporting facilities).

COs were also asked quite explicitly about the wider benefits the armed forces received from a relationship, via the USUs, with the universities. The key issue here was about the relationships that USUs were able to inculcate with students. These students might enjoy their participation in a unit and develop an understanding of military and defence matters which they would then take with them to the civilian workplace. This was seen, from the perspective of current COs, as particularly significant at a time when the armed forces were contracting, and declining numbers of the civilian population were perceived as having knowledge of the armed forces. Alternatively, and crucially, individuals through unit participation could potentially develop (if they did not have this already) an interest in military participation as full-time officers, or part-time through the Reserves. The potential connection with the Reserves was particularly significant in OTC CO minds: as an employer, universities could be the target of armed forces attempts to increase awareness of Reservist opportunities, and USUs had a part to play in that.

The point was also made that the contemporary British armed forces, because of the scale of the reductions through austerity but also reflecting shifts in UK foreign policy and defence missions, was having to learn its place in the world afresh. Part of this process involved establishing new forms of relationship with the civilian world to reflect a new reality, and the USU system was part of that.

### 5.5 Commanding Officer perceptions of the value of the university armed service units

All the COs were asked at the start and the conclusion of their interview to describe what they thought the value of the USUs was, is or could be, and were encouraged to reply in whichever way they wanted. The CO responses provided a great range of explanations on value. These have not been quantified, rather the intention here is to show in narrative form the range of issues that the sample of COs identified as comprising the value of the USUs.

#### 5.5.1. *The value to students as individuals*

The value of the USU experience to students was seen as lying primarily with the skills the USU experience could help students develop, primarily in the form of transferable skills which would enhance employability. These skills included the transferable skills cited in Chapters 3 and 4 by students and by graduates, and we do not repeat them here. The COs, because of their position, articulated how in their view some skills in particular, including the ability to work under pressure, to develop a work ethic, to plan and problem-solve, and to provide leadership, were skills that they thought the armed forces were both seen to develop particularly well through military practice, and which also exported well to the civilian world, particularly the workplace.

Personal development was also thought to be of significant value to individuals, in terms of the self-development and character-building aspect of the USU experience which emerged through a student being taken out of their comfort zone, and in terms of activities which brought increased self-confidence, including activities which might be initially perceived as fun, like adventurous training, but that were not frivolous. Social skills were also seen as being developed, including matters of etiquette, and of being able to engage with a range of different people in diverse social situations.

The USU experience was also thought to develop a sense of good citizenship amongst students, in terms of their development of a sense of responsibility, including social responsibility. This might be developed and manifest through charitable work. Students were taught to look out for others as part of their USU training, and this experience was thought to develop an idea of selfless commitment to others.

The social side of the USU experience for students was also recognised. Students made friends and had access to a smaller group within a larger institution which could help with the transition to university life. The USU experience was thought to be fun, and the significance of enabling the USU experience as an enjoyable one was widely recognised by the COs. The units could also provide access to opportunities not otherwise available to an individual, for reasons of cost or for reasons of general availability. Adventurous training and opportunities for overseas travel were key, but also access to quite specific resources, such as flight and maritime navigation training.

### 5.5.2. *The value to the armed forces*

In contrast to the students and graduates, the COs placed much greater emphasis, when considering the broad question of value, on the value of the USUs to the armed forces. Significance was placed on the visibility of the armed forces which the USUs were thought to enable or enhance, including the utility of being able to draw on USU members to visibly boost the numbers of people in uniform at public events, and the utility of the URNUs in being able to take the P2000 vessels to locations not accessible to larger Royal Navy ships and thus being able to, literally, fly the flag for the Navy. Charity work undertaken by officer cadets was frequently cited as of benefit in terms of increased public awareness and visibility of the units. USUs provided a mechanism for interaction between military and civil society. The units were also beneficial for the armed forces in cases where unit engagement with industry enabled not only the message to be promoted that USU graduates had employability and skills, but that this was a feature of ex-forces personnel as well. The links to universities were part of the value of the USUs in terms of enhanced public visibility, and constituted one particular set of connections amongst many between the armed forces and civilian society, at a time when the multiplicity of those connections was seen to be diminishing.

COs also referred to the argument that the USU experience had longer-term benefits for the armed forces through the passage of USU graduates into the civilian workplace and social world. This was understood in terms of generating individuals with an understanding of both military matters (general defence-mindedness), or more specific understanding about the distinctive roles of the three armed forces, particularly 'air-mindedness' and 'sea-mindedness'. The USUs enabled the armed forces to project a broader view of what the armed forces might do and be within civilian life, beyond the representations prevalent in the media and popular culture.

Recruitment to the armed forces was also an obvious and significant aspect of the value of the units. USUs enabled individuals to make an informed choice about joining the armed forces, to understand how the recruitment process worked and to consider whether an armed forces career was the right choice for them. The value of the USUs also lay in 'de-risking' recruitment for the armed forces by being able to assess an individual's suitability. Recruitment to the Reserves was also understood as benefitting from the existence of USUs in these terms. The USUs also enabled the armed forces to recruit highly educated officers, by definition.

## 5.6 Conclusions: the value of the university armed service units to the armed forces

The individuals interviewed had a range of experience in terms of time spent in command of a unit, and their experiences reflected this. All were positive and enthusiastic about their posting (something evident not only in what was said in the interviews, but also in the way it was said). The COs are key individuals within the USU structure, and although their enthusiasm might be anticipated as a reflection of their professional practice as officers, it is still a point worth making that those in charge of the units have such a high degree of enthusiasm for their work. Some of the COs had little prior knowledge of the units within their service whilst at university or in the earlier stages of their military career (and as one URNU CO said, 'if you had asked me [before becoming CO] I probably wouldn't have seen any benefit in them'), but all were emphatic that there were benefits to students, to universities and to the armed forces from the existence of the USUs. They also clearly enjoyed their specific role in the lives of the students under their command. One of the COs noted, with affection, how:

> 'You're more than a Commanding Officer – you're also a father figure [...] I suggested that part of a pre-requisite to be a Squadron commanding boss was you had to have teenage children, 'cause you knew then how to relate and you knew all the tricks that this lot would get up to and try, the wool they'd try to pull over your eyes.'

The key findings from interviews with COs are as follows (and we note again that we have not included here repetition of points made by students and graduates, all of which were identified by the COs, unprompted, during the interviews).

In terms of the nature of the USU-university relationship, the diversity of types of university from which USUs draw their students and with which they engage, and in turn the range of students attracted to USUs, is a notable feature. As a mechanism for facilitating this relationship, MECs vary in terms of their levels of activity and the utility of those activities to COs. Specific individuals, including but not limited to MEC Chairs, can be invaluable to COs in terms of developing working relationships with specific universities. CO perceptions of the attitudes of Student Unions towards the USUs show a range of responses, and COs are very aware of their role in negotiating these student-armed forces relationships. The informal and ad-hoc relationships that COs may develop with individuals or departments within universities are also an element of the USU-military relationship.

In terms of the value of the USUs to universities, this was thought to lie with the value that units were able to bring to students through the range of USU activities. USUs were seen as being significant in the development of individual students, and as a group with an enhanced skills set; this is turn was thought to reflect back positively on to universities, particularly when those students graduated and went into employment. We perceived that some COs were of the view that universities, both as individual institutions and as the higher education sector, could potentially benefit to a greater degree from the relationship with the armed forces articulated through the USUs, and that universities could potentially reap greater rewards from that relationship than they might do at present.

In terms of the value to the USUs and the armed forces of the relationship with universities, this was seen to be manifest in the recruitment of good students into the units. The association that units had with a particular university might be beneficial in terms of the public image of a particular unit. The ability for the armed forces to potentially recruit good candidates for officer training, either for the Regulars or the Reserves, because of the relationship via USUs was recognised. There was value for the armed forces too in the enhanced visibility for those forces within the universities, and this was notable at a time of reduced public awareness of military forces.

Assessments by COs of the overall value of the USUs emphasised these points about the value to individual students of the experience of the USUs and the value to the armed forces of the existence of the units.

There are two final points to make in conclusion. The first concerns the differences between universities and armed forces in terms of organisational character and culture, levels of central direction versus autonomy, the locus of power for central direction in each institution, the function of chains of command and hierarchies (particularly in terms of the flow of information up and down hierarchical and across horizontal communication chains) and the ways in which both organisations can and do initiate change and react to external changes. Added to this is the relative size of the units compared to the size of the universities with which they engage. Given these factors, it is probably not surprising that the USU-university relationship can present challenges, particularly for individuals put in command of a unit for a limited period of time and facing a very steep learning curve.

The second point concerns the question of the use of scarce financial resources in maintaining the units. It is notable that in the interviews with COs, despite having the opportunity to raise the point, there was very little commentary from COs about the financial costs and quantifiable benefits of the USUs. Where this was mentioned, it was raised as question of possible conflicts over the use of scarce resources within the armed forces, particularly within the context of budgetary cuts. The fact that the question of financial resources was not highlighted is not proof that this issue is far from the minds of COs. Nonetheless, we suggest that it is indicative of the attitudes of the COs interviewed that they were so clearly able to articulate wide-ranging and detailed arguments about the value (and otherwise) of the USUs to the armed forces and to the universities, without reducing the issue to a question of budgets and balance sheets.

CHAPTER 6

# The Universities and the University Armed Service Units

In this chapter, we draw on interviews with representatives from universities to explore university perceptions of the value of the USUs. The analysis is also informed by observations from our interviews with COs about the USU-university relationship, and draws also on the research team's collective and considerable experience of working in higher education and engaging with issues around the USU-university nexus. Further details of the methodology used are given in Chapter 2. Note that in this element of the research, the intention was to generate indicative rather than comprehensive data, hence the small sample of interviewees.

## 6.1 Knowledge of the university armed service units within universities

It was apparent from the start of the research which underpins this book that levels of knowledge about the USUs vary enormously across the higher education sector. As Chapter 1 demonstrated, the reach of the USUs is uneven across the sector; although roughly three quarters of all the member institutions of Universities UK have students participating in units, the proportions from each institution vary. We have also noted the very small size of the total USU population in relation to the overall UK student population. As this chapter will show, levels of understanding about USUs can be very low indeed within the sector,

---

**How to cite this book chapter:**
Woodward, R, Jenkings, K N and Williams, A J. 2015. *The Value of the University Armed Service Units.* Pp. 155–164. London: Ubiquity Press. DOI: http://dx.doi.org/10.5334/baq.f. License: CC-BY 4.0.

and it is important to note at the outset that it is to the credit our interviewees working in senior administrative posts within institutions that they were able to grasp very clearly the issues pertaining to student unit participation, despite professing to have very little knowledge about the units at the outset.

We approached five institutions in a region where we knew students participated in all three service units, asking the academic registrar or equivalent for an interview to discuss issues around USU-university relationship. Academic registrars were approached because these individuals tend to have institutional responsibility for administration and oversight of student services, teaching quality, student progress and careers. Their roles often include a lot more than this, but given the evidence that had emerged from the student survey and the graduate interviews about the value of the USU experience, particularly for transferable skills and employability, we were interested in whether those responsible for these aspects of university education within institutions were alert to these issues. Alternative interviewees could also have included Pro-Vice Chancellors, Deans or an equivalent with senior responsibility for strategic direction of student employability and skills agendas. However, we considered academic registrars to be better placed because of their to day-to-day working knowledge of the ways in which various aspects of the student-orientated administrative services work together (or otherwise) within an institution. We deliberately chose not to interview representatives from MECs because we wanted to get a sense of baseline levels of knowledge in institutions from those in senior administrative positions.

Five academic registrars or equivalent were approached for an interview. One declined our request. This individual stated that he was not aware of his institution's engagement with the armed forces, let alone the USUs, and felt he would not be able to comment at all on the value of the USUs. This was despite the presence of students from this particular university participating in two of the service units, and representation from that university on the local MEC. Four others agreed to interview, although in one case we had to convince the individual concerned that there might be value in research terms to their participation, despite this individual's concerns that they knew very little about the USUs.

This concern about lack of knowledge came through in all the interviews; one respondent said at the outset that 'as far as I am aware, [our university] doesn't have [a unit], and if we do it isn't anything to do with me'. Another was aware of the units from a previous job at a different university in the region, but had not realised that the same unit drew from different universities across the region. This individual had made an effort, prior to the interview, to find out a bit about her current university's role and relationship with the local units, but found little information available. The third interviewee was aware of the units because in a previous role in marketing and student recruitment that university had used information about the units for marketing purposes. The fourth interviewee had been aware of the OTC because of a discussion in their administrative department about representation on an MEC, but had not been aware of the UAS or URNU. None of our interviewees had had USU experience themselves at university, although one had a close relative who had been in the OTC as a student so knew something about the units from that, and one mentioned having been vaguely aware of the OTC whilst themselves a student, because of a friend's involvement.

## 6.2 University armed service units-university communication and liaison

All the individuals we interviewed worked in universities that we knew were represented on the regional MEC. As we have already noted (see Chapter 1), MECs constitute the formal mechanism for managing the USU-university relationship, and many exist under university statute. It is very unusual for universities to make commitments to USUs or provide support beyond the structures of the MEC. Interviewees all said that they were vaguely aware of their MEC, but had no direct experience of seeing it mentioned in any of the administrative committees on which they sat; we gained a sense that the links between MECs and the university administration were not particularly visible.

Given this, it was instructive to assess the points at which central university administration had awareness of the USUs. Because the universities in question were all represented on an MEC, in theory those representatives had a role in reporting back from that MEC and liaising as required over specific issues arising from MEC discussions. In practice, this was not so simple. One registrar was quite frank about the lack of feedback received from their MEC, and thus their own lack of information about how this reporting relationship worked, noting that 'if anyone were to [provide feedback], I would have thought it would have been to me, so I just wonder whether it is particularly well linked in'.

There was uncertainty about what MECs actually did, and thus what information feedback or liaison requirements might actually contribute, and in turn what action or response a university might offer, and from which part of the administration. Although Vice Chancellors and other very senior academic staff with strategic responsibilities were often formally members of an MEC, in practice it was recognised that they did not attend meetings (not least because of time commitments). Note that this might not be the case in all institutions and MECs, and we know of instances (particularly in smaller institutions) where very senior academic staff are active members of their local MEC and are thus able to bring to their university at an executive level any insights or action points developed at MEC level. Given that universities were represented on MECs by named individuals, there were questions about why particular individuals might be nominated for this task. The point was raised by respondents that those who represented the university might be selected to do so on the basis of their military knowledge and engagement (and indeed availability), rather than because their institutional responsibilities or positioning within administrative structures are such that they would be well placed as a conduit for communications within that structure. It was also the case that a number of individuals within a university administration, with different areas of responsibility, might all have remits which touched upon issues raised at MECs about the USUs. So, for example, the individual responsible for liaising with students over Freshers' Fairs and similar events might work in a different part of the administration to those with responsibility for the student careers service. Similarly, those with responsibility for the development of the value-added schemes that many universities are using to provide recognition for student extracurricular activities (usually for employability purposes) may work quite separately to those responsible for the development of graduate and transferable skills within degree programmes.

One respondent noted how she had often been a little ambivalent about the MEC, about 'what it actually was doing [...] to some extent it was just showing solidarity as much as anything else'. There might have been instances where negotiations around individual student issues were discussed (for example, facilitating student management of competing commitments around assessments and USU activities), but this respondent considered that the key function of the MEC was the maintenance of high-level relationships between the university and the armed forces. This is an illuminating observation, because one of the original purposes of MECs was to provide a liaison and assistance function through which students' academic and military commitments (including military commitments which were compulsory) could be managed. From discussion with respondents (and certainly in our own experience[66]), this practical function of MECs seems quite minimal under current university administrative arrangements for student progression and pastoral care, perhaps even negligible.

If the utility of MECs is indeed in the development and maintenance of a high-level relationship, the seniority and area of responsibility for university representatives is important. It was clear from other discussions that where MEC representation was provided by senior management, this certainly gave the impression of enhancing the flow of information between the units and university. Equally, we heard of MEC representation by individuals (both academics and administrative staff) who clearly were very proactive within their own institutions in terms of disseminating information about USUs and (quite crucially) taking forward initiatives around military-university relations for consideration at their universities at senior levels. It is not, therefore, just a question of seniority, but rather about a combination of area of responsibility coupled with proactivity in establishing communications and the flow of information into a university at the appropriate level. Equally, we heard criticisms of

---

[66] Two of the authors of this book have served on their local Military Education Committee, both for two three-year terms.

MECs as quasi-social clubs with little power and responsibility (or enthusiasm and drive) to use their role to develop military-university relationships, and where university representation was dominated by individuals quite distant from key university administrative and academic structures.

## 6.3 Perceptions of the value of university armed service units to students

### *6.3.1. Skills*

It was clear from discussions with the registrars that they could see value in USU participation to the students attending from their university. The list of factors providing value mirrored very closely that provided by students themselves, and by graduates (note that these interviewees had not been briefed on the research findings prior to interview). Factors included the skills students developed to enhance their employability, particularly skills transferable to the workplace and notable on a CV such as time management, team-working, adaptability and negotiation skills. Personal development, resilience and independence were also mentioned. The USUs were seen as providing friendship, fun and social opportunities, a sense of camaraderie and opportunities for travel. Getting paid for participation was noted as useful in a context of high student fees and levels of student debt. It was noted by one interviewee that there was a direct correspondence between the skills the university wished to inculcate in its students, and those developed through the USU experience.

When asked to consider why students might join a unit, the skills development component was seen as key, particularly in the development of skills which might not be an explicit part of a degree programme, or which could be developed in a different way to those developed on a degree programme. The point was made, for example, that the practice of leadership in a peer group of students might be different to that practiced in a military context.

The type of skills developed in a USU might be slightly different to those developed on a degree programme; for example, as well as opportunities for leadership development, there may be opportunities for developing self-confidence and facing challenges that would not occur on a degree programme. There might be opportunities in a military context to be more assertive about achievements than in an academic context. But the point was also made that some skills, such as self-reliance, making judgements, being decisive, organising and planning, and understanding a bigger picture, would also be developed through other extracurricular activities, and that an individual student would not have to join a USU to have the opportunity to develop those skills, which could be achievable through other means. Students organised many activities themselves: one interviewee noted how in their university there was active encouragement by the university for students to do so, and thus for students to have insight into how organisation, team-working and leadership skills developed through clubs and societies could be instrumental in skills development.

As to whether the skills a student developed through their USU experience might help a student with their degree programme, the consensus from our interviewees was that it probably did, but that this would be very hard to quantify. Skills might be applied in different contexts in a degree programme, although some skills were seen as having direct application. Primarily, students had to be able to manage their experience and generate their own motivation. There was always the risk that USU or other activities could provide a distraction. The USU experience was seen as possibly, but probably not directly, of help to a student in terms of progression through their degree programme.

The appeal of the experience to students who might wish to pursue a career in the armed forces was also noted. One interviewee noted that the type of experience offered by a USU might be more appealing to a particular model of student (that is, a direct entrant from school, attending university away from home), and that it would not therefore appeal across a diverse student body, particularly to mature students.

### 6.3.2. Employability

Our respondents were asked whether they thought USU participation made students more employable. Responses indicated that whilst it was hoped that this would be the case, it was the responsibility of the students to make that link and case. Careers services were significant in this regard, and there was discussion about how difficult students sometimes find the task of articulating the applicability of skills to employment situations, whatever the points of origin of those skills. The USU experience certainly might give a student more to talk about at interview or mention on a CV, but the student would have to be able to articulate the value of that experience. The USU experience might show greater life experience which might be seen as enhancing their employability, but again, there were many things that students did which showed this. Indeed, the USU experience was comparable to any other student activity which enhanced employability: the onus was on the student to make the case for the skills developed to have application in an employment context. It probably helped with employability (including the transition to the workplace through familiarity with structure, hierarchy and organisational norms), like many other activities.

### 6.3.3. Students and Reserves deployment

We discussed the issues around the deployment of students as reservists. This was a hypothetical discussion as students are Category B reservists and are not eligible for deployment. We are not aware of any plans within the MoD or armed forces to change this. However, it was a pertinent question to ask, given the fact that the question had been raised as part of wider debates about the expansion of the Reserves, and the fact that OTR training produces officers capable of commissioning into the Army Reserve.

The deployment of students as reservists was, it was thought, potentially possible but in practice very problematic. Students are usually expected to progress through their degree programme in regular stages. Exceptions are students who go on placement elsewhere (usually for a year) as part of their degree programme, and students who have to suspend their studies for medical or personal reasons. These interruptions can be managed administratively, but are recognised as presenting challenges for students. These challenges were seen as applicable in the hypothetical case of student Reserves deployment, compounded by specific factors around military deployment. The timing and duration of a deployment could mean suspension of studies for one or two whole years; the nature of degree programmes is such that learning is sequential, structured by progression through terms, semesters and academic years, and it is virtually impossible for students to drop out and then back in to degree programmes apart from at specific points in that programme. There might be financial implications on return if a student was unable to return directly to university and resume their studies. There may be practical effects in terms of housing. There may be emotional effects in terms of the disruption to peer support networks, quite apart from any emotional effects incurred by the deployment itself. Degree programmes can, and do, change over time, and this could affect a student returner. The consensus was that although in theory deployment with the Reserves could be managed, in practice it would not be in the best interests of students to deploy because of the dislocations which would follow. It would not be impossible, but would certainly be both educationally disruptive and expensive.

## 6.4 The benefits to universities of the university armed service units

We posed the question to our interviewees about the value their university might get from having the link to the USUs. The value was seen to be primarily to the students, and even those interviewees who considered that they had no knowledge of the units articulated very clearly how, in their view, students might benefit from USU participation, and thus how an institution would in turn benefit by facilitating this for students. The enhanced employability of that institution's graduates, particularly through the development of the transferable skills outlined above, were key here: the employability of graduates is one measure by which universities are evaluated (particularly by prospective students using Key Information Sets to decide which universities to apply to), and so where the USU experience was complimentary to the university's mission, then this would be valuable to that university, by definition. The idea was also explored around the fact that engagement with USUs might be seen as part of a university's civic engagement role.

Two further issues were raised by interviewees. The first concerned the question of how a university might be perceived in terms of its promotion of the USUs, for example in its prospectus or web-based marketing literature. The individuals who raised this point were adamant that although the university could and should provide information on opportunities available to students, which would include USUs, they had to avoid being perceived to be promoting specific activities, and particularly if such promotion was seen to be preferential. Essentially, the work of the university was to provide opportunities and information on those opportunities available at that institution, and leave it to students to decide whether or not to take up those activities.

The second issue raised concerned the question of the sensitivity around military-university links. Respondents had differing views on this, reflecting their understandings of their recruitment markets, particularly internationally. For one university, it was thought that there might be issues for international students from countries and contexts with very different attitudes towards military forces, and that it might not be a 'smart selling point' if the university were to portray itself as having strong military ties. In another (very different) university, the perception was that promotion of such links was less of an issue and there had been no issues with international student recruitment at that university (the institution in question had a long tradition of USU presence). In the words of that university representative, 'it's not come to my attention in any way, which suggests it's not problematic in any way at all'. At that university, in any case, the provision of information about USU opportunities was seen as being the responsibility of student organisations rather than the university, which focused its marketing on the academic opportunities available.

Respondents were also asked about the value to the USUs of their relationship with the university. This was seen as lying primarily with the access to students and thus USU recruits that the USU-university relationship facilitated, and that in turn this might provide a source of high-calibre graduates for entry into the armed forces. One respondent discussed how the Army, in particular, had a good relationship with the careers advisory service in that university and would ultimately benefit from the careers development work that the university conducted with its students. Given the social diversity of many universities, the recruitment to USUs and possibly the armed forces from this diverse pool was also thought to be of benefit. Beyond the interviews, we also learned of instances where the value of the USU to the university was either recognised and had practical expression (for example, through the provision of secretarial support for a unit, paid for by that unit but provided and supported through the university), or appeared not to be recognised (for example through reluctance of central university administration and senior academic management to provide support for the local MEC).

Finally, the point was made that there may be value to both USUs and to universities in terms of the links which the relationship could develop in terms of academic research. This echoed a point also raised by the COs. What was absent from any comments by our interviewees was an indication of awareness of existing involvement by the armed forces in occasional staff or student learning activities. COs had mentioned this, and we were aware of such events taking place in at least three of the universities whose representatives we spoke to. Respondents, however, did not raise the topic, suggesting a lack of awareness of such activities.

## 6.5   Conclusions: the value of the university armed service units to universities

In conclusion there are two points to make about the value of the USUs to the universities. The first is to note the lack of knowledge and understanding about the USUs within universities. Although we did not survey academic staff in order to assess this in a rigorous fashion (although such an exercise would not be difficult to undertake), we know from experience and anecdotal evidence that knowledge levels are low, or that knowledge is potentially quite inaccurate. That said, we also know of countless instances where student participants themselves have, in effect, worked as ambassadors for the USUs and the opportunities they offer through student contact with academic staff. The knowledge base is also uneven within university administrative structures, and at the highest levels of senior management. What seems evident to us is that institutional attitudes towards the USUs, which are properly the concern of individual universities, seem in some cases poorly informed about the nature of the USUs. This, we suggest, is not particularly unusual across the sector.

The second point to make is about the most appropriate mechanisms for developing informed debate and decision-making about USUs within universities. We have already noted the role of MECs as a conduit for information and a mechanism for developing university-USU links. At best (and we have come across many examples of this), MECs can provide a forum for the exchange of information and the development of initiatives, particularly where university and USU objectives are clearly aligned, such as around the employability agenda. Through appropriate individuals, a conduit can exist for the flow of information to appropriate points within university administrative systems and senior management levels, and this can help with specific initiatives. At worst, MECs can exist in a bubble beyond the purview of central university administration, with little or no discernible effect or value. The decision on how best to use MECs is one for senior university management. We would suggest, on the basis of evidence collected through this research, that some universities may be missing significant opportunities to make the most of their MECs. That said, our strong sense from the interviews conducted with individuals who were concerned that they knew little or nothing about the USUs, was that they could quite readily imagine what those opportunities might be. Above all else, they indicated that they had no difficulties in imagining what the value of the USU experience might be to students, and to the university, within the parameters outlined above.

CHAPTER 7

# Conclusions: the Value of the University Armed Service Units

This concluding chapter turns to the wider issues raised by the empirical data provided in the preceding chapters, flagging them up for wider debate and discussion. These issues are as follows: the reach and representation of the USUs across the higher education sector; equalities issues, political debate and access to information about the USUs; the comparability of USU and other extracurricular student activities; the USUs and recruitment to the UK armed forces; knowledge of the USUs within the higher education sector; knowledge of USUs amongst employers and reflections on researching the USUs.

## 7.1 The reach of the university armed service units across higher education

It was noted in Chapter 1 and at various points in the presentation of empirical data in subsequent chapters, that the USUs as a whole have good levels of reach across the higher education sector. By this, we mean that access to USU activities is potentially available to students attending the majority of the UK's universities. This is evident, for example, in the lists of participating universities contributing formally to each of the service units (see section 1.2) and the representation in practice indicated by the presence of respondents to our survey (see Appendix 5). However, this reach is very uneven in that some units have a far higher number of students from some universities than others in the same catchment area. We

---

**How to cite this book chapter:**
Woodward, R, Jenkings, K N and Williams, A J. 2015. *The Value of the University Armed Service Units*. Pp. 165–173. London: Ubiquity Press. DOI: http://dx.doi.org/10.5334/baq.g. License: CC-BY 4.0.

have also noted the dominance in representation amongst students from Russell Group universities, and have suggested that in turn this reflects two issues. The first is the patterns of basing and university association, many of which are of very long standing: for some students, it is simply easier in practical terms to attend a USU, and those tend to be Russell Group university students because of these basing patterns. The second is the differential access to information about the USUs across universities, reflecting both recruitment efforts by the units and the extent to which individual units may or may not be enabled to recruit in particular universities (and we return to this below).

In terms of the uneven reach of USUs, it became apparent during the course of this research that there may be wider issues that follow from this, including questions about the effects of unequal access to USU participation on the make-up of the units and thus the USU experience for those participating, and a question about the limited diversity (particularly social diversity) of USUs because of this. Put simply, we would raise the question as to whether USU participation is an elite activity, and if it is, whether that is acceptable to universities, the armed forces and the student body. We should also note that the remit for the research underpinning this book did not include the requirement to adjudicate on the level and geographical spread of USU provision, and USU reach across the sector. Nonetheless, it would appear that the uneven reach of USUs is not just a question of availability or otherwise of the experience to the student population, but is also a question about the reasons for and possible mechanisms to address this issue of uneven reach. Also pertinent to note here is the fact that whilst the higher education sector in the UK has expanded and diversified over the past two decades, levels of USU provision have remained broadly static.

## 7.2 Equalities, politics and access to information about university armed service units

The mechanisms which USUs use for recruitment amongst the student body, the utility of particular recruitment strategies such as Freshers' Fairs and similar, and the politics of USU recruitment on campus have all been noted in this book. The presence or absence of a USU recruitment stall at Student Union events is, of course, a matter entirely for Student Unions. Student Unions may wish to avoid USU representation as part of a wider move to disassociate that union and student body from military organisations or phenomena, in turn as part of a wider political critique of militarism and militarisation. In doing so, however, they may be denying their members access to the resources provided by USUs. These may be resources to which students may not otherwise have access, such as adventurous training or experience of leadership training. We have also noted how different groups have differential access to information about the USUs pre-university and on arrival. Those with knowledge of USUs have a choice of participation. Those without that knowledge are denied the choice, and thus access to the resources that USUs provide.

There are, however, two wider issues to which this limit to student access to information speaks. The first, following an established liberal feminist argument about the causes and perpetuation of gender inequalities, is that restrictions on access to information are more likely to impact on the proportion of women joining USUs than men, given that women are more likely to arrive at university without prior knowledge of the units, and are therefore more likely to be reliant on events such as Freshers' Fairs for information about those units. The restriction of recruitment opportunities may, quite simply, have a disproportionate effect on women as a group, and in turn help to perpetuate existing gender inequalities within the British armed forces.[67] We recognise of course that the question of gender and military participation is a complex one. We would also argue, however, that issues around women's military participation are an essential component of broader debates about what, exactly, civil society wants its armed forces to be, and do.[68] The participation of women in USUs is part of that debate. These arguments could also be made about social class.

The second issue to note here concerns the politics of militarism and militarisation on campus. We should note here our arguments made elsewhere about the necessity of engagement with military organisations in order to develop informed critique of the more abstract issue of militarism, militarisation, its causes and its consequences.[69] As researchers and lecturers working in the field of critical military studies, we are adamant both that the question of the military presence, via USUs on campus, is an appropriate focus for student political debate, and also that this debate needs to be an informed one, structured around evidence and observation rather than supposition and speculation. Exposure to USUs, what they do and what they might represent, would seem to us to be necessary as a means of developing a more informed political debate about military-university links.

## 7.3 The comparability of university armed service units and other extracurricular student activities

As should be clear from the empirical detail provided in this book, students, graduates and unit COs share the view that the USU experience provides for

---

[67] For an overview of the politics of gender and the contemporary British Army, see: **Woodward, R.** and **Winter, T.** (2007). *Sexing the Soldier*. London: Routledge; **Woodward, R.** and **Duncanson, C.** Gender divisions of labour in the contemporary UK armed forces. *New Strategist*. (in press).

[68] See **Duncanson, C.** and **Woodward, R.** Regendering the military: theorising women's military participation. *Security Dialogue* (in press).

[69] See **Rech, M. F., Bos, D., Jenkings, K. N., Williams, A.** and **Woodward, R.** (2015). Geography, military geography and critical military studies. *Critical Military Studies, 1* (1), 47–60.

students both opportunities to undertake specific activities, and a context in which these activities can be used to develop transferable skills which may enhance student employability. We have also noted at a number of points that the USUs are not the only student activity which may facilitate this. This research did not set out to compare the USU experience against other activities in terms of the generation of skills and employability or of levels of student enthusiasm and enjoyment. We would note that this remains an open question at this point in time. Establishing a methodology rigorous enough to capture reliable data on student comparisons between activities would be challenging, not least because of the enormous range of student activities for potential comparison and the difficulties of determining which of these would be appropriate comparators.

However, we would also note the distinctiveness and specificity of the USU experience as a student extracurricular activity. Part of this lies with the range of activities undertaken, from military and adventurous training through to sporting and social activities, and thus the range of potential skills development opportunities that this then provides. Part of this also lies in the combination of those activities, such as the organisation and planning required to initiate a particular adventurous training activity, which in turn may be physically testing, mentally challenging and require significant team interaction. The distinctiveness of the USU experience seems evident.

The military context for USUs is significant here, in terms of the specificity of certain types of skills development, particularly leadership. We have noted throughout this book the emphasis which is placed on the USU experience for leadership development, something widely recognised by student participants. Understandings of what leadership might constitute are significant here. Implicitly framing some discussions of leadership was the idea that conceptualisations of leadership in both military and corporate employment contexts are one and the same, hence the transferability of leadership skills between the two. It is pertinent to note, however, that this is just one of many ways of understanding leadership which reflects a specific understanding of hierarchy and power structures within an organisation. Drilling down to explore exactly what leadership might constitute in different working environments, and how this may or may not correlate with military conceptualisations of leadership, was beyond the scope of this research. However, given the significance of the idea of leadership as a transferable skill developed through USU experience, its presence in graduate skills frameworks, the emphasis on it in employment contexts, and yet the existence of different models for understanding what it is and how it works, this would suggest that closer consideration of leadership as a transferable skill would be valuable. In turn, the comparability of models of leadership development in different student activities may be informative to discussions about the specificity or otherwise of the USU experience for students.

## 7.4 The university armed service units and recruitment to the UK armed forces

The USUs serve an important recruitment function for the UK armed forces, both Regulars and Reserves. The degree to which the service units emphasise this varies between them, and has also varied over time. We were able to assess the significance of the USU experience in shaping student decisions about whether or not to join the armed forces, either Regular or Reserve. This research deliberately did not attempt to assess the views of those who pursued a full-time career with the armed forces about the utility of a USU experience, and we would flag this up as an area of possible future research which may be of interest to the armed forces, and in particular to those charged with officer training. What we were able to assess was the significance of the USU experience in terms of recruitment to the Reserves, and we note the strong relationship here. We have two observations to emphasise here, noting that we do so because of the significance of the Reserves to current debates on the future structure and composition of, in particular, the British Army.

The first follows from discussions with graduates about why, despite having considered the possibility, individuals did not ultimately pursue participation with the Reserves following graduation. This is partly because the idea simply slipped down an individual's list of priorities. It is also partly because of the challenges of combining Reserves participation with employment. Reserves participation requires time commitment. It also rests on a certain amount of locational stability. It is recognised that in the first two to three years after leaving university, graduates may be busy negotiating the challenges of finding and performing a job, moving location, engaging in new social and personal relationships and exploring new leisure activities. It is a time of enormous change. It may not be an appropriate time to consider, in addition to all these challenges, participation in the Reserves, however much an individual may have enjoyed USU participation and might wish to take it forward to the Reserves. It could be suggested that the responsibility for retaining and pursuing an interest in the Reserves, for those inspired to do so by their USU activities, rests solely with the individual and it is their responsibility to initiate Reserves participation when they are ready to do so following transitions from university. Conversely, we would argue that significant responsibility here rests with the armed forces themselves. The mechanisms for maintaining contact and encouraging interest may be varied, and marketing and relationship maintenance strategies may need to be handled carefully. There is some evidence that strategies for keeping potential Reservists 'warm' and in contact are being pursued in the present. Our point here is to note the significance of former USU participants as a potential recruitment pool for the Reserves, and thus part of the potential value of the USUs for the armed forces.

The second observation here is about the direct recruitment of reservists from amongst the student body. We are neither advocating nor cautioning against the targeting of students for Reserves recruitment. This is properly an issue for the armed forces and for students as individuals, capable as adults of making an informed decision about their military participation. What we would note, however, is the care with which recruitment on campus needs to be planned and managed in view of potential central university and Student Union concerns about military engagement with the student body. The challenges of operational deployment aside, it is clear that student participation in the Reserves (as opposed to USUs) can be undertaken and can be relatively unproblematic if academic and military commitments can be coordinated. Following the completion of our data collection, we were provided with evidence of one university that had set up a Reserves troop for student members, and we ourselves have on occasion taught serving reservists. We suggest that the real challenge for the armed forces lies in managing engagement with this potential pool of recruits.

## 7.5 Knowledge of the university armed service units within the higher education sector

We have noted at various points in this book the presence and absence of knowledge and understanding of USUs within the higher education sector. This seems to us to be a significant issue, given what we have already noted about the utility of the USU experience to students who wish to participate for degree progression, the potential correspondence between university objectives for graduate employability and the value of the USU experience in assisting individuals to develop this, and our point about the necessity for debates about the military-university relationship to be informed by evidence and observation rather than by supposition and speculation.

In terms of levels of knowledge of USUs amongst academic staff, we would suggest that, were USUs or universities keen for greater levels of knowledge and awareness in this group, then student advocacy would be the best means to achieve this. This is partly because of the sheer quantity of information which is passed down to academic staff on a daily basis through university hierarchies, and the efficient mechanisms most academics use for very quickly filtering out information which they feel is of no direct relevance to them through the use of the 'delete' button on email systems and the paper recycling bin. Students are the best advocates because it is through personal contact that the communication of student experience is best achieved. Any academic who has had tutorial or pastoral responsibilities and who talks to their students will recognise this. This is quite apart from the opportunities which many students have (and take) on some degree programmes where USU experience might be included as a legitimate discussion point in an educational context, such as a tutorial, seminar or lecture. We would suggest therefore, that if low levels of knowledge about USUs are thought to be problematic, that student participants have a distinct and valuable role to play in disseminating wider information in an informal way in educational contexts.

In terms of levels of knowledge of USUs within universities central administrations, and at the senior executive level, we note both the great range of levels of this and the role of MECs in facilitating this. We note also the issue of MEC membership and university representation on MECs as significant to both the flow of factual information and the development of initiatives involving USU and university collaboration. The decision on whether to engage with USUs, and how to do so, is one for senior university management. Such decisions need to be made on the basis of available information (and this book may be one such source). We note also the role pro-active individuals can (and quite evidently do) play in both providing information and developing relationships such that senior university management can take an informed view of the utility or otherwise of the USUs to their university. We note that this takes time, that it has to happen over periods of time, and that this may pose issues because of continuity and change within unit leadership, MEC membership and changing responsibilities and job remits within universities. Although it may be the responsibility of the service units to initiate and maintain knowledge dissemination across universities, it is certainly the responsibility of universities to have awareness of the USUs, given their responsibilities and duty of care towards students.

## 7.6 Knowledge of university armed service units amongst employers

We have noted in this book student and graduate perceptions of the levels of employer knowledge and understanding of USUs, the transferable skills which USU participation may or may not develop in individuals and the utility of those skills for student employability. We have also noted in passing the point that some employers in some sectors may be more or less favourably inclined towards evidence of employee experience derived from USU participation. We note that this reflects a much bigger and more abstract debate about civil-military relations, attitudes towards defence and military activities and attitudes towards the armed forces, much of which is beyond our scope for discussion here.

Responsibility for communicating the value of the USU experience in terms of employability rests with individual employees, as we have seen. There is an additional point to make here, however, about the responsibility that lies with the armed forces themselves for communicating the transferability of skills derived in military contexts. This is something to which attention is being given in defence circles, as a matter of policy and practice (for example, through the work of the organisation SaBRE[70]), as a matter for direct intervention (for example, through the work of third sector and private recruitment companies specialising in support of ex-forces employees in the civilian labour market, or the brokering of employment for ex-forces employees) and as a matter of communication more generally. On the evidence presented in this book, it would appear that the transmission of information about the potential utility of USU-derived skills may be part of that bigger picture of communication. Although there is no direct link between skills developed through USU participation and skills developed through full military participation, it may be that emergent activities around communication about the latter within the labour market may assist in the communication of the former. We would also note that examples of good practice already exist at the level of some MECs and individuals in developing their own strategies for communication about value of USU-derived skills to employers and businesses in their locality. There may be further research to be done to establish an evidence base around such practices.

### 7.7 Researching the university armed service units

As was noted in the acknowledgements and in Chapter 1, whilst the research underpinning this book was conducted independently from the MoD and armed forces in that it was funded by the ESRC and conducted solely by academics working within higher education, that research benefitted considerably from communication and liaison with individuals and groups working across the defence community.

We draw two key learning points from the experience of doing this research. As we note elsewhere, we are strong advocates of the necessity for military research, particularly research identifying as 'critical' in social science terms, to engage directly with the organisations and institutions which are the focus of empirical exploration, practical critique and critical conceptualisation.[71] Our view on this is shaped also by our knowledge from across the social sciences, arts and humanities, about how and why academics might engage with the military, and what this might facilitate in academic research and writing.[72] Our experience of researching the USUs has reinforced this view on the necessity for researchers of military phenomena to engage directly with military personnel and institutions, particularly where the intention is informed critique.

---

[70] Further details about SaBRE are available at: http://www.sabre.mod.uk/
[71] See **Rech M. F., Bos D., Jenkings K. N., Williams A. J. and Woodward R.** (2015). Geography, military geography and critical military studies. *Critical Military Studies*, 1 (1), 47–60.
[72] See **Williams, J., Jenkings, K. N., Rech, M. and Woodward, R.** (Eds.). (2016). *The Ashgate Research Companion to Military Research Methods*. London: Ashgate.

Second, and following from this, we note that the relationship between academic researchers and their respondents is a two-way street. We are very aware that our research respondents, and a wider group of people within the armed forces and with whom we have discussed the research, have in turn had critical and challenging questions to pose of us and our conceptualisation of the phenomenon under investigation, just as we have had of them and theirs. Furthermore, we are also very aware that the process of conducting this research, particularly the element involving interviews and conversations with serving members of the armed forces, has gone on to provoke debates and exchanges quite separate from the research. Research participants are never passive respondents; the process of engaging in interactional research involving interviews is widely recognised as both productive of analytic insights on data as well as the data itself, and provocative of further thought, commentary and action about the phenomenon under investigation on the part of the research participant. So it has been with this research. We have no way of knowing what the likely effects of this process of interaction might have been, or may be in the future. We hope, however, that the research process itself and any researcher effects in turn have some value in ongoing debates about the value of the USUs.

# Appendix 1

## Questionnaire used for survey of student USU participants, spring 2013

1. Which USU are you a member of? (Please tick only one.)
   - University Royal Naval Unit (go to Q2)
   - Officer Training Corps (go to Q3)
   - University Air Squadron (got to Q4)

2. Which URNU are you a member of? (Please tick only one.)
   - Birmingham URNU
   - Bristol URNU
   - Cambridge URNU
   - Edinburgh URNU
   - Glasgow and Strathclyde URNU
   - Liverpool URNU
   - London URNU
   - Manchester and Salford URNU
   - Northumbrian URNU
   - Oxford URNU
   - Southampton URNU
   - Sussex URNU
   - Wales URNU
   - Yorkshire URNU

3. Which University Officer Training Corps are you a member of (Please tick only one.)
   - Aberdeen UOTC
   - Birmingham UOTC
   - Bristol UOTC
   - Cambridge UOTC (Cambridge)
   - Cambridge UOTC (Norwich)
   - Edinburgh UOTC

- East Midlands UTOC
- Exeter UOTC (Exeter)
- Exeter UOTC (Plymouth)
- Glasgow and Strathclyde UOTC
- Liverpool UOTC (Liverpool)
- Liverpool UOTC (Lancaster)
- London UOTC
- Manchester and Salford UOTC
- Northumbrian UTOC
- Oxford UOTC
- Queens UOTC (Belfast)
- Southampton UTOC
- Tayforth UOTC (Tayforth and Dundee)
- Tayforth UOTC (St Andrews)
- Tayforth UOTC (Stirling)
- Wales UOTC (Aberystwyth)
- Wales UOTC (Bangor)
- Wales UOTC (Cardiff)
- Wales UOTC (Swansea)
- Wales UOTC (Wrexham)
- Yorkshire OTR (Sheffield)
- Yorkshire OTR (York)

4. Which UAS are you a member of? (Please tick only one.)
   - Birmingham – University of Birmingham Air Squadron (UBAS)
   - Bristol University Air Squadron (BUAS)
   - Cambridge University Air Squadron (CUAS)
   - East of Scotland University Air Squadron (ESUAS)
   - East Midlands University Air Squadron (EMUAS)
   - Glasgow and Strathclyde – Universities of Glasgow and Strathclyde Air Squadron (UGSAS)
   - Liverpool University Air Squadron (LUAS)
   - London – University of London Air Squadron (ULAS)
   - Manchester and Salford University Air Squadron (MASUAS)
   - Northumbrian Universities Air Squadron (NUAS)
   - Oxford University Air Squadron (OUAS)
   - Southampton University Air Squadron (SUAS)
   - Wales – University of Wales Air Squadron (UWAS)
   - Yorkshire University Air Squadron (YUAS)

5. Did you consider joining another USU? (Please tick all that apply to you.)
   - No, only the one I am currently in
   - Also the Officer Training Corps

- Also the University Air Squadron
- Also the University Royal Naval Unit

6. Did you actually apply to join another USU? (Please tick all that apply to you.)
   - No, only the one I am currently in
   - Also the Officer Training Corps
   - Also the University Air Squadron
   - Also the University Royal Naval Unit

7. How far in miles is your USU weekly meeting venue from your university? (Please tick only one.)
   - 0–4.9 miles
   - 5–9.9 miles
   - 10–14.9 miles
   - 15–19.9 miles
   - 20–24.9 miles
   - 25–29.9 miles
   - 30 miles or more

8. How do you normally travel to your USU weekly meeting venue? (Please tick only one.)
   - Walk
   - Cycle
   - Bus
   - Train
   - My own car
   - A friend's car
   - Transport provided by USU or university
   - Other (please specify)

9. How long have you been a member of your USU? (Please tick only one.)
   - 0–12 months
   - 13–24 months
   - 25–36 months
   - 36 months plus

10. Thinking about your overall assessment of your experience in your USU to date, has it been… (Please tick only one and write in the box provided.)
    - Mostly negative
    - Mostly positive
    - Both negative and positive in different ways (Please explain your response.)

11. How would you describe the main benefits to you of your USU experience so far? (Please write in the box provided.)

12. In what year of your undergraduate degree did you join your USU? (Please tick only one.)
    - 1st year
    - 2nd year
    - 3rd year
    - 4th year
    - As postgraduate
    - Other (please specify)

13. Why did you join a USU? (Please tick all that apply.)
    - Adventurous training opportunities
    - Armed forces or MoD bursary
    - For the challenge
    - CV enhancement
    - Flying opportunities
    - Interest in the military
    - Pay
    - Sailing/nautical skills
    - Shooting skills
    - Sport
    - Transferable skills
    - University course credits
    - Wanted to develop military skills
    - Other (please specify)

14. Would you recommend joining a USU to other students (Please tick only one and explain why in the box provided.)
    - No
    - Yes
    - Don't know

(Please explain your response.)

15. Are you a member of any other university or Student Union clubs or societies? (Please tick one box and use text box if answering 'Yes'.)
    - No
    - Yes

(If yes, please name them.)

16. Please rate how you are developing the following skills through participation in your USU. (Please tick one of the following for each skill: 'not at all',

'some, but not as much as I would like', 'about as much as I had anticipated', 'more than I had anticipated', 'way beyond my expectations', 'not applicable'.)
- Adaptability
- Budgeting
- Communication skills
- Critical thinking
- Decision-making
- Independence
- Information literacy
- Initiative
- Knowledge of the armed forces
- Leadership skills
- Literacy
- Maturity
- Numeracy
- Occupational awareness (i.e. understanding the nature of a job to guide one's professional development)
- Organisation and planning
- Presentation skills
- Problem-solving
- Project planning
- Self-confidence
- Social skills
- Synthesising information
- Teamwork
- Time management
- Verbal interaction skills

17. Please rate how you are developing the following skills in relation to your degree programme. (Please tick one of the following for each skill: 'not at all', 'some, but not as much as I would like', 'about as much as I had anticipated', 'more than I had anticipated', 'way beyond my expectations', 'not applicable'.)
    - Adaptability
    - Budgeting
    - Communication skills
    - Critical thinking
    - Decision-making
    - Independence
    - Information literacy
    - Initiative
    - Knowledge of the armed forces
    - Leadership skills

- Literacy
- Maturity
- Numeracy
- Occupational awareness (i.e. understanding the nature of a job to guide one's professional development)
- Organisation and planning
- Presentation skills
- Problem-solving
- Project planning
- Self-confidence
- Social skills
- Synthesising information
- Teamwork
- Time management
- Verbal interaction skills

18. Thinking about the skills you are learning through your USU, are you also learning these from: (Please tick all that apply to you.)
    - My degree programme
    - University sports activities
    - Union club or society activity
    - Charity or other voluntary work
    - Paid employment
    - Personal hobbies or interests
    - Nowhere else
    - Other (please specify)

19. Has being in a USU helped you progress through your university degree? (Please tick one only. If yes, please expand on how it has helped in the box below.)
    - No
    - Yes

20. Has being in a USU been detrimental to progress through your university degree? (Please tick one only. If yes, please expand on how it has helped in the box below.)
    - No
    - Yes (please specify)

21. Can your USU activities be used as credits towards your university degree? (Please tick one only, and if 'yes', please specify how in the text box.)
    - No
    - Don't know
    - Yes (please specify)

22. Can your USU activities be used to acquire a recognised formal civilian qualification? (Please tick one only, and if 'yes', please specify how in the text box.)
    - No
    - Don't know
    - Yes (please specify)

23. Has joining a USU impacted on your future career choices? (Please tick one only, and if 'yes', please specify how in the text box.)
    - No
    - Yes (please specify)

24. Do you think being in a USU will help you with getting a graduate job? (Please tick one only, and if 'yes', please specify how in the text box.)
    - No
    - Yes (please explain your answer)

25. Do you think being in a USU will help you with getting promoted in a graduate job? (Please tick one only, and if 'yes', please specify how in the text box.)
    - No
    - Yes (please explain your answer)

26. Before you came to university, you may have considered a career in the armed forces. Which of the following best applies to you? (Please tick only one.)
    - I never considered joining the armed forces
    - I thought about joining the armed forces but took no positive action
    - I made inquiries about joining the armed forces but took no further action
    - I attended a recruitment event run by an armed forces recruiting team, but took no further action
    - I applied for MoD/armed forces university sponsorship
    - I made a formal commitment prior to going to university to enter the armed forces on graduation
    - Other (please specify)

27. We are interested in whether people in USUs become interested in joining the Regular or Reserve armed forces following graduation. Which of these best describes you? (Please tick only one.)
    - I was intending to join the Regular armed forces (full-time) prior to joining my USU, and still am.
    - I was intending to join the Reserve armed forces (part-time) prior to joining my USU, and still am.

- I was not intending to join the Regular or Reserve armed forces, and am still not.
- I was intending to join the Regular armed forces (full-time) but am now intending to join the Reserve armed forces (part-time).
- I was intending to join the Reserve armed forces (part-time) but am now intending to join the Regular armed forces (full-time).
- I was intending to join the Regular armed forces (full-time), but am no longer intending to join any armed forces.
- I was intending to join the Reserve armed forces (part-time), but am no longer intending join any armed forces.
- I was not intending to join the armed forces, but now intend to join the Regular armed forces (full-time).
- I was not intending to join the armed forces, but now intend to join the Reserve armed forces (part-time).
- Other (please specify)

28. Have you applied for any graduate jobs or post-graduation training programmes that will lead to employment when you complete your degree? (Please tick all that apply to you.)
    - No
    - Yes, armed forces
    - Yes, public sector (including civil service, NHS and local government)
    - Yes, public sector (other)
    - Yes, private sector defence industry or defence-related
    - Yes, private sector but not defence industry (e.g. accountancy, banking, engineering, media, etc.)
    - Yes, third or not-for-profit sector (e.g. charities)
    - Yes, other (please specify)

29. When applying for a graduate position, have you ever decided not to mention your USU experience? (Please tick one box and if 'yes' or 'no', use the text box to explain your reason.)
    - I have not yet applied for any graduate positions.
    - No, I have always mentioned it.
    - Yes, I have sometimes omitted it from my CV or application.

30. If you have been to an interview for a graduate employment position, did the topic of your USU experience come up in the interview? (Please tick all that apply to you.)
    - I have not yet been to any interviews for graduate employment
    - No, it was not mentioned.
    - Yes, in passing.
    - Yes, I raised it.
    - Yes, I was asked about it.

If you have discussed your USU participation in a job interview, please tell us about the nature of the discussion(s) in the text box.

31. Were you aware of USUs before arriving at university? (Please tick one box and use the text book if applicable.)
    - No
    - Yes, but it was NOT a factor in my choice of university
    - Yes, and it was a factor in my choice of university (Using the text box, please explain how.)

32. How did you first find out about the USU you eventually joined? (Please tick only one.)
    - Cadets (UK military)
    - Careers service – armed forces
    - Careers service – school
    - Careers service – University
    - Email from Student Union
    - Email direct from USU
    - Family
    - Friends
    - Freshers' Fair
    - Leafleting
    - University website
    - Student Union website
    - USU website
    - Other students
    - Other (please specify)

33. We are interested in whether your experiences since joining a USU have affected your view of the British armed forces. Which statement best describes you? (Please tick only one.)
    - Unchanged and remains positive
    - Unchanged and remains negative
    - Changed and is now positive
    - Changed and is now negative
    - Other (please specify)

34. What was your age on 31st March 2013?
    - 18
    - 19
    - 20
    - 21
    - 22
    - 23

- 24
- 25 or older

35. At school, were you a member of, or did you participate in, any of the following organisations: (Please tick all that apply to you.)
    - Cubs
    - Brownies
    - Scouts
    - Guides
    - Venture Scouts
    - Sea Scouts
    - Boys' Brigade
    - Girls' Brigade
    - Armed forces cadets
    - Other organisations (please specify)

36. Where did you study for your A levels or equivalent? (Please tick only one.)
    - State school as a non-boarder
    - State school as a boarder
    - Further education or Sixth Form college as a non-boarder
    - Further education or Sixth Form college as a boarder
    - Independent sector (fee-paying) school or college as a boarder
    - Independent sector (fee-paying) school or college as a non-boarder
    - Other (please specify)

37. Which A level (or equivalent) subjects and grades did you get? (Complete as many as apply to you.)

38. Which of the following best describes you after completing A levels or equivalent? (Please tick only one.)
    - After A levels, I went directly to university
    - After A levels, I gook a gap year and mainly travelled
    - After A levels, I took a gap year and mainly worked
    - After A levels, I took a permanent job and later decided to go to university
    - After A levels, I was unemployed and so decided to go to university
    - Other (please specify)

39. Which university do you attend? (Please give the name in the text box.)

40. What is the title of the degree programme on which you are currently registered? (Please give the name in the text box.)

41. What is the qualification you are studying for? (Please tick only one.)
    - Bachelor's degree
    - Four-year degree leading to a Masters qualification (e.g. MEng.)
    - Post-graduate diploma
    - Master's degree
    - Doctorate

42. Has USU participation caused you to change either degree subject and/or university? (Please tick one box, and explain the change if applicable in the text box.)
    - No
    - Yes, changed degree subject but stayed at the same university.
    - Yes, changed university but not degree subject.
    - Yes, changed both university and degree subject.

43. Have any of your relatives been members of a USU? (Please tick all that apply.)
    - Sibling (brother or sister, including via new parental relationship)
    - Parent (or equivalent in position of parental authority)
    - Grandparent
    - Other close family member (e.g. aunt, uncle, cousin, etc.)
    - None

44. Have any of your relatives been members of the armed forces? (Please tick all that apply.)
    - Sibling (brother or sister, including via new parental relationship)
    - Parent (or equivalent in position of parental authority)
    - Grandparent
    - Other close family member (e.g. aunt, uncle, cousin, etc.)
    - None

45. Are you… (Please tick only one.)
    - Female
    - Male
    - Other

# Appendix 2

## Semi-structured interview schedule for graduate interviews

1. What do you think the value of the University Armed Service Units is?
2. Where did you go to university?
3. What year did you start university?
4. What subject did you study?
5. Which University Service Unit did you join?
6. How long were you in this unit?
7. Did you stay linked to the Armed Forces in any way when you left?
8. Did you go straight to a job or further studies?
9. Could you give me an overview of your career history so far?
10. Was there any reason why you did not join the Armed Forces?
11. Had you ever intended to join the Armed Forces?
12. How much emphasis did you place on your experience in the OTC/URNU/UAS in job applications?
13. Did you have different application strategies for different types of employer?
14. Did you ever not put/omit that you had been in a USU on your CV?
15. Can you recall how your USU experience was discussed at interview?
16. Did being in a USU help you in getting your first job?
17. Did being in a USU help you in performing in your job?
18. Did you pick up skills from the USU which you had not picked up from your university course?
19. When recruiting people, do you take into consideration membership of the USU and the military?
20. Does being in a USU ever get discussed with colleagues at work?
21. Does being in a USU ever get discussed with clients?
22. In what other aspects of your life has being in a USU influenced you?
23. How has being in a USU influenced your career development?
24. Has being in a USU given you a positive or negative regard for the Armed Forces?

25. Have you been influential towards others' regard for the Armed Forces?
26. Are you typical of people who were in the USU?
27. Did you ever join the TA or Reserves?
28. How did you find out about the USU before you joined?
29. Had you been in the cadets or similar organisation?
30. Do you have members of the family or friends in the USU?
31. Did being in the USU prepare you for the workplace in ways that your university course did not?
32. What aspects of the USU experience have stayed with you?
33. What networks has the USU allowed you to participate in?
34. Again, what do you think the value of the USUs is?
35. What value do you think that the USU got from you?
36. Is there anything that you would like to add?

# Appendix 3

### Semi-structured interview schedule for Commanding Officer interviews

1. What do you think is the value of the USUs?
2. How long have you been CO?
3. How long is the posting?
4. Did you volunteer/how were you appointed?
5. Can you provide an overview of your career to date?
6. Did you go to university?
7. What is your remit as CO?
8. Does your remit cover Regular forces?
9. Does your remit cover Reserve forces?
10. What is your relationship to the universities?
11. What is the value of being linked to the universities?
12. What is the value to the USU from the universities?
13. What value do the regular forces get from the USUs?
14. What value do the reserve forces get from the USUs?
15. How do you recruit USU members?
16. What is the value of USUs for students?
17. Why do students actually join?
18. What commitments do students make?
19. What commitments do USUs make to students?
20. What commitments do universities make to the USUs?
21. What skills do USU members obtain?
22. How do these skills differ from university courses?
23. Do USU skills help students at university?
24. Can students get formal qualifications through their USU?
25. Can students get course credits?
26. Does being in a USU help with getting a job?
27. Does being in a USU help with transition to the work place?
28. Do you stay in contact with alumni?

29. Do you recruit from alumni?
30. Does being in a USU give students a positive or negative regard for the armed forces?
31. Does being in a USU make students influential towards others about the armed forces?
32. Again, what is the value of the USUs?
33. Is there anything you would like to add?

# Appendix 4

## Semi-structured interview schedule for university representative interviews

1. What is the value of the USUs?
2. What is your job title and area of responsibility?
3. How long have you been in post?
4. What was your knowledge of the USUs before this interview?
5. Where you in a USU at university?
6. Did you know about USUs when at university?
7. What can you tell me about the USUs and their relationships with the MEC?
8. What do universities get from having USUs?
9. What can you tell me about Students Unions and the USUs?
10. What do you think the value is for USUs of having a relationship with the university?
11. What is the value for students of joining a USU?
12. Why do students join a USU?
13. What would be the issues at stake if USU students were deployed as Reservists?
14. What are the commitments the university makes to USUs?
15. What skills do students get from USUs?
16. Do the skills students get from USUs differ from those on academic courses?
17. Do these skills help students on their course?
18. Can students get a qualification from their USU activities?
19. Can students get course credits for their degree from USU activities?
20. Does being in a USU help with getting a job?
21. Does the USU experience help with student transition to the workplace?
22. How does your university provide information on the USUs?
23. Are there any issues around international students and the USUs?
24. Again, what is the value of the USUs?
25. Is there anything you would like to add?

# Appendix 5

## Student survey participation by university and service unit

Note: in order to protect respondent anonymity (because of the small numbers participating from some universities), the table shows only the presence ('*') of respondents to the survey in universities and units, and not the number of those respondents from each university and unit. Names in square brackets denote the location of that university's main campus, where this is not immediately evident in the university's name.

| University | OTC | UAS | URNU | Higher education mission group | USU |
|---|---|---|---|---|---|
| University of Aberdeen | * | * | * |  | Aberdeen UOTC<br>East of Scotland UAS<br>Edinburgh URNU |
| Abertay University [Dundee] | * | * | – | GuildHE, | Tayforth UOTC<br>East of Scotland UAS |
| Aberystwyth University | * | * | – |  | Wales OTC (Aberystwyth)<br>Wales UAS |
| Anglia Ruskin University | * | * | – |  | Cambridge UOTC<br>Cambridge UAS |
| Aston University [Birmingham] | * | * | * |  | Birmingham UOTC<br>Birmingham UAS<br>Birmingham URNU |
| Bangor University | * | * | – |  | Wales OTC (Bangor)<br>Liverpool UAS |

(*Continued*)

| University | OTC | UAS | URNU | Higher education mission group | USU |
|---|---|---|---|---|---|
| University of Bath | * | * | * |  | Bristol UOTC<br>Bristol UAS<br>Bristol URNU |
| Bath Spa University | * | – | * |  | Bristol UOTC<br>Bristol URNU |
| Birmingham City University | * | * | * |  | Birmingham UOTC<br>Birmingham UAS<br>Birmingham URNU |
| University of Birmingham | * | * | * | Russell Group | Birmingham UOTC<br>Birmingham UAS<br>Birmingham URNU |
| University College Birmingham | * | – | – | GuildHE | Birmingham UOTC |
| Bournemouth University | * | * | – | University Alliance | Southampton UOTC<br>Southampton UAS |
| University of Bradford | – | – | * |  | Yorkshire URNU |
| University of Brighton | – | – | * |  | Sussex URNU |
| Brighton & Sussex Medical School | – | * | * |  | London UAS<br>Sussex URNU |
| University of Bristol | * | * | * | Russell Group | Bristol UOTC<br>Bristol UAS<br>Bristol URNU |
| Brunel University London | – | * | – |  | London UAS |
| CAFRE College of Agriculture Food and Rural Enterprise, Loughry, [Belfast] | * | – | – |  | Queen's UOTC |
| University of Cambridge | * | * | * | Russell Group | Cambridge UOTC<br>Cambridge UAS<br>Cambridge URNU |

Appendix 5    193

| University | OTC | UAS | URNU | Higher education mission group | USU |
|---|---|---|---|---|---|
| Cardiff University | * | * | * | Russell Group | Wales UOTC (Cardiff) Wales UAS Wales URNU |
| Cardiff Metropolitan University | – | * | * |  | Wales UAS Wales URNU |
| University of Chester | – | * | – |  | Liverpool UAS |
| University of Chichester | * | * | – | GuildHE | Southampton UOTC (Brighton) Southampton UAS |
| City University London | – | * | * |  | London UAS London URNU |
| College of Law (University of London) | * | – | – |  | London OTC |
| Coventry University | * | * | – | University Alliance | Birmingham UOTC Birmingham UAS |
| De Montfort University [Leicester] | * | * | * |  | East Midlands UOTC East Midlands UAS Birmingham URNU |
| University of Derby | * | – | – |  | East Midlands UOTC |
| University of Dundee | * | * | – |  | Tayforth UOTC East of Scotland UAS |
| Durham University | * | * | * | Russell Group | Northumbrian UOTC Northumbrian UAS Northumbrian URNU |
| Edge Hill University [Ormskirk, Lancashire] | * | * | – |  | Liverpool UOTC Liverpool UAS |
| University of Edinburgh | * | * | – | Russell Group | City of Edinburgh UOTC East of Scotland UAS |
| Edinburgh Napier University | – | * | – |  | East of Scotland UAS |

(*Continued*)

| University | OTC | UAS | URNU | Higher education mission group | USU |
|---|---|---|---|---|---|
| University of Exeter | * | * | * | Russell Group | Exeter UOTC<br>Bristol UAS<br>Bristol URNU |
| University of Glasgow | * | * | * | Russell Group | Glasgow & Strathclyde UOTC<br>Glasgow UAS<br>Glasgow URNU |
| Glasgow Caledonian University | * | * | * |  | Glasgow & Strathclyde UOTC<br>Glasgow UAS<br>Glasgow URNU |
| Glyndŵr University (Wrexham) | * | – | – | GuildHE | Wales OTC (Chester) |
| University of Greenwich | – | – | * | University Alliance | London URNU |
| Harper Adams University | * | – | – | GuildHE | Birmingham UOTC |
| Heriot-Watt University [Edinburgh] | * | * | – |  | City of Edinburgh UOTC<br>East of Scotland UAS |
| University of Hertfordshire [Hatfield] | – | * | – |  | London UAS |
| University of Huddersfield | * | – | – | University Alliance | Yorkshire Officer Training Regiment |
| University of Hull | * | * | – |  | Yorkshire Officer Training Regiment<br>Yorkshire UAS |
| Imperial College London | – | * | * | Russell Group | London UAS<br>London URNU |
| Keele University | * | * | – |  | Birmingham UOTC<br>Birmingham UAS |
| University of Kent | – | * | – |  | London UAS |
| Kings College London | – | * | * | Russell Group | London UAS<br>London URNU |
| Kingston University | – | * | – | University Alliance | London UAS |

Appendix 5    195

| University | OTC | UAS | URNU | Higher education mission group | USU |
|---|---|---|---|---|---|
| Lancaster University | * | * | * |  | Liverpool UOTC (Lancaster det.) Liverpool UAS Liverpool URNU |
| University of Leeds | * | * | * | Russell Group | Yorkshire Officer Training Regiment Yorkshire UAS Yorkshire URNU |
| Leeds Beckett University [formerly Leeds Met] | * | * | – |  | Yorkshire Officer Training Regiment Yorkshire UAS |
| University of Leicester | * | * | – |  | East Midlands UOTC East Midlands UAS |
| University of Lincoln | * | * | – | University Alliance | East Midlands UOTC East Midlands UAS |
| University of Liverpool | * | * | * | Russell Group | Liverpool UOTC Liverpool UAS Liverpool URNU |
| Liverpool Hope University | – | * | – |  | Liverpool UAS |
| Liverpool John Moores University | * | – | * | University Alliance | Liverpool UOTC Liverpool URNU |
| London Metropolitan University | – | * | – |  | London UAS |
| London School of Economics | – | * | * | Russell Group | London UAS London URNU |
| Loughborough University | * | * | * |  | East Midlands UOTC East Midlands UAS Birmingham URNU |
| University of Manchester | * | * | * | Russell Group | Manchester and Salford UOTC Manchester UAS Manchester URNU |
| Manchester Metropolitan University | – | * | * | University Alliance | Manchester UAS Manchester URNU |

(*Continued*)

| University | OTC | UAS | URNU | Higher education mission group | USU |
|---|---|---|---|---|---|
| Newcastle University | * | * | * | Russell Group | Northumbrian UOTC<br>Northumbrian UAS<br>Northumbrian URNU |
| University of Northampton | * | – | – | | East Midlands UOTC |
| Northumbria University [Newcastle] | * | * | * | University Alliance | Northumbrian UOTC<br>Northumbrian UAS<br>Northumbrian URNU |
| University of Nottingham | * | * | * | Russell Group | East Midlands UOTC<br>East Midlands UAS<br>URNU[1] |
| Nottingham Trent University | * | * | – | University Alliance | East UOTC<br>East Midlands UAS |
| University of Oxford | * | * | * | Russell Group | Oxford UOTC<br>Oxford UAS<br>Oxford URNU |
| Oxford Brookes University | * | * | * | University Alliance | Oxford UOTC<br>Oxford UAS<br>Oxford URNU |
| Peninsular College of Medicine and Dentistry [Plymouth] | * | – | – | | Exeter UOTC |
| Plymouth University | * | – | – | University Alliance | Exeter UOTC |
| University of Portsmouth | * | * | – | University Alliance | Southampton UOTC<br>Southampton UAS |
| Queen Margaret University [Edinburgh] | – | * | * | | East of Scotland UAS<br>Edinburgh URNU |
| Queen Mary University of London | – | * | * | Russell Group | London UAS<br>London URNU |
| Queen's University Belfast | * | * | – | Russell Group | Queen's UOTC<br>Manchester UAS[2] |
| University of Reading | * | * | * | | Oxford UOTC<br>Oxford UAS<br>Oxford URNU |

Appendix 5    197

| University | OTC | UAS | URNU | Higher education mission group | USU |
|---|---|---|---|---|---|
| Robert Gordon University [Aberdeen] | * | * | * |  | Aberdeen UOTC<br>East of Scotland UAS<br>Edinburgh URNU |
| Royal Agricultural University [Cirencester] | * | – | – | GuildHE | Oxford UOTC |
| Royal Holloway University of London | – | * | * |  | London UAS<br>London URNU |
| University of Salford | * | * | * | University Alliance | Manchester and Salford UOTC<br>Manchester UAS<br>Manchester URNU |
| University of Sheffield | * | * | * | Russell Group | Yorkshire Officer Training Regiment<br>Yorkshire UAS<br>Yorkshire URNU |
| Sheffield Hallam University | * | – | – | University Alliance | Yorkshire Officer Training Regiment |
| University of Southampton | * | * | * | Russell Group | Southampton UOTC<br>Southampton UAS<br>Southampton URNU |
| Southampton Solent University | * | * | – | GuildHE | Southampton UOTC<br>Southampton UAS |
| University of St Andrews | * | * | – |  | Tayforth UOTC<br>East of Scotland UAS |
| University of St Mark and St John Plymouth | * | * | – | GuildHE | Exeter UOTC<br>Bristol UAS |
| St Mary's University [Twickenham] | – | – | * | GuildHE | London URNU |
| Staffordshire University [Stoke on Trent] | * | * | – |  | Birmingham UOTC<br>Birmingham UAS |
| University of Stirling | * | * | – |  | Tayforth UOTC<br>Glasgow UAS |

(*Continued*)

| University | OTC | UAS | URNU | Higher education mission group | USU |
|---|---|---|---|---|---|
| University of Strathclyde | * | * | * |  | Glasgow and Strathclyde UOTC<br>Glasgow UAS<br>Glasgow URNU |
| University of Sunderland | * | * | * |  | Northumbrian UOTC<br>Northumbrian UAS<br>Northumbrian URNU |
| University of Surrey [Guildford] | – | * | – |  | London UAS |
| University of Sussex [Brighton] | – | – | * |  | Sussex URNU |
| Swansea University | * | * | * |  | Wales UOTC (Swansea)<br>Wales UAS<br>Wales URNU |
| Teesside University | * | * | – | University Alliance | Northumbrian UOTC<br>Northumbrian UAS |
| UCL University College London | – | * | * | Russell Group | London UAS<br>London URNU |
| UCLAN University of Central Lancashire [Preston] | * | * | * |  | Liverpool UOTC (Lancaster det.)<br>Liverpool UAS<br>Manchester URNU |
| UEA University of East Anglia [Norwich] | * | * | * | University Alliance | Cambridge UOTC<br>Cambridge UAS<br>Cambridge URNU |
| University of Ulster [Belfast] | * | – | – |  | Queen's UOTC |
| USW: University of South Wales, (formerly University of Glamorgan and University of Newport, to April 2013) | * | * | * | University Alliance | Wales UOTC (Cardiff)<br>Wales UAS<br>Wales URNU |

Appendix 5    199

| University | OTC | UAS | URNU | Higher education mission group | USU |
|---|---|---|---|---|---|
| University of Wales Trinity Saint David (formerly Swansea Met, and University Wales Lampeter) | * | – | – |  | Wales UOTC (Swansea) |
| UWE: University of the West of England [Bristol] | * | * | * |  | Bristol UOTC<br>Bristol UAS<br>Bristol URNU |
| UWS University of the West of Scotland [Paisley] | – | * | – |  | Glasgow UAS |
| University of Warwick | * | * | * | Russell Group | Birmingham UOTC<br>Birmingham UAS<br>Birmingham URNU |
| University of Winchester | * | – | – | GuildHE | Southampton OTC |
| University of Wolverhampton | * | – | – |  | Birmingham UOTC |
| University of Worcester | * | – | – | GuildHE | Birmingham UOTC |
| University of York | * | * | – | Russell Group | Yorkshire Officer Training Regiment<br>Yorkshire UAS |
| York St John University | * | – | – | GuildHE | Yorkshire Officer Training Regiment |

[1] Name of URNU not given in original response.
[2] Indicated in original questionnaire response; note the distance between Manchester and Belfast.

# Appendix 6

Students' assessments of skills development through university armed service unit participation

| Skill (USU) | Not at all | Some but not as much as I would have liked | About as much as I had anticipated | More than I had anticipated | Way beyond my expectations |
|---|---|---|---|---|---|
| *Adaptability* | | | | | |
| OTC | 1 | 3 | 32 | 49 | 13 |
| UAS | 0 | 2 | 27 | 51 | 18 |
| URNU | 0 | 5 | 31 | 45 | 17 |
| *Budgeting* | | | | | |
| OTC | 22 | 15 | 36 | 11 | 3 |
| UAS | 14 | 12 | 42 | 18 | 4 |
| URNU | 19 | 10 | 44 | 11 | 5 |
| *Communication skills* | | | | | |
| OTC | 0 | 3 | 28 | 45 | 23 |
| UAS | 0 | 3 | 17 | 49 | 26 |
| URNU | 0 | 3 | 20 | 49 | 26 |
| *Critical thinking* | | | | | |
| OTC | 2 | 6 | 28 | 46 | 17 |
| UAS | 1 | 8 | 29 | 44 | 17 |
| URNU | 1 | 7 | 29 | 42 | 18 |

| Skill (USU) | Not at all | Some but not as much as I would have liked | About as much as I had anticipated | More than I had anticipated | Way beyond my expectations |
|---|---|---|---|---|---|
| *Decision-making* | | | | | |
| OTC | 1 | 4 | 20 | 46 | 28 |
| UAS | 0 | 4 | 22 | 48 | 25 |
| URNU | 0 | 7 | 20 | 43 | 27 |
| *Independence* | | | | | |
| OTC | 1 | 6 | 27 | 41 | 21 |
| UAS | 1 | 3 | 23 | 39 | 32 |
| URNU | 2 | 5 | 29 | 35 | 27 |
| *Information literacy* | | | | | |
| OTC | 8 | 11 | 44 | 24 | 6 |
| UAS | 4 | 7 | 49 | 29 | 5 |
| URNU | 6 | 9 | 42 | 27 | 8 |
| *Initiative* | | | | | |
| OTC | 1 | 5 | 27 | 42 | 23 |
| UAS | 0 | 3 | 23 | 45 | 28 |
| URNU | 1 | 4 | 24 | 44 | 25 |
| *Knowledge of the Armed Forces* | | | | | |
| OTC | 0 | 6 | 27 | 36 | 30 |
| UAS | 0 | 5 | 25 | 31 | 37 |
| URNU | 0 | 6 | 24 | 35 | 33 |
| *Leadership skills* | | | | | |
| OTC | 1 | 6 | 20 | 41 | 31 |
| UAS | 0 | 5 | 20 | 38 | 35 |
| URNU | 1 | 7 | 16 | 42 | 33 |
| *Literacy* | | | | | |
| OTC | 21 | 9 | 46 | 10 | 2 |
| UAS | 11 | 7 | 52 | 14 | 4 |
| URNU | 16 | 6 | 48 | 9 | 5 |

(*Continued*)

| Skill (USU) | Not at all | Some but not as much as I would have liked | About as much as I had anticipated | More than I had anticipated | Way beyond my expectations |
|---|---|---|---|---|---|
| *Maturity* | | | | | |
| OTC | 3 | 5 | 34 | 39 | 17 |
| UAS | 2 | 4 | 30 | 41 | 22 |
| URNU | 1 | 4 | 38 | 38 | 17 |
| *Numeracy* | | | | | |
| OTC | 19 | 11 | 44 | 11 | 2 |
| UAS | 13 | 13 | 44 | 14 | 2 |
| URNU | 14 | 8 | 45 | 14 | 4 |
| *Occupational awareness* | | | | | |
| OTC | 2 | 7 | 31 | 38 | 21 |
| UAS | 0 | 5 | 28 | 39 | 26 |
| URNU | 2 | 5 | 32 | 29 | 29 |
| *Organisation & planning* | | | | | |
| OTC | 1 | 5 | 22 | 43 | 28 |
| UAS | 0 | 2 | 20 | 41 | 36 |
| URNU | 1 | 3 | 21 | 41 | 32 |
| *Presentation skills* | | | | | |
| OTC | 6 | 11 | 31 | 34 | 16 |
| UAS | 2 | 7 | 23 | 38 | 28 |
| URNU | 3 | 4 | 22 | 43 | 27 |
| *Problem-solving* | | | | | |
| OTC | 2 | 7 | 32 | 42 | 16 |
| UAS | 1 | 5 | 31 | 40 | 22 |
| URNU | 0 | 7 | 30 | 39 | 23 |
| *Project planning* | | | | | |
| OTC | 4 | 8 | 34 | 36 | 15 |
| UAS | 1 | 6 | 28 | 40 | 22 |
| URNU | 2 | 10 | 27 | 39 | 18 |

| Skill (USU) | Not at all | Some but not as much as I would have liked | About as much as I had anticipated | More than I had anticipated | Way beyond my expectations |
|---|---|---|---|---|---|
| *Self-confidence* | | | | | |
| OTC | 1 | 2 | 22 | 38 | 34 |
| UAS | 1 | 3 | 20 | 38 | 36 |
| URNU | 1 | 1 | 22 | 37 | 37 |
| *Social skills* | | | | | |
| OTC | 1 | 2 | 28 | 42 | 25 |
| UAS | 0 | 2 | 25 | 41 | 30 |
| URNU | 0 | 2 | 26 | 39 | 29 |
| *Synthesising information* | | | | | |
| OTC | 2 | 7 | 42 | 35 | 10 |
| UAS | 2 | 4 | 46 | 36 | 10 |
| URNU | 2 | 6 | 39 | 36 | 14 |
| *Teamwork* | | | | | |
| OTC | 1 | 2 | 26 | 42 | 28 |
| UAS | 0 | 2 | 26 | 43 | 27 |
| URNU | 0 | 2 | 24 | 39 | 33 |
| *Time management* | | | | | |
| OTC | 1 | 6 | 25 | 37 | 29 |
| UAS | 1 | 2 | 24 | 36 | 35 |
| URNU | 1 | 4 | 30 | 35 | 29 |
| *Verbal interaction skills* | | | | | |
| OTC | 1 | 4 | 33 | 42 | 17 |
| UAS | 0 | 1 | 33 | 40 | 24 |
| URNU | 0 | 2 | 29 | 40 | 25 |

# Appendix 7

## Students' assessments of skills development through degree programme

| Skill (University) | Not at all | Some but not as much as I would have liked | About as much as I had anticipated | More than I had anticipated | Way beyond my expectations |
|---|---|---|---|---|---|
| *Adaptability* | | | | | |
| OTC | 11 | 22 | 40 | 20 | 3 |
| UAS | 7 | 21 | 44 | 22 | 3 |
| URNU | 8 | 18 | 41 | 23 | 6 |
| *Budgeting* | | | | | |
| OTC | 28 | 16 | 29 | 14 | 4 |
| UAS | 22 | 14 | 33 | 19 | 4 |
| URNU | 26 | 14 | 31 | 11 | 6 |
| *Communication skills* | | | | | |
| OTC | 7 | 22 | 36 | 26 | 7 |
| UAS | 6 | 25 | 37 | 24 | 7 |
| URNU | 5 | 24 | 34 | 27 | 8 |
| *Critical thinking* | | | | | |
| OTC | 4 | 15 | 31 | 34 | 14 |
| UAS | 3 | 14 | 37 | 32 | 13 |
| URNU | 3 | 14 | 37 | 32 | 13 |

| Skill (University) | Not at all | Some but not as much as I would have liked | About as much as I had anticipated | More than I had anticipated | Way beyond my expectations |
|---|---|---|---|---|---|
| *Decision-making* | | | | | |
| OTC | 8 | 22 | 39 | 22 | 6 |
| UAS | 7 | 21 | 44 | 21 | 7 |
| URNU | 6 | 21 | 38 | 24 | 8 |
| *Independence* | | | | | |
| OTC | 5 | 11 | 34 | 31 | 17 |
| UAS | 2 | 8 | 38 | 30 | 20 |
| URNU | 5 | 13 | 31 | 34 | 15 |
| *Information literacy* | | | | | |
| OTC | 4 | 10 | 35 | 36 | 12 |
| UAS | 3 | 7 | 39 | 36 | 13 |
| URNU | 2 | 7 | 37 | 35 | 17 |
| *Initiative* | | | | | |
| OTC | 8 | 19 | 37 | 27 | 6 |
| UAS | 6 | 20 | 42 | 23 | 7 |
| URNU | 9 | 16 | 35 | 29 | 8 |
| *Knowledge of the Armed Forces* | | | | | |
| OTC | 53 | 6 | 11 | 5 | 3 |
| UAS | 62 | 8 | 9 | 4 | 2 |
| URNU | 58 | 6 | 8 | 5 | 1 |
| *Leadership skills* | | | | | |
| OTC | 31 | 24 | 22 | 12 | 4 |
| UAS | 30 | 29 | 22 | 10 | 5 |
| URNU | 31 | 31 | 18 | 11 | 5 |
| *Literacy* | | | | | |
| OTC | 8 | 11 | 43 | 24 | 8 |
| UAS | 7 | 11 | 49 | 23 | 7 |
| URNU | 7 | 13 | 43 | 24 | 9 |

(*Continued*)

| Skill (University) | Not at all | Some but not as much as I would have liked | About as much as I had anticipated | More than I had anticipated | Way beyond my expectations |
|---|---|---|---|---|---|
| *Maturity* | | | | | |
| OTC | 8 | 11 | 43 | 25 | 11 |
| UAS | 4 | 9 | 46 | 28 | 10 |
| URNU | 7 | 11 | 41 | 25 | 11 |
| *Numeracy* | | | | | |
| OTC | 16 | 11 | 35 | 19 | 11 |
| UAS | 11 | 10 | 34 | 24 | 17 |
| URNU | 15 | 8 | 35 | 20 | 16 |
| *Occupational awareness* | | | | | |
| OTC | 10 | 16 | 33 | 25 | 13 |
| UAS | 10 | 17 | 34 | 26 | 10 |
| URNU | 11 | 18 | 27 | 23 | 15 |
| *Organisation & planning* | | | | | |
| OTC | 5 | 14 | 38 | 30 | 10 |
| UAS | 4 | 12 | 43 | 30 | 10 |
| URNU | 4 | 12 | 37 | 29 | 16 |
| *Presentation skills* | | | | | |
| OTC | 5 | 15 | 36 | 32 | 11 |
| UAS | 6 | 18 | 34 | 31 | 11 |
| URNU | 0 | 16 | 28 | 38 | 11 |
| *Problem-solving* | | | | | |
| OTC | 7 | 15 | 40 | 26 | 10 |
| UAS | 4 | 15 | 37 | 28 | 14 |
| URNU | 6 | 15 | 35 | 27 | 14 |
| *Project planning* | | | | | |
| OTC | 7 | 12 | 39 | 31 | 8 |
| UAS | 7 | 15 | 38 | 29 | 10 |
| URNU | 8 | 14 | 34 | 28 | 12 |

| Skill (University) | Not at all | Some but not as much as I would have liked | About as much as I had anticipated | More than I had anticipated | Way beyond my expectations |
|---|---|---|---|---|---|
| *Self-confidence* | | | | | |
| OTC | 8 | 17 | 42 | 24 | 7 |
| UAS | 6 | 16 | 46 | 22 | 9 |
| URNU | 9 | 19 | 41 | 20 | 7 |
| *Social skills* | | | | | |
| OTC | 9 | 18 | 39 | 22 | 9 |
| UAS | 7 | 18 | 39 | 26 | 8 |
| URNU | 11 | 19 | 38 | 21 | 8 |
| *Synthesising information* | | | | | |
| OTC | 5 | 9 | 43 | 31 | 10 |
| UAS | 3 | 7 | 48 | 27 | 13 |
| URNU | 4 | 8 | 39 | 31 | 14 |
| *Teamwork* | | | | | |
| OTC | 11 | 21 | 35 | 24 | 6 |
| UAS | 7 | 23 | 35 | 27 | 6 |
| URNU | 11 | 23 | 27 | 26 | 9 |
| *Time management* | | | | | |
| OTC | 5 | 15 | 36 | 29 | 13 |
| UAS | 3 | 10 | 36 | 33 | 18 |
| URNU | 4 | 9 | 39 | 31 | 14 |
| *Verbal interaction skills* | | | | | |
| OTC | 6 | 17 | 44 | 24 | 6 |
| UAS | 5 | 14 | 46 | 24 | 8 |
| URNU | 6 | 14 | 38 | 30 | 8 |